The Web of Leadership:
The Presidency in
Higher Education

A VOLUME IN
CONTEMPORARY ETHNOGRAPHIC STUDIES

Editor: Jaber F. Gubrium, *Department of Sociology, University of Florida*

CONTEMPORARY ETHNOGRAPHIC STUDIES

Editor: **Jaber F. Gubrium**
Department of Sociology
University of Florida

Oldtimers and Alzheimer's: The Descriptive Organization of Senility
Jaber F. Gubrium, *Marquette University*

Becomimg Doctors: The Professionalization of Medical Students
Jack Haas and William Shaffir, *McMaster University*

The Web of Leadership: The Presidency in Higher Education
William G. Tierney, *Pennsylvania State University*

**Hearts and Minds, Water and Fish: The IRA and INLA
in a Northern Irish Ghetto**
Jeffrey A. Sluka, *Massey University, New Zealand*

Caring Strangers: The Sociology of Intergenerational Relations
Dale J. Jaffe, *University of Wisconsin, Milwaukee*

A Paradoxical Community: The Emergence of a Social World
Haim Hazan, *Tel-Aviv University*

The Web of Leadership:
The Presidency in Higher Education

by **WILLIAM G. TIERNEY**

Center for the Study of
Higher Education
Pennsylvania State University

 **JAI PRESS INC.**

Greenwich, Connecticut   *London, England*

Library of Congress Cataloging-in-Publication Data

Tierney, William G.
    The web of leadership.

    (Contemporary ethnographic studies)
    Bibliography: p.
    Includes index.
    1. Universities and colleges—United States—Administration—
Case studies. 2. College presidents—United States—Case
studies. 3. Educational anthropology—United States—Case
studies. 4. Organizational behavior—Case studies. I. Title.
II. Series.
LB2341.T59   1988   378'.111   88-13180
ISBN 0-89232-959-9

Copyright© 1988 JAI PRESS INC.
55 Old Post Road, No. 2
Greenwich, Connecticut 06836

JAI PRESS LTD.
3 Henrietta Street
London WC2E 8LU
England

ISBN NUMBER: 0-89232-959-9

Library of Congress Catalog Card Number: 88-13180

Manufactured in the United States of America

CONTENTS

Preface   xiii

Actors and Roles Mentioned in Text   xv

Introduction   xvii

PART I.   FRAMING LEADERSHIP

Introduction   3

I.   The President's Chair   5
Previous Frames of Reference   6
   General Theory   6
   Organizational Theory   8
   Collegial Theory   10
Critique of Previous Work and
an Alternative Approach   12
   Historical Context   12
   Ambiguity of the Concept   13
   Measures and Values   14
An Alternative Frame   15
   Time   18
   Space   19
   Communication   20
   Power   22
Methodology   24

II.   Historical Framework   31
History of the College   32
   Sisters of Mother Mary   32
   The Early Years   36
   The Recent Past   42

New President, New Time 45
  Changes 45
  Problems 48
  Administrative Solutions 51
Ways of Seeing 53
  History of Change 57
  The Curriculum 58
  Ceremonies and Traditions 60

PART II. ACTORS AND THEIR ROLES

Introduction 65

III. Primary Groups 69
Midmanagement 69
Board of Trustees 79
Faculty 85
Executive Committee 96

IV. Secondary Groups 111
Sisters of Mother Mary 111
Alumni 114
Students 117
Staff 121

PART III. LEADERSHIP SCENES AND SCRIPTS

Introduction 127

V. Administrative Council 129
October 25 131
December 15 135
February 28 137
March 22 139
April 17 143
May 17 146

VI.	**Daily Life**	**149**
	Morning	149
	Private Space/Public Greetings	149
	Time	151
	Literacy in the President's Office	153
	Informal Encounters	154
	Address Forms	156
	The Territory of Leadership	157
	Midmorning	160
	Gestures	160
	Seasonal Activities	161
	Communicating with Constituents	162
	Afternoon	163
	Humor	163
	Informal Decision Making	164
	Messages	165
	Late Afternoon	166
VII.	**The Presidency**	**169**
	The College Presidency	169
	Interviews with the President	174
	Woman/Sister	175
	Nomination to CMM	177
	Life at CMM	178
	College Leadership	178
	The Past Year	179
	Analysis	181

PART IV. INTERPRETING LEADERSHIP

	Introduction	**187**
VIII.	**The Context of Time, Space, and Communication**	**189**
	Time	189
	Formality/Informality	189
	Past Events; Future Plans	189
	Seasonal and Ceremonial Time	190

Space   192
Public Space   192
Private Space   193
Communication   194
Written Discourse   194
Oral Discourse   197

IX. **Conclusion**   **203**
Contextualizing Leadership   204
Historical Context   204
Competing Theories   207
Measures and Values   209
Method   210
Referents of Power   212
Time   213
Space   214
Communication   215

Appendix A: A Note on Method   **219**
Observation and Study   219
Method of Transcription/Analysis   223
The Ethnographer as Friend   224

Appendix B: Spatial Diagrams   **227**
President's Office   228
Administrative Offices   229
Campus   230

References   **231**

Index   **239**

This would be our business, to show them each thus transfixed as between the stars' trillions of javelins and of each the transfixions: but it is beyond my human power to do. The most I can do—the most I can hope to do—is to make a number of physical entities as plain and vivid as possible, and to make a few guesses, a few conjectures; and to leave to you much of the burden of realizing in each of them what I have wanted to make clear of them as a whole: how each is itself; and how each is a shapener.

James Agee, *Let Us Now Praise Famous Men*

Preface

This work originated out of an interest to understand leadership in higher education. As an in-depth look at one president at a small liberal arts college, the study used an anthropological framework and field methods to uncover how leadership operates within a cultural milieu. The investigation attempts neither to pass judgment on the actions of individuals nor to create a framework wherein heroes and villains exist. Instead, I integrate the daily activities of a college community and its president with its historical consciousness and the environmental factors that surround decision making in the 1980s.

I spent 30 hours each week during the academic year 1983/84 conducting the ethnography. A large amount of time was spent observing the daily activities of the President, attending college meetings and ceremonies, and interviewing other key actors within the organization such as deans and faculty members. My purpose was to understand how they viewed their work and how leadership affected that work. Within the text names of all individuals (except the child, Clarissa) are pseudonyms, as is the name of the institution, College of Mother Mary (CMM).

One of my favorite "listening posts" for the college community was in the hall of the administration building, immediately outside of the President's office. Periodically throughout the year I sat on the couch and watched and participated in the drama which is about to unfold for the reader. I saw entrances and exits, as well as acts, expressions, and events, that the actors communicated to one another. Often, the youngest member of College of Mother Mary wandered into the hall on unsteady legs.

Clarissa was the infant daughter of the Director of Financial Aid. During the course of the year I watched Clarissa move from a crawling position to a wobbly two-step, and then finally to a comfortable walk. My learning about the institution and ideas concerning leadership and organizational culture progressed similarly.

As one learns inductively, one also can benefit from individuals who pose questions or provide necessary enlightenment and encouragement. My thanks go to Lew Mayhew, Shirley Heath, David Tyack, Dan McLaughlin, Ellen Chaffee, and Rolf Norgaard. Their comments and criticism have fundamentally altered my ways of seeing and conducting research. I could not have worked with better colleagues and human beings.

One also learns from daily experience and from observing the minutiae of everyday life. Indeed, one conclusion reached in this work is that we necessarily need to uncover daily practices and discourse if we are to successfully interpret organizational reality. Thus, I owe a great debt to the people of College of Mother Mary. What was oftentimes a trying and difficult year for them turned out to be a year of unique engagement for me. Virtually everyone at CMM provided me with helpful advice, encouragement, and, oftentimes, friendship. I thank all of them, especially the President, Sister Vera, who allowed me to be her shadow for a year.

In early fall 1984, the former President, Sister Barbara Therese, died at the age of 73. She, too, provided counsel and friendship during the course of the year. It is to the oldest and youngest members of the college community that I dedicate this work. For the study speaks of time and a new way to consider leadership and the culture of an organization. From our elders we gain knowledge of the past, and from the young we gain hope for the future. For Clarissa and Sister Barbara Therese.

William G. Tierney

Actors and Roles Mentioned in Text

Executive Committee

Sister Vera Regan	President
Patrick O'Connell	Academic Vice President (AVP)
Tim Leary	Vice President for College Affairs (Development)
Sister Joan Rinelli	Vice President for Student Affairs
Dan Blue-Smith	Faculty Senate Chair and Dean of the Faculty-elect

Board of Trustees

Mr. Sanger	Jim Yoshihira
Tim Thompson	J. Francis Hanrahan

Faculty

Sue Ann Simmer	English
Bobbi Trumble	English
Louie Canova	Business Department Chairperson

Joe Calabrese	Business
Jake Barnes	Drama Department Chairperson
Dr. Beckett	Physics

Midmanagers

Tom Brady	Director of Facilities
Dave Falconieri	Director of Admissions
Dan Grant	Director of Business Affairs
Molly Dish	Alumni Director
Jane DeSelm	Dean of Students

Others

Sister Barbara Therese (BT)	Chancellor and previous President
Sister Mary Therese (MT)	Director of International Research and former Academic Vice President
Sally	President's secretary
Marty	Student

The scenes take place at College of Mother Mary (CMM) in Rosewood, California from August 1983 through May 1984.

Introduction

After my last interview with Sister Vera in July, I walked to the courtyard where Sue Ann Simmer waited. Another faculty member of College of Mother Mary talked with her as I approached and a student wandered by and said, "Hello, Professor Simmer. I hope you're having a good summer." "I sure am," said Sue Ann, and then greeted me with, "After all that happened this year we all deserve a good summer." We had arranged to have lunch and as we walked toward her car she brought me up-to-date on the summer's activities. "Did you hear what he [the Academic Vice President] has done now?" asked Sue Ann. "I think you were at the Curriculum Committee when we approved the new Computer Studies major. He told no one, but he has ordered Dana [the registrar] to take any mention of it out of the new catalogue. Before he went on vacation last week he called Eleanor in from the hallway—he shouted to her from his desk—and told her he had decided to postpone the major." Sue Ann shook her head back and forth and as we reached the car she said, "Typical. Nothing's changed. They've learned nothing. That's just what we've seen all year long. I don't look forward to next year."

A few weeks prior to our meeting the administration had issued contracts, and the day Sue Ann's contract arrived she brought it to the President's office. Sue Ann remarked:

> I'd talked with Vera about my load for next year already. I just can't teach four classes, sit on Rank and Tenure, chair the English Department, and chair Academic Standards. And now they want me to sit on the accreditation committee. I asked her to reduce my teaching load to three and she agreed.

> Anyway, I thought I'd make a joke, so I brought over the contract the day it arrived and went to her office. Well, of course, I had to walk seven feet into the room to even see if she was there. She wasn't. Sally [the president's secretary] told me that Vera had gone to the bank.
>
> As Sally and I were talking, I saw Vera pull up and park in her space, so I waited. She entered, head down, and walked straight to her desk. She must have passed me by about 12 inches and didn't say anything. Nothing. I thought I'd still make a joke so I said, "Sister, I hear you've been to the bank." Well, she just looked over to Sally and I thought she was going to shoot her. I said, "It really wasn't necessary, Sister," and she just looked quizzical. I said, "Well, Sister, I thought you went to the bank to give me a special reward for being the first to return my contract signed, sealed, and delivered—see," and I held it up to her. Well, then, she smiled and said, "Thank you." I told her, "Look, Sister, I've signed it in green—for a reason."
>
> She looked at it, my signature signed in green ink, and I said, "Green's the sign of hope, Sister. It's hope for next year."

Sue Ann's comments accurately mirror the tenor of people's attitudes during the summer. The hoped-for decline in tension had not arrived; rather, people spoke about a lull in the storm. Sister Joan Rinelli, the Vice President for Student Affairs, commented in mid-July, "I can't believe that next year will be worse than last, but it will. Vera and O'Connell (the Academic Vice President) just don't see. There will be real bloodletting this fall. I told that Executive Committee that this year just might be my last." Dan Blue-Smith, a faculty member, mentioned how his optimism had been tempered: "O'Connell is a smart guy. I admire his knowledge and know-how, but the way he deals with people," said Dan, shaking his head.

This work takes as its point of departure the experiences of those intimately involved in leading and managing College of Mother Mary. Its purpose is to develop an ethnography of leadership that provides "thicker description" (Geertz 1973) than current theories on leadership. As evidenced by the opening comments, the college lived through a year fraught with crisis and conflict. Leadership, and the participants' understanding of it, is central to unlocking the dramatic puzzle of the institution's problems. Throughout the year the actors communicated their sense of crisis through an array of symbols based, in part, on an individual's or group's perception of the history of the institution, and how its leaders perform.

College of Mother Mary differed greatly in 1984 from the institution chartered to offer Associate of Arts degrees in 1868. Nevertheless, the actors continued to communicate an identity and a sense of underlying purpose through their collective interpretation of institutional mission. Founded as a college for young women on the West Coast, the college saw its mission as providing a religiously oriented education based on a liberal arts curriculum. Although the college admitted all religious denominations and nationalities, CMM existed primarily for American Catholic women. Faculty and administrators were overwhelmingly from the Sisters of Mother Mary, and the staff were primarily lay Catholics from the surrounding parishes.

In the last quarter century the college has seen a rapid transformation. There has been a persistent increase in lay faculty, administration, and staff. In the 1920s the college relocated 30 miles to the north. In the 1950s it began granting the Bachelor of Arts degree. The 1960s brought with them a comprehensive evening division and the admission of men. In the 1970s the institution added a graduate division.

From the outset of the research, college personnel admitted they faced numerous problems. In an institution where the liberal arts once reigned, business now accounts for half of the majors. Catholic ceremonies and the religious presence have been greatly reduced. Less than one-half of the student body are Catholic. One-third of the students are from foreign countries. The attrition rate stands at 73 percent versus a national average of 50 percent. There has been an almost constant seven-year decline in full-time equivalency (FTE) enrollment. In 1983/84 starting salaries for assistant professors were $17,000 and for staff they were $10,000. Administrators found it increasingly difficult to balance the budget on tuition-driven revenue. In the previous year, they were forced to tap the remaining excess income from the school's endowment to balance the budget.

Since Sister Vera assumed the presidency in 1980, there has been a rapid turnover in key staffing positions—admissions, finance, and the academic vice president (AVP)—to name but a few areas. Sister Vera succeeded a nun who had been president for 24 years. As one might expect, the styles and characteristics of Sister Vera and her predecessor, Sister Barbara Therese, differed greatly. As the drama unfolds we find that the actors at the college had an implicit knowledge of how they expected a college president to act, both as a decision maker and as a colleague with whom they interacted on a daily basis. Their perception of leadership came in large part from their contextual understanding of the institution and their acquaintance with the previous president. As becomes apparent in the following example, the discrepancy between the two leaders' styles marks a broad transition in organizational culture.

One morning Sister Vera arrived at her office just as the previous president entered the same door. They both walked down the hallway. Within a space of 12 minutes, Sister Vera entered the corridor, looked neither up nor down it, entered her office, greeted her secretary, and nodded to me. During the same period Sister Barbara stopped in seven offices and had interchanges with 13 different people. "Good morning, dear," she said in one office. "The bouquet looks rather dreary there, dear," she said in another. "I hope you have a good weekend," she said to me, and replied to a faculty member, "Oh yes, Mary's party was really quite fun. I wish you had been there."

That morning both individuals operated in different roles and contexts. That is, Sister Vera was an embattled president who entered a building rife with dissension, whereas Sister Barbara was a partially retired chancellor who no longer carried the burdens of the presidential office. Surely, we can expect both individuals to behave differently toward different groups. Nevertheless, their manner that morning indicates how each interacted with the college community. Indeed, many individuals pointed to examples such as the one provided as typical of the differences between the two women. Extending beyond nuances of social interaction, these differences include radically divergent styles of leadership and decision making.

Under Sister Barbara, decision-making power rested in a two-person administration—the President and Academic Dean. A host of other individuals contributed their services, such as the Dean of Students, Registrar, and Admissions Director. These people had tasks to do, they voiced opinions in committees or to the Academic Dean, but they played no active decision-making role in the college's formal organizational hierarchy. Sister Vera saw the need to change this "family-like" attitude toward decision making, and created an Executive Committee. The Academic Dean became the Academic Vice President, the Dean of Students became the Vice

President for Student Affairs, the part-time development consultant became the Vice President for College Relations, and the Director of Finance became the Vice President for Finance. Words like "midmanagement" and "salary scale" came into use, and an organizational blueprint evolved that could easily be diagrammed and understood on paper. The Executive Committee met in closed-door sessions with the President once a week, and people came to realize that committees, too, operated as organizational structures. Consequently, College of Mother Mary not only experienced a turnover in key staffing positions, but also a rapid change and proliferation of organizational roles.

The study uses the dramaturgical metaphor to portray the web of organizational relationships in which leaders move and function. By way of this metaphor, the reader grasps not only the problems different individuals and groups face in a changing environment but also the human element inherent in organizational roles. As a theater-in-the-round, the work allows the reader to view and analyze the actors in their interactions with one another.

This study questions the assumption that present actions are the sum of past histories, or that one can understand decision making and its outcomes by holding that the truth about a situation resides within interactions alone. We view organizations as discrete entities that create their own history through a series of patterns, ceremonies, and signals. Further, organizations change with the environment and the actions of individuals within the system.

The approach advanced in this book considers organizations in a light distinctly different from previous theories of leadership. We speak neither of organizations that change due to a heroic individual's actions, nor of individuals situated in organizations without reference to history, nor of organizations as historical products of progress. Thus, the method informing this study approaches organizations not by considering historical progress, or the lack of it, but by viewing how actions occur.

Past research has entertained two contradictory notions: either leaders are all powerful and the organization exists in their shadow, or leaders merely fulfill functionally defined roles in which they are powerless to change organizational reality. Most leadership theories and applied studies examine leaders within a particular setting, attribute characteristics to them, posit possible avenues by which they can lead, and then seek to contextualize leadership before finally determining how much of an input individuals can have on an institution. The conclusion ultimately relies on a conception of an individual's ability to change societal reality.

In an effort to depart from the many preconceptions that plague previous work, this study seeks to understand leadership by observing how events occur and how symbols are used. Evidence obtained from formal meetings, interviews, informal observations, and discursive analyses of presidential communication developed into patterns that guided the research. The portrayal of the crisis and conflict at College of Mother Mary reflects a situation wherein different actors feel, speak, and act as if a "we-they" atmosphere prevailed in the college. To conclude, however, that there are heroes or villains in this piece is inaccurate. To provide the reader with a list of traits or characteristics that a president must use to avoid similar situations places leadership within contexts that are either misinformed or ill-advised. A sounder theoretical under-standing of leadership requires that we question the presumption that if a leader exhibits skill in the use of a particular trait, then he or she will be a successful leader. This study situates leadership and the actors involved in the investigation within a cultural context. As a result we view leadership in a transformative matrix influenced by a wide variety of practices, not by a short list of identifiable traits. Time, space, and communication provide three referent points for understanding this matrix.

Time involves not only the historical context within which the college operates but also the formal use of planned meetings and ceremonies and the many informal contacts a leader uses throughout the day. The administrative meeting structure arranged by Sister Vera and Sister Barbara's informal communicative style are but two examples of how leaders can structure time. Space connotes areas where groups of people come together for a variety of activities that are either private or public in nature. Space receives mention as another form that demonstrates power, and influences how people perceive one another's relationships. At the outset of this introduction, Sue Ann Simmer commented on where the President parked her car, and how she had to walk "seven feet into her office" to see if Sister Vera was there. These are spatial indicators that demand analysis. The third referent point on this matrix engages us in an exploration of communication. Within the manifold relationships of the college, discursive codes and symbolic actions shape collectively shared patterns and actions. As we have seen, the greeting styles of Sister Vera and her predecessor differ dramatically. Communication produces differing patterns which can at the same time impose a new practice on the organization as well as maintain or lose control of the situation. Communication, then, is another process whereby people form meanings about the organization and about one another.

This work is divided into four parts. As a theatergoer generally has some knowledge of a play before it begins, Part I orients the reader to previous research on leadership, the theoretical frame developed in the history, and current context of the institution. Part II provides the action for the drama. Different actors and groups of the college come onstage as problems and proposed solutions unfold. Part III is a textual analysis of the drama, and provides additional leadership scenes through which the actors move. Part IV returns to a discussion of time, space, and communication and outlines the uses of these three coordinates by the actors. A discussion of how the interpretive framework used here can best be applied to previous studies of leadership research ensues, after which we briefly consider directions for research on leadership.

Part I

Framing Leadership

Introduction

Part I provides the reader with the necessary background—theoretical and historical—to understand the drama that occurs. Chapter I begins with a discussion of leadership from three different theoretical perspectives—general, organizational, and collegial. Each perspective elaborates on the definition of leadership, the measures the theorists used, and how they undertook the study. This is followed by a critique of the shortcomings of previous work done on leadership that suggests an alternative way to study the problem. The third part of this chapter begins with an epistemological discussion about how leaders construct and conceive of their worlds, and then considers leadership within that context. The fourth part of the chapter uses the methodology of anthropology—ethnography—as the means for undertaking the study of leadership within the purview of the social construction of reality.

Chapter II provides a historical perspective on the College of Mother Mary. The chapter opens with a discussion of the college's founding in 1868 and continues up to the present. The second part considers the current problems that beset CMM, and places those problems within the larger context of higher education in the 1980s and the more specific context of a Catholic institution that operates within specified patterns, traditions, and ceremonies. Finally, the third part offers three situations that the actors faced during the course of the year. These situations enable us to see how different groups, such as faculty and administration, viewed problems and solutions from quite different perspectives.

Chapter I

The President's Chair

Late one afternoon an uncharacteristic quiet settled in the hallway and in the President's office. Normally, the building was a hub of activity and noise, with students, administrators, staff, and faculty moving throughout the setting. At four o'clock, the Director of Financial Aid's husband arrived across the hall with their young child, Clarissa. Clarissa recently learned to walk, and she wandered into Sister Vera's office on unsteady feet. "Hi, hon," said Sister Vera. "I bet you want to sit in my chair, don't you. Just like last time. Yes. Here now, let me twirl you around." Sister Vera picked up the child and placed her in the black chair behind the desk, and slowly moved the chair around and around. "Now you know what it feels like to be President, Clarissa. You're in the President's seat, now. Do you like it? You can keep it if you want." Shortly thereafter the child climbed down from the chair and waved good-bye to Sister Vera. "Well, you didn't stay very long, Clarissa. I guess you don't like that seat either, huh? Bye-bye, Clarissa."

Who sits in the President's chair and how one conceives of the chair vary significantly depending upon how one views the locus of leadership. What empowers the chair? Is it the chair itself that provides power, or is the chair merely a wooden object with the "great man" who sits in the chair creating its power? Is the chair of a college president different from the seat of a chief executive officer of a business? Depending upon the paradigm and context from which a theorist operates, differences occur in the conception of a president's chair and the use and influence of leadership within a setting. The thesis of this work is that levels of action and

5

discourse constitute leadership in ways dramatically different from previous theories.

PREVIOUS FRAMES OF REFERENCE

Three frames of reference inform the discussion about theories of leadership. Moving from the broad to the specific, we first consider general theories of leadership that involve overarching explanations in a variety of contexts, forms, and functions. Second, the literature on organizations is examined for more focused reference to leadership theories in modern organizations. Third, we consider a specific organization—a collegiate institution—and discuss how writers have viewed leadership and the college presidency.

General Theory

In times of crisis or chaos a common conception is that people turn to individuals endowed with heroic qualitites who will lift them out of their dilemma and discover solutions that are otherwise unachievable. Everyone can list people they consider to be such individuals: Mohandas Gandhi helped form a nation through nonviolence, Abraham Lincoln guided a young nation through a war, and Martin Luther King sought to bring social justice to a people. The list continues ad infinitum as we scan the horizons of history for individuals who seemingly played a vital role for their country, an idea, or their time.

Initially, discussions of leadership focused on the individual and attributed his or her greatness to heroic qualities or particular traits. Carlyle's "[t]he history of what man has accomplished in this world ... is at bottom the History of the Great Men who have worked here" (Carlyle 1897, p. 1) and Aristotle's "[f]rom the hour of their birth some are marked out for subjection, and others for command" appear as all-encompassing statements that cut across time, situation, and environmental influences. In this light, leadership is a preordained quality, and an understanding of historical events, an explanation of the causes of war and peace, or the success of particular institutions can best be explained by a discussion of heroic individuals. The implication for accepting these ideas is that when an institution is in crisis, or when a war arises, similar men and women will come forth to guide people away from the abyss. Leadership thus defined is an overarching and time-free concept, applicable to all situations and contexts without reference to those who are led.

James MacGregor Burns provides a more recent attempt to define and understand leadership in a similarly broad, overarching context. "Leadership over human beings is exercised when persons with certain motives and purposes mobilize, in competition or conflict with other institutional, political, psychological and other resources so as to arouse, engage, and satisfy the motives of followers. This is done in order to realize goals held mutually by both leaders and followers" (1978, p. 18). Burns makes a valuable contribution to an understanding of his definition by pointing out the differences between *transactional* and *transformational* leadership. He views transactional leadership as a bargaining process, a give-and-take, so that compromises are made because of the transactional leadership of an individual. Transformational leadership exists when individuals "shape, alter, or elevate the values and goals of followers through the vital teaching role" (1978, p. 425). A Gandhi or a Martin Luther King fits the latter form, while a Lyndon Johnson can be seen as the transactor par excellence when one talks about sending legislation through the halls of Congress.

Burns also discusses the types of leadership roles open to an individual within the transactional-transformational forms. Individuals have many possible avenues open to them whereby they exert influence: bureaucratic, revolutionary, reform-oriented, intellectual, and moral. Further, Burns provides insight into social factors that can influence an individual's rise to power, such as personal background, psychological make-up, intellectual capabilities, and the time in which the individual lives.

The forms and types of leadership that Burns employs give helpful information when we consider the individual. Indeed, Burns arrived at this theory by studying leaders throughout history. Because his theory is broad-based, it also can be considered in a wide variety of contexts. As will be shown, Burns's model of leadership can be applied to organizational and collegial theories of how individuals lead. While Burns's theory is recent, it is not characteristic of most of the research over the last 15 years. His work is a close, if not more refined, fit to that of theorists of an earlier era who sought to define leadership in all-encompassing terms. Characteristic of much of the recent research is a movement away from broad-based theory and toward discussion of particular organizational aspects of leadership.

Organizational Theory

While leadership within an organization is one type of role discussed by Burns, the literature on organizations is full of theories, models, and propositions about how leaders lead, the effects of leadership, and the determinants of group dynamics. Halpin's (1966) *Initiating Structure* and *Consideration* scales and Fiedler's (1976) *contingency theory of leadership* offer the two most commonly discussed approaches to leadership in this field. What follows is a discussion of each theory, how these theories are measured, and criticism that has been directed at each theory from within the field.

According to Halpin, the two most important dimensions of leadership behavior are "initiating structure and consideration." Initiating structure refers to the leader's behavior in creating and explaining "well-defined patterns of organization, channels of communication, and methods of procedure" (Cunningham 1973, p. 4) for the followers. Consideration refers to how the leader carries out tasks to enhance "friendship, mutual trust, respect, and warmth" on the part of the followers. Halpin acknowledges that these two behaviors are the products of both individual and situational factors, and that the effective leader may need to adopt different behavior patterns in different situations. Nevertheless, he does not conceptualize in any systematic way the situational conditions that may affect the relationship between leader behavior and effectiveness. Despite this limitation, Halpin's work is a milestone in the study of leadership in nontrait terms.

Studies of Halpin's theory have made extensive use of the Leader Behavior Description Questionnaire (LBDQ) as a measurement device. The LBDQ measures subordinates' perceptions of their leaders' actual behavior. The questionnaire consists of two scales for measuring this behavior—*Initiating Structure* and *Consideration*. Each scale contains 20 short descriptive statements of ways in which the leader behaves. The members of the leader's group indicate the frequency with which the leader engages in each behavior by selecting one of five adverbs: always, often, occasionally, seldom, or never. Although the LBDQ has been frequently used to study leadership, its suitability as a measuring instrument has been questioned (Charters 1964). The principal criticism of this instrument has to do with validity; there is little, if any, evidence that the LBDQ measures what it purports to measure.

Fiedler's contingency theory of leadership recognizes the importance of the situation or context in which leadership occurs. Fiedler conceptualizes how the characteristics of the leader and the situation interact to determine leader effectiveness. The essence of the theory is that effective leadership is dependent upon the fit between the motivation of the leader and the favorableness of the situation in which the leader exists and performs. Specifically, Fiedler argues that relationship-motivated leaders will be more effective than task-motivated leaders in situations of moderate favorableness. The reverse holds in highly favorable situations; under those situational circumstances Fiedler expects a task-motivated leader to be more effective than a relationship-motivated leader. The degree to which a situation is favorable depends upon: (1) the quality of the leader-member relations—the warmer and friendlier, the more favorable; (2) the nature of the tasks performed by the subordinate—the more structured, the more favorable; and (3) the positional power of the leader—the greater the positional power, the more favorable.

This theory has two main shortcomings. First, the theory fails to offer any meaningful explanations for the specified relationships. For example, Fiedler asserts that task-motivated leaders will be more effective than relationship-motivated leaders when leader-member relations are friendly, the tasks performed by subordinates are highly structured, and the positional power of the leader is relatively great. Unfortunately, Fiedler never explains why the task-motivated leader is more likely to be effective than the relationship-motivated leader under these circumstances. Since the major premises of the theory have not been explicated, it is impossible for researchers to test the theory's underlying assumptions, and thereby gauge its soundness as a theory. Also, the theory has very weak empirical support in both educational and noneducational settings. Data offered in support of the theory are often in the hypothesized direction but fail to attain statistical significance.

The studies that follow Fiedler's approach to leadership rely on the Least Preferred Co-Worker (LPC) Scale. The LPC instrument measures the esteem in which leaders hold the person with whom they have had the most difficulty in getting a job done. The leader describes this person by a variety of adjectival pairs such as pleasant-unpleasant, helpful-frustrating, and gloomy-cheerful. The conceptual meaning of these scores has changed over time. Most recently, Fiedler interprets the LPC as an index of a leader's motivational hierarchy; high scores reflect a relationship-motivated leader while low scores indicate a task-motivated leader. This measure is even more suspect than Halpin's LBDQ because it lacks test-retest reliability and construct, content, predictive, and concurrent validity. The low test-retest reliability is particularly damaging, since Fiedler regards the motivational orientation of the leader as a stable characteristic.

While both Halpin's and Fiedler's studies have been criticized as lacking empirical support, both theorists have helped generate further thought about possible ways of understanding leadership. More specifically, these studies have made a significant contribution to understanding the nature of leadership within a specific organization at a specific point in time. The studies have focused on the leader and tried to determine the psychological, situational, and behavioral characteristics that provide for leadership. While no conclusive, consensual agreement has been reached about the nature of leadership, these approaches have succeeded in moving the discussion of leadership away from the "Great Person" trait concept and toward a contextual understanding of leadership.

Collegial Theory

The college presidency of the early twentieth century is viewed differently than the beleaguered chief of the college campus in the 1980s. Indeed, Professor March's "organized anarchy" model of college administration has gained wide credence among students of college governance. March characterizes the modern institution of higher education as an organization that has problematic goals, an unclear technology, and fluid participation. He elaborates: "The American college or university is a prototypic, organized anarchy. It doesn't know what it is doing. Its goals are either vague or in dispute. Its technology is familiar, but not understood. Its major participants wander in and out of the organization" (March and Cohen 1974, p. 3).

The contrast with the way other theorists describe presidents and colleges from another era is stark. "Great individuals ... make a college great" (Dodds 1962, p. 13). "Upon the college presidents of the country, more than upon any other group of persons, falls the responsibility for the well-being of higher education" (Stoke 1959, p. vii). Finally, "Only a president can effectively combine tradition and vigor to gain an understanding of, and response from, the complex of cooperating constituencies" (Brown 1969, p. 19). Brown and the other students of this persuasion see a college as operating in the long shadow of a great person, and individual effort can effect much change.

We have, then, a view of a college directed by, in William Moore's (1971) words, a "blind man on a freeway," and another view that subscribes to the "Great Person" theory of leadership. One question that can be asked is how the same institution had at one point in time a leader who was able to create great changes, and at another point in time a leader who presided over anarchy. Burns's notion of forms and types of leadership can help provide an answer.

Certainly there are form and type differences between the founder of a liberal arts college who has carte blanche to create a curriculum, faculty, and student type, and the president who leads an institution with a hundred-year history, fiscal problems, and an organizational saga set before he or she entered office. One individual can be seen as a transformer, where individual charisma can play an important role, while the other individual is one who leads within a bureaucracy in a transactional form. Simply stated: the life history of an organization demands different kinds of leaders. Burns disagrees with March and maintains that leadership, although difficult, is possible within a bureaucracy. March, on the other hand, feels it is quite difficult for an individual to create change in an organization. The outcomes "of the university do not much depend on the college president. His capabilities are limited, and his response is limited by his capabilities" (March and Cohen 1974, p. 45). If March is correct, one should not expect great changes to come from the president's office. J. Douglas Brown's views, however, speak for a reemergence of presidential power and authority, based on impressions of presidents of an earlier time.

It is interesting to note that theorists of both persuasions arrived at their conclusions by using similar methodologies. While March was more systematic in understanding the daily activities of college presidents, March, Brown, and the other mentioned theorists created their models by studying in-depth portraits of individual presidents from a specific time. Again, the different time periods and individuals studied could account for the different answers reached concerning the effectiveness of a college president.

We have seen that there are theories that intertwine, overlap, or conflict with one another. The Great Person theory of leadership is essentially how Brown describes a college leader. Bureaucratic transactional leadership helps explain March's organized anarchy. The contingency theory of leadership, however, conflicts with the idea that a college can exist in the "long shadow of a great man." All of these theories of leadership examine the individual within a particular setting, attribute characteristics to the individual, posit possible avenues by which he or she can lead, and then seek to contextualize leadership, before finally determining how much of an input the individual can have in an institution. The conclusion ultimately relies on a conception of the individual's ability or inability to change societal reality. Further exploration of the assumptions and theoretical underpinnings of much of the research on leadership gives rise to three distinct problems.

CRITIQUE OF PREVIOUS WORK AND AN ALTERNATIVE APPROACH

Historical Context

Most research on leadership is either time-bound or time-free. The work of Professor March fits quite well the conception of a college president during the troubled times of the late 1960s. Similarly, the leadership behavior of an individual in a contrived group setting may also fit that particular group quite well. To generalize from either of these settings, however, appears flawed if one takes into account that individuals, groups, and institutions have distinct histories by which they define themselves. As Berger and Luckmann note:

> Institutions further imply historicity and control. Reciprocal typifications of actions are built up in the course of a shared history. They cannot be created instantaneously. Institutions always have a history, of which they are the products. It is impossible to understand any institution adequately without an understanding of the historical process in which it was produced (1966, pp. 54-55).

Surely, March's conception of a college president as a "driver out of control on an icy patch of freeway" would not apply to men like White, Jordan, or Harper—men of an earlier era. At the same time, leadership in a contrived group—members of an experimental psychology class, for example—does not take into account the possibility that members define themselves, and their leader, in terms of a commonly held ideology or belief system acquired in an institution over time. One thesis of this book is that an educational organization will often have a common binding ideology, and to ignore this fact is to misinterpret how leadership functions. Burton Clark speaks about this common belief system: "Believers define themselves by their organizational affiliation, and in their bond to other believers they share an intense sense of the unique" (1980, p. 605). To discuss leadership divorced from its historical context appears to neglect an important aspect of how one reaches a common definition of leadership. Accordingly, we should not be surprised that the definition of leadership is highly ambiguous, and lacks consensual understanding.

Ambiguity of the Concept

Thomas Carlyle and James MacGregor Burns are examples of writers who spoke of leadership within a broad framework. Halpin, on the other hand, looks at two specific variables—*Initiating Structure* and *Consideration*—and defines a leader's success within the confines of those variables. A successful leader to Fiedler is an individual who has positive relations with his or her subordinates and can structure tasks in a clear, precise manner. Obviously, it does not necessarily follow that an individual adept at structuring tasks or who is considerate of subordinates' feelings is also someone who Carlyle or Burns would characterize as a successful leader.

There has been little agreement on the concept of leadership. In the last 20 years the field has seen a narrowing of the conceptual base and a movement toward understanding particular aspects of leader behavior. The road to clarity has been away from the overarching concept of leadership that Aristotle had in mind. While researchers have dropped the desire to generalize about leadership, they still seek to generalize about the specific aspects of leadership they have chosen to study. The particular variables studied, however, may have no meaning once removed from the historical context in which they have been considered. Furthermore, the measures and values used to study leadership, in general, may have little, or no, validity when studying educational organizations.

Measures and Values

Alex Bavelas states: "It is obviously impossible to define 'good leaders' without reference to a system of values" (1977, p. 325). It is necessary to amend his statement to include "and agreement as to what determinants should be measured." For example, most of the work that has been done with the contingency model of leadership concerns *interacting* groups—air force bomber crews or basketball teams, for example. These groups work closely together, and group cohesion is a necessity if the task is to be accomplished. Presumably, defining leadership effectiveness within these groups is relatively easy. A basketball team that wins many games, or a B-29 bomber crew that hits its targets, can be deemed successful.

Two problems arise when we try to apply this terminology to educational organizations. First, most educational organizations are not interacting, but *coacting* groups. Although a common task is present (teaching students, for example), group cohesion is not a necessity for the success of the group. Each group member in a loosely coordinated system with ambiguous goals does his or her task without the necessary support or work demanded in interacting groups.

Second, educational organizations do not have one end result that can define a leader's success. That is, a college president who makes the institution financially stable, but in so doing engenders faculty rebellion might not be deemed a "successful" leader. Education has a multiplicity of outcomes that defy a single measuring scale. Further, the process of education can often be as important as the outcomes. A college president who demands academic excellence by rote learning may be deemed a failure by an institution that wants students to question their values in the process of reaching the mastery of specific skills. Thus, within education one needs to consider not only how to measure a leader's effectiveness in terms of a multiplicity of goals, but also by the methods the leader takes to achieve those end results. What one needs, then, is to undertake a much more fine-grained and detailed analysis of leadership than has previously been done.

AN ALTERNATIVE FRAME

We stray momentarily from the discussion of leadership in higher education in order to consider how people construct societal reality. That is, rather than discuss an individual's ability or inability to create change we first need to place that individual within a societal web of consciousness. The investigation turns itself away from two assumptions: (1) present actions are merely the sum of past histories and (2) one can understand decision making and their outcomes by assuming that the truth of the situation resides within interactions. This analysis agrees with Pierre Bourdieu when he states:

> We are insisting ... that "interpersonal" relations are never, except in appearance, individual-to-individual relationships and that the truth of the interaction is never entirely contained in the interaction. This is what social psychology and interaction or ethnomethodology forget when, reducing the objective structure of their interaction in a particular situation and group, they seek to explain everything that occurs in an experimental or observed interaction in terms of the experimentally controlled characteristics of the situation such as the relative spatial positions of the participants or the nature of the channels used (1979, p. 81).

That which binds people together is based neither on interactionist principles nor on psychological variations that offer individual-based interpretations of situations. What is needed is a way of orchestrating the sociological, psychological, political, economic, and even religious forces into a single vision. The understanding of objective structures of consciousness and their relationships to organizations requires a broader framework than that of interactionist methodology. An alternative view of societal consciousness posits that there is within an organization a dialectical process between historical structures and individual interpretations of those structures.

Historical structures integrate past experiences, functioning not as a unilinear progression, but rather as a matrix of perceptions and actions that link objective and cognitive tasks. Actors within an organization appear in an interconnected web of relationships that existed prior to the individual's entrance into the organization, and the individual's interpretation and action upon that structure. For example, a college with a hundred-year history will have a system of the way the actors decide tasks and decisions that may be implicit within the organizational web. A new actor who enters the organization will need to learn how the system functions while the organization undergoes a transformation, however minute, because of the entrance of a new actor. In this light, systems of classification of the social order are created out of an arbitrariness dependent upon a subjective interpretation of the natural world. Consciousness of daily life and knowledge of history enable individuals to act according to particular forms of codes and discourse. Individuals live in what they conceive to be an ordered world and make sense of this world through subjective interpretations of the objective structure. Structure, thus defined, relates to the individual elements which the system determines to be the complete set of possible elements for the organization.

Organizations large and small create their own histories. As individuals function in organizational activities they adopt a full range of behaviors to which the organization has given sanction and legitimacy. Organizations, whether they be rigidly prescriptive such as, for example, the army or loosely affiliated such as a business, control, direct, and modify the behaviors of their members. Such control is neither mechanistic nor unidirectional. Each individual interacts in discrete ways and places an individual interpretation on whatever role the organization mandates.

Again, individuals do not merely exist according to interactionist principles. Greater structures are imposed upon them. Codes of style and action, the different languages members of these organizations use, dress, ceremonies, stories, and other cultural artifacts necessarily form and shape the way individuals act within an organization. Institutions, by the very fact of their existence, control human conduct by setting up predefined patterns of conduct which channel it in one direction as against the many other directions that would theoretically be possible (Berger and Luckmann 1967, p. 55). Yet an historical structure is not an endless progression of lifeless facts that imposes itself on present-day actors. This interpretation rejects a reified historical past that is either static or mechanically placed upon people.

Organizations change, bend, are altered, by environmental influences and the actions of the individuals within the objective system. It is this dialectical relationship between the objective structure and individual consciousness that produces change within the organization. Individuals live within countless organizations, and the experiences within one organization undoubtedly can pose alternative avenues for restructuring another organization.

The framework discussed here views organizations in a light distinctly different from that of those theories previously discussed. This view neither speaks of organizations that change because of a heroic individual's actions, nor does it see individuals constrained by a Weberian straitjacket. There is neither an individual situated in an organization without reference to history, nor are there organizations which are merely historical products of progress. An alternative way of viewing an organization is not by considering historical "progress," or the inability to make progress, but by a consideration of the way actions occur. As Michel Foucault, the French philosopher, stated: "I don't say that humanity doesn't progress. I say that it is bad method to pose the problem as: 'How is it that we have progressed?' The problem is: how do things happen. And what happens now is not necessarily better or more advanced, or better understood than what happened in the past" (1980, p. 50).

When one views an organization from the perspective of "how things happen," one anticipates the problems that confront previous work on leadership. If we look at the organization as a matrix of forces, we necessarily incorporate the history of the institution into the study. Conceptual clarity comes not from a preformed construct but rather by way of the actors' interpretation of leadership. To uncover how events occur, one investigates not only the final results but also the measures and values used to achieve those results. From the vantage point of the alternative frame three points guide the interpretation: time, space, and communication. We discuss time in order to consider the historical context of the institution. Spatial relationships demonstrate nonverbal ways that individuals interact with one another. Communication refers to how the actors' discursive practices constitute leadership. Finally, a discussion of power, as a value-laden construct, accentuates the practices of time, space, and communication that outline "how things happen."

Time

The repetition of an act, the entropy of the organism, and the rate at which the organism repeats the act and/or dies, all provide markers for an understanding of how things happen. A linear model of reality which places acts within set chunks of demarcated periods is bereft of a sense of how change takes place. Within this view one is forced to see time, and the acts that occur within it, as a continuous movement, as a succession of epochal durations, advancing in a unilinear progression.

Instead of a cyclical or unilinear model of time, an alternative portrait is to view time as a pendulum, discontinuous, with a succession of alternations and full stops. We distinguish intervals not as time zones set in hours or days, but as periods created in social life by society. The Western idea that people fill in blocks of time, that a particular day or time period is when we must fulfill a given act, has confused the matter so that we see time ordering life rather than viewing a community's life as a series of interconnected—and freeswinging—pendulums.

An organization exists not only by the internal structures and cycles of itself, but also by its connection to, and intertwining with, the larger societal, political, social, and economic structure. In an investigation of leadership it is critical to consider how these different pendulums interconnect with and overlap one another. To continue the metaphor: a grandfather clock has a wide swinging mechanism, and it is only at the most extreme ends of the community pendulum that crisis occurs, yet throughout the swinging of the mechanism change undoubtedly appears. This view takes into account how the larger society tempers and mediates change. The generative transformation of organizational structures takes place not because an individual—a "leader"—wills that change, but depends on the larger societal context with which the organization is connected. To ask if a system undergoes radical change with the elevation of a new person to the presidency, for example, is not helpful; we must think of the epochs themselves and understand how they order time. To believe that change is a universal due to an individual's actions is to deny the complex interplay and interrelationships among the organization, the larger social history, and the placement of the actors within the organization. In educational organizations one needs to consider not only how to measure a leader's effectiveness in terms of a multiplicity of goals, but also by the methods the leader takes to achieve those end results.

Space

Different spheres of space—public and private—suggest different meanings to organizational participants. Public space refers to areas where groups of people come together for any number of activities (informal meeting areas such as a mailroom, for example, or specified function areas such as a library, or lunchroom). Public areas are spatial domains that no one individual "owns." Public space provides areas where most often status differentials do not automatically occur.

Private space concerns areas that organizational participants cede to an individual or group of individuals. An individual's office is the best example of a private area that "belongs" to one actor. A meeting room where one group regularly meets and the table and chairs are set in a specified way is another example of private space.

Obviously, examples can also appear where public space is used privately, or vice versa. Two individuals can regularly sit at a specific location in a public area such as a lunchroom so that organizational participants cede the area to the two individuals as private space. Conversely, an individual whose work area has changed from a room with walls to one without walls most likely has seen a spatial transformation from private to public space of his/her domain.

Physical gestures, such as winking and nodding to someone or patting an individual on the back, are private examples conducted publicly as signs of support or interpersonal recognition. An individual's clothes or where one parks a car, sits, and walks are additional spatial forms that connote nonverbal "signs of power, and influence how people perceive of one another's relationships." Body language and spatial patterns lend the reader a fuller understanding of "how things happen" than if one concentrated solely on oral discourse.

Communication

The investigation of communicative codes and operations rests on the belief that within this web of relationships communicative forms enable a collectively shared pattern of symbols and actions to occur that produce "how things happen." Communication (and language lies within this domain) does not structure organizational life, but is an act, an event, by the participants within the organization.

How individuals use language—how they communicate with one another—frames their understanding of reality. Louis Pondy speaks of Martin Luther King's ability, for example, not by speaking of his "dream," but by speaking of his ability to articulate that dream:

> The real power of Martin Luther King was not only that he had a dream, but that he could describe it, that it became public, and therefore accessible to millions of people ... If the leader can put it into words, then the meaning of what the group is doing becomes a *social* fact. The meaning can then be exchanged, talked about, modified, amplified, and used for internal processing of information (1978, pp. 94-95; his emphasis).

By studying how a leader communicates to different constituencies one can then comprehend how the organization structures its reality and perceives leadership. Through the analysis of communication we gain an understanding of the coordinates of the institution, how language affects the actions of the organization, and what the leader's position is within these coordinates.

Clearly, an analysis of discourse within the modern organization will not only look at oral methods of communication, but also at written artifacts that exemplify how people communicate with one another in writing. This form of analysis explicates how written and oral codes interact, contradict, or support one another as the actors transmit messages. Communication also rests not only on words, but on a host of unspoken acts and events.

Similarly, when we undertake an analysis of "how things happen," we enter into a dialectic that forces us to ask how things do not happen. That is to say, to investigate language, processes of decision making, or the decisions themselves is only half of the story. The silence that occurs within a system can provide as much insight about what happens as can the analysis of the stated actions of actors within the organization. Simply put, the researcher needs to record more than that a college president conferred with three vice presidents before making a decision. It is also imperative to consider those whose voices were not heard and those decisions that were not made.

To speak of systematic change in this manner orients the interpretation of an organization—and leadership within it—away from individualistic renditions of how things happen and toward a more comprehensive analysis. Bourdieu states in *Men and Machines*:

> A certain type of pessimist functionalism which imputes the effects of domination to a single, central will, makes it impossible to see the contribution the agents (including the dominated ones) make, willingly or knowingly or not, to the process of domination, through the relationship between their dispositions—linked to the social conditions in which they were produced and the expectations and interests entailed by their positions within the fields of struggle for which words like state, church, or party are shorthand terms (1981, p. 308).

The crux of the matter is to view the organizational determinants of time, space, and communication as components of a systemic power structure wherein individuals struggle for power. To reiterate, the analysis of time allows for the view of an organization as an ongoing tale with a particular history that is dynamic rather than frozen. Spatial patterns provide nonverbal clues about organizational dynamics. The study of communication demonstrates how linguistic techniques come together to produce organizational perceptions and decisions. In order to study how things happen we look at the myriad of relationships and transformations at work within the organization that make available to the actors the manifold power relations that make up organizational reality.

Power

Through an analysis of time, space, and communication a researcher can begin to delineate the structure of power, and, hence, leadership within that structure. The purpose, again, is not to show how political practices determine the meaning and form of an organization, but rather to unpack how history gives place to definite types of discourse within which political practices occur.

Power neither exists by socially induced traits nor resides outside of a set discourse of interconnected elements. Foucault writes:

> The important thing is not to attempt some kind of deduction of power starting from its centre and aimed at the discovery of the extent to which it permeates into the base, of the degree to which it reproduces itself down to and including the most molecular elements of society. One must rather conduct an ascending analysis of power, starting, that is, from its infinitesimal mechanisms, which each have their own techniques and tactics, and then see how these mechanisms of power have been—and continue to be—utilized (1980, p. 99).

In this light there are as many forms of power as there are types of relationships. All groups and individuals within a constituted organization exercise and are subjected to mechanisms of power. Certain categories of people—students, for example—have little ability to exercise power, but nevertheless few members of groups do not find some means of exercising power if only over one another. Power, therefore, is not to be identified with a role or an individual, in that the role, or governing apparatus of an organization, is only the end result of the multiplicity of networks and interconnected links of an organization. It is the task of this analysis to analyze the operation of these networks and links.

Referring to the discussion of time, we analyze the operation of power not as static, unchanging, or divorced from time, but rather as an unceasing struggle wherein relations to power are transformed, strengthened, or possibly reversed. The ubiquity of power demonstrates itself throughout organizational processes and decisions. This form of analysis points the discussion away from accepting leader-follower relations, or a preconfigured study of who holds the power and who it is who must follow. Foucault offers four principles which guide this form of analysis: (1) rule of immanence, (2) rule of continuous variations, (3) rule of double conditioning, and (4) rule of the tactical polyvalence of discourse (1980, pp. 185-186).

The *rule of immanence* relates to how this discussion of power began; to speak of an organization is to speak of power, and, hence, we cannot isolate the idea of power from the organization. One needs to consider leadership not as a characteristic of an individual, but instead look to the local centers within which power resides. In a continuation of that idea, the *rule of continuous variations* moves the study of power away from leader-follower relations or the concept that certain individuals are innately powerful. Instead of discussing power in a distributive form, we look at the organization as a "matrix of transformation" wherein power resides.

The *rule of double conditioning* speaks for an historical understanding of the situation. The study of an organization necessarily must view the relationships and processes and not isolate particular variables for study. This rule refers to more than simply the scale (microscopic, macroscopic) with which one studies the organization. "This process should be seen," says Foucault, "not as a mere difference of scale, but rather as the double conditioning of a strategy by specific tactics and of tactics by an overall strategy" (1980, p. 186). That is, to study a situation one does not set up a dialectic wherein false analogies lie, but rather attempts to delineate how particular aspects of an organization relate to the larger societal frame.

Finally, the *rule of the tactical polyvalence of discourses* refers to the section on communication previously discussed. Discourse produces, transmits, and reinforces power as well as undermines it. Neither is there a uniformity to discourse nor can the communicative processes of leader and follower be isolated. Discourse derives from a multiplicity of elements that intersect in a complex, unstable way, "as instruments and effects of power, but also as points of resistance" (Foucault 1980, p. 186).

Prior to a consideration of the method one uses to undertake a study of this alternative frame, a brief summary is in order. An organization has an ideology based upon its history, individual interpretations of that history, and the environmental influences of the moment. Structures are neither static nor progressive but rather a matrix within which transformations occur. One studies these transformations by analyzing communication in order to understand "how things happen." Communication refers to how the actors within the organization transmit messages, which necessarily includes more than a study of oral language. The study of how things happen demands a study of how things do not happen, and which actors are not included in particular processes and decisions.

The underlying assumption of this work is that power lies throughout the system and does not reside in a single role or individual. One cannot differentiate a study of an organization and a study of power in an organization—to speak of an organization is to speak of power. To understand how an organization assembles itself and operates one must look at the organization as a matrix—a web—within which power resides.

It is now possible to unite this discussion of an alternative analysis of organizations with leadership in higher education. This alternative perspective allows a study of college leadership that moves away from interactionist or individual-based studies. A hierarchical discussion of "haves" and "have-nots" is inappropriate due to the rule of immanence. Power exists throughout the organization and must be studied in a holistic sense. Leadership, as a social construct, is a variation of power that interconnects with the distributive forms of power. The historical conditioning of the organization, as well as individual interpretations of that history and present acts, demands an interpretation focused not on individual action but on a broader framework. Finally, the investigation of leadership occurs through the communicative processes of the organization. The question, then, is which methodology is most helpful in order to interpret how things happen within this matrix of transformation of an organization of higher education.

METHODOLOGY

Anthropology as a discipline provides a methodology which operates within the context that has been discussed. Ethnographic research attempts to record and describe culturally significant behavior of a particular people. Conklin notes the description

> requires a long period of intimate study and residence in a small, well-defined community, knowledge of the spoken language, and the employment of a wide range of observational techniques including prolonged face-to-face contacts with members of the local group, direct participation in some of the group's activities, and a greater emphasis on intensive work with informants, than on the use of documentary or survey data (1968, p. 173).

The ethnographer looks at settings from a cultural perspective rather than a physiological or psychological one, and the researcher makes a rigorous attempt to stay value-free. The research discussed in the first part of this chapter has tried to prove or disprove a particular theory; ethnographic work, however, attempts to enter the situation without biases and seeks to understand the situation as the participants see it. A strength of ethnography is the multiple methods it employs to gain a perspective on the situation. Participant observation, formal and informal interviewing, and content analysis provide the ethnographer with a multitude of ways of understanding and describing the situation.

There has been almost no formal ethnographic research done in the field of higher education. In many respects it is paradoxical that higher education has escaped ethnographic studies. Erving Goffman (1961) describes *total institutions* as organizations where all aspects of life occur in the same place and under the same authority; each member carries out daily activities in the same proximity as a large group of members; the activities are highly scheduled and coordinated; and there is a single script designed for the organization. Prisons, boarding schools, and residential universities are examples of total institutions.

Colleges and universities also have set geographic boundaries in which its clientele live and work. While there are not generational-kinship similarities comparable to those in a tribal village, there is a generational cross-section, and some people—faculty or administrators—may reside within the community until death. Thus, it appears that institutions of higher education are appropriate settings for ethnographic study. The question then turns to how one states the problem so that the definition of ethnography will be upheld. If we return to the interpretation of ethnography previously given it will be helpful to apply that definition to a university or college setting. Ethnographic research calls for:

1. *"a long period of intimate study and residence ..."*
   The researcher would be best suited to spend an academic year at the institution in order to observe a full "season" of the unit of analysis. Shorter periods of time that stretch beyond one season also allow the researcher constantly to reevaluate the findings and data. What is not desired is "blitzkreig ethnography" (Rist 1979) where one person spends a minimal amount of time at the research site and never returns. While one short visit to an institution may be helpful for many reasons, that visit defies the definition given here.

2. *" ... in a small, well-defined community ..."*
   Residential institutions that have geographic boundaries and fit Goffman's term of total institutions appear best-suited for study. Multiplex institutions with upward of 10,000 students do not seem appropriate for a study by a single researcher; there is simply too much to record and observe. Conversely, commuter institutions that rely largely on part-time staff also would not fit within the definition. The imperative is for the researcher to observe a set number of people participating in a wide range of activities. If the institution is too large the researcher will not get an understanding of the clientele; if the institution is too unstructured or loosely defined, the researcher will not see the clientele participating in a wide set of activities.

3. *" ... knowledge of the spoken language ..."*
   The ethnographer must have the ability to comprehend the technology in use at the institution, as well as how the governance structure, financial undertaking, and a wide range of other activities operate. As an anthropologist enters the field with an understanding for terms such as "kinship" or "ritual," so must the researcher for higher education

understand the operative words in collegiate institutions. In addition, the ethnographers should have a feel for "traditional" ethnography so that they have an understanding of the theoretical implications and assumptions of the research tool.

4. " *... and the employment of a wide range of observational techniques.*"
   As stated, participant observation, unstructured interviews, and a wealth of other data collection methods need to be employed by the researcher. Ethnography demands talking with as many different groups as possible—administrators, faculty, students, and staff, for example—while at the same time working with a few individuals from different constituencies in-depth. The observational techniques should account not only for the major events of the group such as graduation, Board of Trustees meetings, and the like, but also the petty, mundane affairs of everyday life. The researcher needs to make sense of the organizational "web" not only from his or her standpoint but also from the view of the people within the web. That is, the researcher must understand the life of the "village" not only from an etic standpoint, but also how the natives themselves view their web.

Reference has been made to a "cultural understanding of the problem," and the problem as it has been defined concerns a modern organization. Prior to discussing the organization itself we must define *culture*, and within that definition, *organizational culture*. One of the many interpretations of culture is by Clifford Geertz, who says, "Man is an animal suspended in webs of significance he himself has spun. I take culture to be those webs, and the analysis of it to be therefore not an experimental science in search of law, but an interpretive one in search of meaning" (1973, p. 5). The researcher approaches the institution to be studied as if it were an interconnected web that cannot be understood unless one looks not only at the structure and natural laws of that web, but also at the actors' interpretation of the web itself.

Organizational culture, then, is the study of particular webs of significance within a organizational setting. That is, we look at an organization as a traditional anthropologist would study a particular village or clan. The researcher tries not to preform questions and assumptions, but works from a cultural model that implies the actors within the social setting have a historical consciousness, an ideology, and a way of doing things. Obvious differences occur when one compares modern organizations and those studied by traditional anthropologists. When one thinks of ethnographic work, a tribe or village comes to mind that has definite geographic boundaries where at least three different generations of people live. An ethnographic study in an institutional setting, however, cannot be defined by a structured geographic boundary; nor will it have generational kinship similarities to that of a traditional tribal group. Yet, as shown, ethnographic research can adapt itself to collegiate institutions, and Goffman's sense of a total institution is a close fit to certain colleges and universities.

The question arises concerning to what extent the use of anthropology and its method enables the researcher to answer questions that previous studies have either neglected or have been unable to answer. As stated, studies of leadership in higher education most often neglect the historical context of leadership, environmental influences, and how the institutional web is formed and altered. Further, previous studies have failed to capture the way a leader reflects and incorporates the ideology of an institution. Good ethnography, however, explores the complexity of real life and attempts understandings of those questions that previous studies have left unanswered.

The attempt to define leadership holistically and within the web of the social construction of reality will be aided if the institution has a particular ideology. Within the myriad institutions of higher education this book has used as its setting a college that, in the words of John Higham, has "an explicit system of general beliefs that give large bodies of people a common identity and purpose, a common program of action, and a standard for self-criticism" (1974, p. 10). The institution must necessarily have a unique history and background and see itself as having a distinct purpose. Burton Clark defines a college with a distinctive purpose in the following way:

All organizations have a social role, but only some have seized their role in the purposive way that we can call a mission. Then, among those that have been strongly purposive, only some are able to sustain and develop the mission over time to the point of success and acclaim. The mission is then transformed into an embracing saga. We are able to speak, then, of colleges (and other organizations) that become legendary, even heroic figures on the social stage (1970, p. 10).

To reiterate: the purpose of this study is to gain an understanding of how an institution constructs its ideology and, within that ideology, how leadership operates. The study investigates how such an institution arose, how people use a saga to create a sustained movement, and how leaders work within the cultural framework. A small liberal arts college with a clearly defined purpose fits the frame better than a large public institution, for example, where a broadly held ideology or common purpose may not exist. The intent is not to undertake a study of leadership that can be generalized to all institutions of higher education; rather the intense study of one institution provides information previously unavailable that will ultimately allow for a closer reading and interpretation of leadership than has previously been done. Further, the paradigm from which the investigation operates obviates problems that other theories encounter. Rather than decontextualize leadership, the study refers to time, space, and communication as a means to frame leadership within a socially constructed setting so that we see how the actors themselves defined leadership and how they came to believe and act the way they did. The "thick description" (Geertz 1973) of one institution opens the way for a comparative understanding of leadership both within the field of higher education and within a broader context. Geertz states:

> The relevance of historical fact for sociological analysis does not rest on the proposition that there is nothing in the present but the past, which is not true, or on easy analogies between extinct institutions and the way we live now. It rests on the perception that though both the structure and the expressions of social life change, the inner necessities that animate it do not. Thrones may be out of fashion, and pageantry too; but political authority still requires a cultural frame in which to define itself and advance its claim, and so does opposition to it (1983, pp. 142-143).

We turn, then, to the distinctive College of Mother Mary (CMM) and first consider a historical sketch of the institution.

Chapter II

Historical Framework

A certain sense of history hovers about the college as its actors prepare for the drama. Individuals within the organization naturally refer to history as they go about their daily business. As with any history, it is selective history. This chapter shows how the college interprets its past in order to demonstrate how subjective interpretations of an objective structure come into play as the drama unfolds.

The chapter looks at College of Mother Mary within the context of collegiate institutions of the 1980s. We consider the macro pendulum of time in order to see the contextualized present. We further discuss how people communicate this sense of the past to audiences in the present. Specifically, how do actors use their historical knowledge to act on their present? How does history objectify personal experience such that leadership roles become circumscribed by environmental forces? Here is an institution that struggles to develop a distinctive saga that meets the needs of its constituencies in the 1980s. In part, its past determines the way the actors conceive of the struggle, and how they will—or will not—eventually define their collectively shared knowledge as a saga.

HISTORY OF THE COLLEGE

Sisters of Mother Mary

The Sisters of Mother Mary, the Order which founded the college, began in France during the closing years of the eighteenth century. Two women, one a peasant and the other an aristocrat, joined forces in response to the needs of their times and a calling from God to establish an Order of Sisters dedicated to teaching girls. The peasant woman, Catherine LaFarge, often receives mention as the force and strength of the movement. An historian of the Order began her work by saying, "When a group assembles to do a great work for God and Country, there is ever back of the movement a dominating factor, a man or woman who crystallizes in the *self* the highest ideals of the age, who gathers up in a forceful personality the best of the past and present, who meets the future with that unerring sense which we, for the lack of a better term, call vision" (Mother Mary [Sisters of] 1926, p. 1).

Because of the political climate of the time, the women needed to transfer their order from France to Belgium. The peasant woman arrived in Belgium physically paralyzed, yet actively ambitious to help spread the word of God. Two of her expressions have been passed down during the years to exemplify the basic premise of the Order: "I must have many little souls to teach them to love the Good God," and "Teach them what they need to know about life." These sayings point toward the religiosity of the Order, as well as the importance of teaching for the Sisters of Mother Mary.

In 1804, on the Feast of the Sacred Heart, Blessed Catherine LaFarge regained the strength of her limbs after the Order had initiated a novena in her honor. Soon after this event the Order grew rapidly so that 15 houses had been established by the time of her death in 1816. Since its inception the Order has been administered and staffed by women to teach women. It differed in three respects from other religious orders: it was ungraded, unbound to the Office of the Church, and uncloistered. Most orders had two grades of nuns—choir and lay—which accounted for status differentials within the Order. Within the Sisters of Mother Mary there were no grades, and all women were equal. Because they were not cloistered, they did not constantly pray the orders of the Church. At that time the cloistering of religious women was far more common than an Order's dedicating itself to the teaching of a previously untaught group—girls, particularly poor girls.

The Order sent its first group of nuns to America in 1840. They arrived in New York and traveled overland to Ohio where they opened classes in January 1841. Before the year was out a well-known missionary who worked on the West Coast had stopped by the school to investigate the willingness of the Sisters to found a congregation among the Indian tribes in the Pacific Northwest. Although the priest met with a positive reception, the Order's leaders noted that much work remained to be done in Ohio. For the priest to establish a second congregation in America he had to talk with the Belgian Mother Superior.

In 1842 the priest returned to his native Belgium and received a hero's welcome. His letters and work among American Indians were well known in Europe and with the Sisters of Mother Mary. His request that the Sisters send a small group with him to the western coast of America was initially met with some resistance from the Bishop and the head of the Order. Obviously, sending European women to an "uncivilized" part of the world caused consternation on the part of those who made the decision; nevertheless, they finally acceded to the priest's persuasive arguments. In late 1843, accompanied by the priest and a few other religious men, six Sisters set sail for America. Although the Bishop and Mother Superior had hesitated about sending young women to America, the young Sisters' enthusiasm was unbridled. They went to America to teach girls who had never had the opportunity to hear God's words, and that meant living in places that demanded self-sacrifice.

As soon as they left, the Sisters realized what the romantic picture of self-sacifice actually meant. Turbulent ocean waters almost capsized the ship. They laid anchor in Valparaiso and had the ship fumigated, whereupon 1400 rats died. A hurricane struck as they rounded Patagonia which almost made the ship strike the rocky shores. Finally, as they approached the port of destination they mistakenly entered a shallow channel of 3 fathoms—when it should have been 30—and everyone aboard prepared for a shipwreck. They arrived unharmed, but one of the priests later wrote, "We escaped by miracle."

The Sisters existed in America amid malaria and squalid living conditions. Due to a lack of workmen, they built their own house and chapel and immediately began teaching Indians. Life in the Northwest was initially all they had hoped for in that they were able to teach those who had never before experienced Christianity. Within a year of their arrival they had opened a thriving boarding school. The six Sisters who came from Belgium initially did all of the work. There were hardships. Wild animals such as mountain lions and wolves constantly invaded the little settlement and made off with fowl and pigs. One of the Sisters wrote of their daily existence: "While some of us were busy in the interior of the house, others were occupied with out-door work, digging ditches, setting an orchard, making roads, irrigating our vegetable garden. The method of the last occupation was as follows: we put a large barrel on a wheel barrow which we rolled down to the stream, filled, and rolled back. This we repeated again and again" (Mother Mary [Sisters of] 1926, p. 85).

In 1846 another contingent of Sisters left the Mother House to work in America. The six Sisters arrived after an equally adventuresome voyage with fresh supplies—books, tools, leather, linen, coffee, sugar, and a stove. No sooner had they arrived than a fire swept through the buildings and destroyed the entire mission. By 1848 they had partially rebuilt the settlement, and they had begun another mission in a nearby town. Problems arose, however, during the next two years which made Sister Jean Marie, the head of the mission, contemplate a move to California. The murder of a Protestant minister and 12 other people by Indians created a climate of fear and mistrust. Catholic missionaries came under suspicion because they lived and worked among the Indians. In the annals of the day an author reported:

> These accusations ... aroused the deepest and intensest prejudice against the Bishop and the Catholic Church generally, and the excitement became so great that the American volunteers, on leaving the valley in pursuit of the Indians, said that their first shots would be for the Bishop and his priests. For several months feeling ran so high that the Catholic churches and institutions were in danger of being burned (Mother Mary [Sisters of] 1926, p. 113).

The gold rush, the destruction of their mission, anti-Catholic sentiment, and unsanitary living conditions helped lure Sister Jean Marie to the sunny climate of California. Throughout their stay in the Northwest the Sisters had been in communication with the Mother House by written correspondence. Although the Sisters in Ohio and other American towns were distant from Europe, communication usually could be achieved within a few months. The Sisters in the Pacific Northwest, however, had to rely on the sporadic trips of cargo ships. Consequently, communication between the Mother House and this newest congregation was infrequent. The sisters had a freedom in decision making that existed in no other congregation. While local priests offered advice, the Sisters as often as not disregarded it.

Although the missions had attracted many children, Sister Jean Marie was content neither with the anti-Catholic atmosphere of the Northwest nor with the continued substandard living conditions. She had transmitted her dissatisfaction to the Mother Superior in Europe, and the advice from Europe was to make the best of things. The Mother Superior gave no one authority to move south. In 1851 yet another contingent of Sisters left Europe for the West Coast. Sister Jean Marie and another Sister traveled to California to meet them. Like the other Sisters sent to the West Coast, the new group's plans had been to work in the Northwest. When they arrived they found that Sister Jean Marie had other ideas; these women settled in the capital of California.

While in California, Sister Jean Marie had consulted with people about establishing a congregation. One person with whom she talked was a priest who recently had established a men's college. He assured Sister Jean Marie that there was a great need for a dedicated group of Sisters to establish schools and a college for women. Without consent from the Mother Superior in Belgium, and with much dissent from the congregation in the Northwest, Sister Jean Marie decided to move the congregation south. Rather than risk asking for advice from the Mother House and receiving a negative response, Sister Jean Marie simply informed the Mother Superior of her decision. Faced with a *fait accompli*, the Mother Superior accepted the decision, but also realized that a replacement for the strong-willed Sister Jean Marie had to be found. Decisions and advice had to come from Europe, and the western province had far surpassed its authority in its move to California. Even the bishop under whose authority they worked in the Northwest was unaware of their plans until they had been made definite.

Almost immediately upon their arrival in California in 1851, the Sisters planned for the creation of a college. The initial years in California may have been physically easier than those in the Northwest, but they were not without difficulty. Lack of finances and little knowledge of native languages were two major obstacles for the Sisters. The authoritarian will of Sister Jean Marie added to the trouble. Finally, they received word from Belgium that Sister Jean Marie had to leave the West Coast and return to Ohio; another less confrontational and more popular woman took charge of the western branch. They again set up houses, chapel, and school and attracted primarily settlers' children and poor Spanish-speaking girls. By this time the Sisters of Mother Mary had established other congregations throughout the world. The missions in the Pacific islands and South America occasionally sent one of their girls to California in order for them to be novices in the Order.

The Early Years

Beginnings. By 1868 the Sisters had established themselves sufficiently to begin a program that provided women with a two-year degree of higher learning. The state charter for the College of Mother Mary in 1868 made the college one of the first collegiate institutions on the West Coast. The college was the first institution for women west of the Rockies, and preceded any other college opened by the Sisters of Mother Mary in America by 14 years.

At that time in the United States the seeds of educational training for women had taken root. The work of Emma Willard at Waterbury and Troy, Catherine Beecher at Hartford, and Mary Lyon at Mount Holyoke, had successfully demonstrated to skeptics the capability of the female mind for coursework in higher education. Within 20 years after the Civil War coeducational institutions had been opened, as well as collegiate institutions for women such as Vassar, Smith, and Bryn Mawr.

While the development of the female intellect was definitely a goal of the College of Mother Mary (CMM), the main purpose of the institution was to enable Catholic girls to further their understanding of and devotion to God. CMM's aim was not to establish an early outpost of feminism; its goal was the furtherance of Catholic doctrine. At the same time an institution administered, taught, and attended solely by women was extraordinary both for the region and the times. Moreover, since its inception, religious freedom has been a cornerstone of CMM's principles. The first Board of Trustees meeting in 1868 stated: "The Catholic Religion shall be the only one professed by the Ladies of this Institution but there shall be no interference with the religious principles of those who profess a different creed; nor shall a scholar be allowed to conform to the Catholic religion without a written or verbal permission of her parents." We have, then, an institution founded for religious principles that accepted other religious opinions.

By 1870 the Sisters had established missions throughout California, and the academy and college remained in the capital. Two hundred and sixty-two boarders attended the academy, and it is difficult to differentiate between those who were college students and those who were not. At that time higher education throughout the country did not have the strict age and entrance requirements that stand as benchmarks for admission today. Harvard University, for example, had the best medical school in the country, yet when Charles Eliot assumed the presidency he discovered the following: "Any youth of honorable character could gain admission by registering and paying the admission fee. ... Large numbers ... could hardly sign their names to the register, and had difficulty in reading the simplest writing" (Cotton 1926, p. 127). Eliot proceeded to raise admission requirements, and he did it with the extensive financial support of men like Rockefeller and Morgan.

CMM had no such financial support. The Sisters arrived in California penniless, and the Mother House was unable to provide any substantial monetary support. Throughout their history the Sisters have survived financially at the college through the generous support of interested benefactors and alumni. Nevertheless, CMM slowly materialized into recognizable buildings and grounds. The Sisters had established the college in the small capital which within 20 years had taken on the trappings of a major western city. By the turn of the century College of Mother Mary no longer found itself in the secluded outskirts of a small city, but rather right in the middle of a bustling business district of warehouses and stores.

The CMM student in the latter part of the nineteenth century received recitation in theology, history, rhetoric, and Latin. The main components of the curriculum were music, elocution, and poetry. By the turn of the century courses in geology, mathematics, botany, and chemistry had been added. Recitations gradually gave way to lecture courses such as "Mental Philosophy," and the teachers challenged CMM students to use their minds not merely for memorization, but also for inductive analysis. From the outset, CMM was much more than a finishing school for daughters of the well-to-do. Emphasis remained on how to act like a Catholic lady, but curricular changes constantly pointed to the Sisters of Mother Mary's desire to increase intellectual curiosity and development.

The Sisters of Mother Mary, and hence the college, had their roots in a European tradition of structured guidelines and rules about how one defines education and the correct way for young women to act in society. In some respects CMM may have had more in common with an American military academy than its western counterparts such as Stanford University and the University of California at Berkeley. Students lived in a semicloistered environment where they could not leave the campus except at Christmas. In order for a young woman to visit her home once a month on Saturdays, she had to receive special permission from the Sisters. The college permitted the parents of a student to visit on Thursday afternoons, yet these visits had to be concluded by four o'clock. The "superioress" of the institution first read letters sent to and from students. Sisters confiscated any "romantic novels" students may have smuggled into the college, and the Sisters reprimanded parents for letting their child read such works. Daily prayer and mass existed for everyone.

Uniforms were the rule of the day. The Sisters created an atmosphere of modesty and unworldliness that gradually changed with the times. Gloves, hats, jewelry, the color of the trim of a girl's dress, were all points of concern and debate among students and administrators. Physical exercise, "gymnastic lessons" and waltzes made their way onto the campus, but only under strict supervision. The Sisters taught the girls sports such as lawn tennis and "hoops." Student entertainment meant the playing of musical instruments, performance of classical plays, and readings from the Bible.

As with most institutions of higher learning at that time, the administration of the college was minimal. The Board of Trustees were Sisters of the Order, and the head of the congregation doubled as president of the college. By the turn of the century, a question arose with regard to whether or not CMM should become a four-year institution offering the B.A. degree. The main point mitigating against the opening of a four-year college was the Sisters' hesitation in conforming to state requirements and accreditation standards. The Sisters felt their obligation to meet particular standards came from the Mother House and, ultimately, Rome; the demands of the state were intrusive and superfluous. If they had to meet those demands in order to become a four-year college they would remain with a two-year program that offered an A.A. degree for Catholic women.

At a trustees' meeting shortly after the turn of the century, much discussion focused on what form of higher education women should have after they finished their degree at CMM. Although some Sisters spoke up for making CMM a four-year institution, two actions ended discussion on the advisability of expanding CMM. First, as had happened with the Order's settlement in the Northwest, an unexpected storm destroyed much of the campus, and much effort had to be put into rebuilding, rather than creating new programs. Second, a letter arrived from Belgium that called for the withdrawal from accreditation because it would "open the way to higher education in an atmosphere in which faith might be lost" (McNamee 1967, p. 240). For the moment, the Sisters redirected their efforts toward creating more educational programs on the secondary level and strengthening the two-year A.A. degree.

By 1920 the "all-round training" at CMM ended with a two-year degree. Although the college included more than 10 buildings, many of these remained damaged from the disaster of the storm. The college also found itself in an area of the city unfit for young women—the commercial and business district. The middle-upper class neighborhood where they had founded the college had been transformed into an industrial area. Sister Anthony, head of the Order and President of the college, decided that the city's burgeoning size, coupled with industries surrounding CMM, necessitated the college's relocation.

Move to Rosewood. In casting about for a new college site, Sister Anthony settled on the former mansion of a wealthy Californian, Thomas Belchamp. Originally built as a summer house in 1865, the Belchamps sold the building in 1875. By 1920 it had passed into the hands of an individual who made the mansion into a sanatorium for mental patients. The Sisters had been made aware of the property by a neighbor, Father Dougherty, a priest who ran a school for boys. He had tired of seeing patients wandering about the property, and he hoped that the land was a suitable site for CMM. Sister Anthony immediately liked the facilities. In late 1920 an adjoining 52 acre tract of land was made available for $17,000. The Belchamp property cost $75,000. Sister Anthony borrowed $100,000 from the bank and settled the deal in February 1922.

The Sisters had hoped that they might realize as much as $4 million and at least $1 million from the sale of their own property. With the extra income they planned to pay off the loan and remodel the Belchamp estate. Sale of the property did not go as expected; the advice they had gotten from bankers and lawyers proved erroneous. The last parcel of land was not sold until 1944, and the total value they received was close to $4,000,000. During the spring of 1922, using a car and a coach, the College of Mother Mary moved to its present site in Rosewood, California. In addition to the mansion, the entire estate consisted of 100 acres, including servant quarters and maintenance buildings.

From 1922 until 1952 the Sisters converted the property from one useful for the wealthy or the insane into a college campus for women. Instruction continued in the arts and sciences. A representative curriculum from those years included: English Composition, European and American History, Biology, Chemistry, Algebra, Trigonometry, and Theology. The college slowly added male instructors, but the overwhelming majority of faculty remained Sisters. As the years passed, the budget and salary schedule for the faculty and administration of CMM did not accurately reflect the costs of the institution. At that time, salary schedules and retirement benefits did not exist in most institutions, and CMM was no exception. Because the Sisters ran the college, and those who received payment were Sisters, the cash flow did not show the college's true income and expense. The few lay people who worked for CMM usually learned about the job through the parish bulletin, or through the Catholic community by word-of-mouth. Salaries for the lay staff, relative to other institutions, were low. Once they had moved to Belchamp, plans got underway for additional buildings to house the students and Sisters. By 1952 much of the land on the campus was still uninhabitable; a small mountain loomed over the eastern side of the dormitory effectively making half of the property scenic, but not appropriate for construction by mid-twentieth-century standards.

Students continued to come to CMM from foreign countries such as Japan, but the vast majority of students graduated from the Sister of Mother Mary's California high schools. These high schools acted as feeder schools, supplying a steady stream of girls to the college, so that there was little need for an admissions office. These students were primarily middle and upper middle class children whose parents expected them to marry shortly after college. Parents intended college to strengthen Catholic values and increase knowledge and preparation for their child's marriage. The young women were served dinner in Belchamp Hall, evening clothes were *de rigueur*. Formal events such as the Inaugural Tea and Founder's Day provided opportunities for Belchamp Hall to return to its original purpose as a palace for entertainment.

The city of Rosewood had literally grown up around the Belchamp estate, yet the "town and gown" animosity that surrounds many institutions of higher learning in the United States never existed at CMM. Adjacent to the college property is the Sisters' elementary and high school. The town gradually grew into a bedroom community for a large metropolitan area. Although there is a Catholic grade school, high school, and college, one could not say that the town particularly was influenced by the Sisters of Mother Mary. Rosewood existed as a sleepy town which accommodated the college neither by disdain nor welcome.

In the 1950s higher education in the United States prepared for an "impending tidal wave of students" (Thompson 1954). The influx of returning veterans who took advantage of the GI Bill, combined with a prosperous economy, created a period of rapid growth and expansion for collegiate institutions. Colleges throughout America rapidly expanded facilities and faculty in order to meet the increased demand.

Because the tidal wave pertained to returning veterans, CMM did not experience the rapid growth of its student body. The college nevertheless entered the 1950s secure with its past, comfortable with its present, and optimistic about its future. A sense of security derived from the past because participants knew what kind of institution CMM was, what the goals and mission were, who the clientele was, and who had the talent and knowledge to manage the curriculum.

The security of the 1950s was in stark comparison to the poverty of the past. Since the Sisters' arrival in California the college had been destroyed by storm, and it had moved. The initial years at Belchamp found crowded work and living space and improper teaching facilities. When they first moved into Belchamp, for example, the stoves did not work, so the Sisters ended up cooking their meals out on the front lawn. In contrast, by the early 1950s the college had enough space to live, work, and teach; a stable clientele; a continued sense of identity and purpose; and finances that were more stable than they had ever been.

In 1952 the Board of Trustees decided to become a four-year institution awarding the B.A. degree. Anticipated state interference never materialized. In fact, the college received a ringing endorsement from the accreditation association as soon as it applied for membership as a four-year institution. At this time the beginning of an administrative structure distinct from the religious congregation took place. In 1956 the Sisters of Mother Mary appointed an individual from their community whose main responsibility was to act as president of CMM. The 1960s saw the skeletal framework of a dean of students, and an admissions office. Prior to 1960 the college had had little need for an admissions staff due to its small size and its stable pool of applicants from the parochial schools. As the prevailing climate had changed for CMM in 1922, so did the areas where CMM had its high schools in the 1960s. What were once middle and upper class neighborhoods transformed into working class areas. Whereas CMM students once were the richest in town, the Sisters increasingly found an applicant pool that could not afford private college tuition. The collegiate atmosphere of the 1960s was also drastically different than anything higher education previously had experienced. CMM's clientele had changed, and so had the desire of young women to attend an all women's Catholic college.

The Recent Past

If one were to look for a benchmark on which to place the beginnings of the modern era of the college one could point to the ascendancy of Sister Barbara Therese as President of the college in 1956. Her appointment came not from the nomination of a search committee to the Board of Trustees, but rather from the superior of the province. In Sister Barbara's words, "I was told that I was to go to—it wasn't a choice you understand, the way I'm saying this, there was no choice—that I had been chosen to be president of the college in the fall of 1956" (Reiss 1982, p. 80). This individual's term of office lasted for 24 years—the longest term of office for any college president in California. Many people maintain that if one wants to mark the accomplishments of Sister Barbara as President all one need do is look around the campus. From 1956 until her resignation in 1980, the college added the following buildings: a residence hall, library, dining hall, early learning center, graduate apartments, church, classrooms, and a retirement home for the Sisters. In order to undertake the building projects, she first had to have the mountain that divided the campus dynamited. Workmen trucked the sand and gravel away, which helped build a nearby freeway. In short, the physical appearance of the campus changed dramatically as of 1956.

The late 1950s marked the inclusion of an evening division for the college's students, the early 1960s saw graduate programs begin, and 1969 earmarked the formal acceptance of male students. The evening division began as a result of the realization that no institutions in the area offered classes in the evening. The program was for part-time students and included both men and women who had completed their college degrees and wanted additional coursework in another area, or individuals who wanted to finish an uncompleted B.A. degree. An outgrowth of the evening division were programs off-campus for business and industries. Eventually the college disbanded these programs due to pressure for quality control from the accreditation agency. Finally, extensions of the undergraduate programs afforded the inclusion of master's degrees in business, teaching, and a few programs in the liberal arts during the 1970s.

The acceptance of male students does not seem to have created much dissension among the congregation; rather, the administration accepted the change as an economic necessity. Other Catholic men's colleges in the area had decided to go coed. The evening division already had prepared the way for men to attend CMM. An enrollment drop in the late 1960s added further incentive to reach out to a previously untapped area. When they decided to go coed, CMM became the first Catholic women's college in the area to do so.

As has been shown previously, the college believed in religious freedom. Throughout the 1960s more lay teachers and staff worked at CMM, and, again, there was no consistent policy of first seeking Catholics for these positions. At the same time, there was a constant demand for people who accurately reflected the values of the institution. Sister Barbara reflected:

> All of those in charge of personnel were encouraged to show, to explain, what we had done in the past, what we would want for the future. We want our colleagues to understand what we are trying to do, not to talk against any religious background but to develop together a value system that will be a strength for people in the future ... There has to be a fine strong moral aim and moral ethics, and in the understanding of the basic philosophy of people and the political situations of the world. If you don't care at all about that, then you are not going to carry a value system through your institution, and that is what we are trying to do here (Reiss 1982, p. 102).

The socialization of students and faculty to this value system occurred in many ways. The longest serving—and still active—faculty member of the college has mentioned committee work as one way of inculcating the values of the institution into its newer members. "The Administrative Council has always been one way to inculcate to younger faculty members what it is we are doing. That committee provided a broad overview of the college, and frequently undertook the task of reassessing the aims of the institution." Traditions such as Inaugural Teas, "candle passing" (where a young woman who was to be married passed a candle at supper to her friends), Honors and Founder's Day, spoke to formal events wherein they explicated the values of the college. At the start of each school year a short retreat offered new and continuing students a moment to reflect on the kind of institution they attended.

The transmission of values, however, came about most obviously from the Sisters and lay faculty. The present longest serving professor's father taught at the institution, and long-term lay professors have been mentioned consistently as embodiments of the tradition and ethic of the college. Many Sisters of Mother

Mary who did not work at CMM lived in Belchamp, so that there existed a visible presence of people who embodied the values of the Sisters of Mother Mary and, hence, the college.

The turmoil of the 1960s saw the rapid decline of people entering religious life and, consequently, fewer Sisters to staff, teach, and live at CMM. The homogeneity of students from a primarily Catholic background also dramatically changed. The inclusion of males, an increasing international audience from a variety of religious backgrounds, and a large number of part-time students who came to CMM not for values but for practical coursework in subjects such as business accounting, created a vastly different admissions pool.

A struggle from this point onward concerned the identity of the institution with its past, and how one creates a viable collegiate institution for an entirely different clientele. The 1960s saw the abandonment of dress requirements, explicit traditions, the formality of parietals, and other socializing ways of the college. While admissions, funding patterns, and the students and faculty themselves demanded these changes, no one could predict how the institutional values and history would be changed, altered, or continued. That is, public institutions or state colleges also underwent the rapid series of changes mentioned above. But because they lacked the coherence of a distinctive ideology and value system, the changes did not so dramatically affect a school's mission. Thus, the institution Sister Vera Regan inherited in 1980 differed radically from the two-year college that had moved to Rosewood in 1922 and the institution Sister Barbara guided in 1956.

NEW PRESIDENT, NEW TIME

Changes

The job of president had changed dramatically since the quarter century when Sister Barbara Therese had assumed the office. From the outset, the processes and actions of the president in an institution of the 1980s differed from those of a president in 1956. Sister Barbara had gotten a phone call telling her to go to Rosewood and become president; Sister Vera applied for the position and went through a rigorous review by the search committee—

the first such committee in the institution's history. On December 13, 1978 the Board of Trustees passed a motion that said, "The president of College of Mother Mary shall be a Sister of Mother Mary," which thereby laid out the framework for the search committee. Faculty, administrators, board members, and students became involved in the selection of the new president.

After her selection, Sister Vera "interned" for six months with Sister Barbara. The two of them shared the same office, and as Sister Barbara made her exit, Sister Vera prepared for the work ahead. At her conferral she had invited the Faculty Senate president to be on the stage with her, along with departmental chairs and the chief administrators. There was both symbolism and annointment in her action in that the formation of the Faculty Senate initially represented an alien body to the college and to the previous president. The faculty formed the Senate in 1976. The attendance at meetings had been sparse, sometimes as few as five. Nevertheless, the Senate represented a group that wanted its demands, concerns, and voice heard. Until 1983 the Senate's main concerns were salary and benefits.

Even as the Faculty Senate continued to develop, its inclusion on the stage with Sister Vera represented how far institutional governance had come. Identifiable groups such as "staff," "faculty," and "administration" were now evident, whereas the CMM of 1956 had primarily one group of people leading it—the Sisters of Mother Mary. There were now "exempt" and "nonexempt" staff, for example, and personnel benefits had been written in order to meet the needs of married people. Salary scales and a step schedule replaced individual bargaining over contracts. The addition of male faculty and administrators had continued over the years until a rough parity had been achieved during the 1970s. The 1970 and 1975 accreditation reports stated that because the college had gone coeducational it was imperative that the administration and faculty reflect that diversity. The faculty in 1984 still had roughly a dozen Sisters, but the overwhelming majority of professors were lay, and no religion predominated.

Although faces have changed over time, the faculty has continued its trademark as a group of concerned scholars where teaching is the main activity. Research is minimal, but evident from a productive few, and the esprit de corps is extraordinarily high. After seven years of teaching at CMM, one faculty member reflected, "When I came here I couldn't believe that a place that had such low salaries could have such high morale." The college has attracted well-qualified faculty members due to its location in a large metropolitan area and its proximity to other major educational research centers where a faculty member's spouse may teach or work. Over 80 percent of the full-time faculty hold doctorates, and when position announcements are advertised it is not uncommon to receive over 50 applications.

There has also been a transformation of the Board of Trustees. Sister Barbara gradually changed the group's composition from one primarily composed of Sisters, to that of lay and Sisters. Tim Leary, Vice President for College Affairs, successfully captured the types of "ideal citizens" one wants for a Board of Trustees. Board members raised funds on behalf of the college, informed themselves as to the strengths and weaknesses of the college, and contributed money of their own for college projects. By 1983 over half of the Board members were wealthy businessmen from the area.

The decision-making apparatus of committees created a vastly changed atmosphere in which to make decisions. Whereas Sister Barbara initially could create policy and make unilateral decisions on her own, by 1984 the citizens of the college had grown to believe in the concept of shared decision making, and the ratification of ideas, plans, and projects through the committee structure. Everyone agreed that oftentimes Sister Barbara had acted without the advice and consent of a particular committee. There are many examples of the President acting against the wishes of a particular committee in order to raise tuition or hold the line on salaries. People pointed to other examples, however, when the Academic Dean occasionally lost a battle about academic policy at a curriculum meeting, or she incorporated an idea into policy with which she personally disagreed. The perception of decision making as Sister Vera assumed office, however, was that ideas and plans came through committees, the president at times did exercise her power of the veto, and the main function of the president was to establish ties with the outside community and to raise funds for the institution.

The student body the President greeted in 1980 was much more diverse than the students of 1956. In addition to the new audience of men, one-third of the students were international, and older students accounted for a quarter of the population. Forty percent of the students were Catholic, and the rest of the student body represented a wide range of religious affiliations. Most obviously, the size of the college had increased. CMM had grown from a full-time equivalency (FTE) of 200 in 1956, to an FTE of 940 in 1984. Fifty percent of the student body were transfers from other local institutions—often junior colleges. Although general education requirements have been maintained, and the college still sees itself as a liberal arts college, over half of the students are business majors. The college continues to stress humanistic values in its curriculum, but vocational, practical courses such as cost accounting and finance have become equally, if not more, important.

As the college grew, so did the city of Rosewood. Neither city nor college expanded because of the other, but rather for similar reasons. Rosewood became a bedroom community for the metropolitan area. The relations of the city and college remained proper, if not distant. The community occasionally attended CMM plays or musical events, and it housed some CMM students, yet Rosewood never had the flavor of a college town. At the same time, there have never been any disagreeable relations between the city and college that one finds in many "town and gown" situations.

Problems

Because of the changes at CMM and in the surrounding environment, the institution encountered many new problems. A retention study completed in 1983 reported that 73 percent of the incoming students did not graduate from the college. The worst retention rates were in majors that were once the bulwark of CMM—music and theater. Fine arts classes had become the most expensive courses in the college. The business department, although generating the bulk of tuition revenue for the college, saw three different department chairs from 1980 to 1983, and the low salary scale—$17,000 to $30,000—had been incapable of attracting and retaining a stable, sizeable core of full-time, permanent, qualified instructors. Coupled with the retention problem was the decline in enrollment. The last seven years, up to and including 1983, saw an almost constant decline in the FTE of CMM. In 1980/81 CMM reached a FTE high of 1100 students, and in 1983/84 there was an FTE of 940. The prediction for 1984/85 was a 10 percent drop in enrollment.

In 1983 the college had to use money from its endowment to balance the proposed 1983/84 budget. Formal development efforts had not existed when Sister Barbara became President. The college's principal donations came from wealthy alumni or a nun's family. Sister Barbara had received federal, state, and foundation support on an almost ad hoc basis. Her personal charm and graciousness opened doors to foundations that provided the funds for CMM's building projects. Tim Leary gave shape and direction to fund-raising. An affable Irishman with a good sense of humor, Leary served the president as first among equals, and was Sister Vera's closest confidant at the college. Nevertheless, the college remained heavily financed by tuition, and its dependence on tuition had increased in the last few years. In 1984/85, for example, the administration predicted that tuition would account for 73 percent of its revenue, whereas in the previous year tuition generated 70 percent of CMM's income. As the attrition rates soared and enrollment dropped, the institution faced a difficult financial future.

Prior to academic year 1983/84 a common view of administration-faculty relations was one of high cooperation and consensus. A study conducted by the National Center for Higher Education Management Systems (NCHEMS), for example, provided the pseudonym "Harmony College" to reflect the atmosphere of the institution. The author of the report on "Harmony College" stated:

> Another kind of flexibility arises from the faculty attitude toward change. They, like others at Harmony, welcome any change that will improve their ability to serve students. When it became clear that the home economics program was no longer viable, for example, even the home economics faculty concurred in the decision. The general attitude in faculty meetings was described by one member as, "How could the administration cope with this situation?" rather than focusing on issues of faculty welfare (Chaffee 1983, p. 87).

Since Sister Vera took over in 1980 a series of administrative staffing changes have occurred; forced or voluntary resignations have taken place in key administrative positions. The Academic Vice President, a Sister who worked at CMM for 30 years, "voluntarily" resigned and became Director of Institutional Research. Sister Vera fired the Director of the Evening Division and a Sister who was Director of International Students. The Admissions Director of 10 years resigned. The Vice President for Finance, appointed by Sister Vera after serving as chair of the business department, resigned in frustration after he was unable to implement a series of fiscal changes. Sister Vera fired the Comptroller and replaced him with another man who has since assumed responsibility for the fiscal matters of the institution, although he does not have the title of Vice President and does not attend the Executive Committee.

The previous President remains on campus in the office of Chancellor. The Vice President for College Relations has assumed a full-time position, although he commonly spends no more than 25 hours a week at CMM because he is a consultant at other colleges. Finally, in June 1983, Patrick O'Connell, an Irishman, became Academic Vice President. Dr. O'Connell had been Academic Dean at an institution not unlike College of Mother Mary on the East Coast. As a professor and administrator he was well versed in the literature of higher education, and he brought to CMM the experience and know-how of a seasoned professional. Throughout the year he worked long hours trying to implement his program for change conceived from a perspective wider than that of the college.

Three major events occurred in the fall of 1983 for which no one had been prepared. First, in September, the man in charge of finance had a serious heart attack that made it impossible for him to work; he eventually returned in January. Second, in October the city of Rosewood initiated a $15 million dollar tax assessment for storm drainage pipes throughout the city. The city council assessed CMM's share to be $500,000—an amount far beyond what the college could pay. Third, in December the county historical society demanded renovations on Belchamp Hall that would cost half a million dollars if the college wanted to convert the hall into the planned administrative center. Previously, the college thought the renovation would be under $30,000; the final figure agreed upon was $100,000.

The year under study has seen an inordinate amount of conflict, crisis, and, to some, chaos. Virtually everyone agrees that CMM has never experienced a year like 1983/84. Two faculty members resigned, in part because of the conflict at CMM. Early in the year another faculty member, Dr. Beckett, abruptly announced his resignation from all committee and administrative work because he could not support the proposed changes. In his words, "I am resigning to warn you that dedicated teachers and many students will be leaving this college if the decisions as to reorganization (and computerization) stand as they are now. I will continue to serve the students of this college to the best of my ability." He posted a copy of his letter on the bulletin board outside of his office for faculty, staff, and students to read. One month later he received a letter from the President—initiated by the AVP—stating that because he could no longer support the policies of the college, his contract at the end of the year would not be renewed.

Administrative Solutions

The Executive Committee—the three Vice Presidents and the President—attempted various solutions to the problems that beset CMM throughout the year. The new Academic Vice President initiated a series of programmatic alterations that provided the basis for much dissent. With the president's approval, Patrick O'Connell overrode the recommendations of an Advisory Council on Computers for a computer science major. Instead, CMM plans to incorporate computer learning throughout its curricula. He merged the Evening Division with the rest of the college, abolished January Intersession, and made plans for a Week-End College to begin in the fall of 1984. He mandated that the 23 departments of the college merge into five curricular divisions. Each department had had a chairperson who had a reduced teaching load to administer the department, even though some departments consisted of one person. O'Connell's mandate originally caused much consternation on the part of the faculty who saw their turf eroding in front of them; by December 1983, however, the Faculty Senate voted for the divisional change.

O'Connell hinted that some majors and small master's degree programs, such as French and music, might be abolished in the near future. The Graduate Committee drew up a list of criteria wherein they investigated graduate degree programs. The AVP overrode their criteria and told them to draw up other guidelines. The Committee for Academic Standards objected to O'Connell's unilateral decision to allow some students on probation to continue at CMM. The Library Committee voted not to incorporate the media center into the library, but when the AVP threatened the librarian with sanction for not supporting administration policy, the changes proceeded according to plan. O'Connell told the Rank and Tenure Committee that they should not give tenure or promote faculty due to budgetary considerations, when the committee had always operated without regard to fiscal considerations—as is the national norm for such committees. Whereas the previous AVP had sat on committees, O'Connell tried to remove himself from them so that committee results could then pass to his desk. At that point he would decide whether to pursue them with the president, or veto them. Finally, he initiated an off-campus program without the approval or knowledge of any committee or faculty.

O'Connell announced in the early fall that a 20 percent increase in enrollment was necessary for the coming year. The Budget and Finance Committee, acting with this projection in mind, voted for a 4 percent increase in tuition—well below the national average—in order to make it easier for admissions to recruit students. By January, O'Connell had changed his projections so that the college actually received no increase in FTE when they took all factors such as attrition and retention into account. By February, however, at the initial budgetary planning meeting he had revised his projection so that in actuality a 20 percent drop in enrollment was forecast for the next year. This 20 percent drop, coupled with the meager 4 percent increase in tuition, accounted for an initial difference of $1 million between planned expenditures and income. The Executive Committee revised their estimates to forecast only a 10 percent drop in enrollment, and called on the Admissions Director to get another 40 students for the fall.

Major development efforts included a gymnasium and the extensive renovation of a building to turn it into an art center. The administration thought that a gym was one way of attracting students to CMM. Initial estimates for the gym were $2 million, but by the spring of 1983 the costs amounted to $3 million. Tim Leary had raised half a million dollars for the art studio, and the administration planned for the art department to move into the building in the fall of 1984. By early spring, however, they realized they had underestimated the costs of such a building; the architect's plans came in at three times the expected cost. By summer, no work had begun, and no plans had been made to raise additional funds. The board decided to delay any decision for procuring additional funds.

The President created an Executive Task Force consisting of two board members, two faculty, and two administrators to draw up alternative proposals for outside revenue. By late spring, however, no concrete plans had been suggested other than to hire a consultant to look into the matter. As mentioned, the college has been 70 percent tuition driven, and 30 percent derives from alternative revenue sources, primarily through Leary's efforts. Extensive comments were made about reducing the dependency of the college on tuition revenue and the advisability of increasing development efforts, such as a capital campaign. The President and Executive Committee consistently rejected these suggestions while they sought alternative sources of revenue.

WAYS OF SEEING

As we shall see, the Faculty Senate took on an entirely new role and function, and became the focal point for faculty opinion. In February it drew up a six-page letter of grievance and sent it to the President and Executive Committee. After much consideration the faculty decided not to send the letter to the Board of Trustees until they had exhausted all avenues of communication with the administration. Two weeks later the President and AVP addressed the Faculty Senate to try to calm the crisis; the response was overwhelmingly negative. By late spring morale was at an all-time low, and "Harmony College" had dissolved into a we-they situation between faculty and administrators, with staff and midmanagers glumly participating from the sidelines. An open revenue meeting in March dissolved into an angry interchange between the chaplain and AVP over the proliferation of administrative positions at the college. Several midlevel directors and faculty privately indicated that they were actively searching for jobs elsewhere either because they had lost faith in administrative decision making or because they felt the college was not the place it once had been.

For the faculty, their stated reasons for conflict with the administration were not that they objected to change and they wanted things the "way they were," but rather with the processes for change. In the letter of grievance the faculty provided examples to illustrate the processes the AVP had taken to achieve end results. These processes, the faculty held, contravened the stated norms of the college and pointed to three issues: the role of the AVP, the role of the executive veto, and the role of the handbook. The stated rules and guidelines for the faculty and administrators did not provide for the actions that have been mentioned—redrawing guidelines, abolishing programs, creating a managerial structure which took into account the ability of the AVP and President to veto measures approved in committee.

For the administration's part, they perceived dissension to stem from the faculty's fear of change. The President pointed out to the faculty that she felt the college was in crisis and she had tried to communicate that feeling in several different ways, most obviously by using endowment funds to balance the previous year's budget. The AVP and President never felt that the problem was one of communication. Instead, the issue was the resistance of the "old guard" on the faculty who had created an atmosphere of "group think" where individuals were afraid to break away from the pack and admit that the administration's solutions were necessary. Sister Vera and Patrick O'Connell consistently maintained that in the end their plans actually increased faculty power and voice, and that the "good old days" were nothing more than a romanticized version of how decisions were made during the reign of Sister Barbara and her academic dean, Sister Mary Therese.

When one reads minutes of past committee meetings, however, one finds striking differences between people's perceptions about how they made decisions and how decisions actually were made. For example, Sister Vera and Dr. O'Connell were much criticized for abolishing Winter Session without consulting the faculty. Again, faculty pointed to the handbook as the way to abolish programs through a collegial, committee-oriented process. Yet Sister Barbara's academic dean created and abolished many programs without discussing those decisions with the faculty. Off-campus programs, *ACE*, a nurse-training seminar, are examples of decisions the AVP made without consulting the faculty. The registrar can point to students who, although the Academic

Standards Committee flunked them, remained at CMM because Sister Mary Therese did not act on their decision. At one point the chair of the Pastoral Studies master's program thought the graduate degree should be abolished, but he could never get on the Curriculum Committee's agenda because the AVP strongly liked the program.

Clearly, democratic decision making was not the hallmark of Sister Barbara's regime, although people constantly talked about the past as if decisions were consensually oriented. Throughout the year faculty talked about Sister Barbara's decisions in the following way:

> Her very conservative philosophy may have in the long run kept the college going. She didn't take chances. The way she ran things may seem funny to you now. People bargained individually for contracts. The better bargainer you were, the better you came out. I was personally treated very well, but that's because I was a good bargainer, and because I'm a man. She and Mary Therese really ran the show. They made decisions down in Belchamp over supper—that's really how things got decided. They are products of the old system of authority, and I wasn't critical because that's what they knew. I often disagreed with Mary Therese, but man, I respect her. She has worked so hard for this school that even though things were not as democratic as we would have liked, you got by. BT and MT always listened. They made arbitrary decisions, sure, but they were able to stimulate us to do our best. We had ideas and they heard them.

The speaker's comments point out several recurring themes voiced by other individuals. People refer to the former autocratic leadership, but acknowledged that it never impeded what they wanted to do. Even faculty members who arrived after Sister Vera became president comment how "decisions were made in Belchamp late at night." Dedication and hard work are qualities people admired, but foremost among comments made by interviewees was that "BT and MT really listened. We had ideas and they heard them."

Another individual spoke of the current changes in a similar form:

> We run much the way a family grocery store would run, and the personality of a person shapes the way we act, rather than a process someone put in place. BT was the matriarch, and as she would toddle down the hall she was gracious. Sister Vera doesn't want to be a matriarch. The place exists over time through a process. She's trying to put in a process. We ran by

an oral tradition, and that's fine if the elders have passed along their knowledge. That old process has broken down, and now we need a new process.

Thus, in one part the college struggles to implement a new process for the 1980s.

College of Mother Mary is beset by many of the problems that exist for higher education in the United States for the remainder of the twentieth century. Declining enrollments, increased consumerism on the part of its clientele, and decreased support from the federal government, do not bode well for tuition driven, private, liberal arts colleges such as CMM. The methods for financial stability that once worked no longer can be applied. Reliance on traditional methods of recruitment spell financial disaster for an institution in an area where many private and public institutions exist. The opportunity for students to attend less expensive public institutions, or to begin their coursework in community colleges and then transfer to a four-year college are not of concern to the private liberal arts college if its traditional market remains unchanged. As mentioned, however, the high schools where CMM used to get the bulk of its constituents now place students in less expensive institutions. Not only do declining enrollments spell financial trouble for institutions in the immediate present, but they also forecast future financial troubles. That is, a smaller body translates into fewer alumni capable of donating funds to the college. Transfer students also have less affiliation with a college they attended to complete a degree and will be less willing to donate funds.

There is a double bind at work with regard to the "distinctiveness" with which CMM sees itself. On the one hand, the Admissions Office constantly makes reference to high school students who say they do not want to attend a "girls' finishing school" even though the institution went coed over 15 years ago. Further, many students no longer seek a degree in the liberal arts because it will not get them a job. The value-oriented approach to education on which a liberal arts college prides itself may only be seen as cumbersome to the 18-year-old student who is ever aware of the difficulties of entering the job market and to the adult student who is in the job market and needs specific skills to remain in that market.

On the other hand, the distinctiveness of the institution is what makes it successful. The mission of CMM as a Catholic institution dedicated to a liberating education previously defined the activities, goals, and processes of the institution. Since the inception of the college, the participants—students, staff, faculty, and the president—worked from a premise about what is important, and how to achieve what is important. The unity of mission came in part from the homogeneity of clientele and an ideological orientation that attracted a particular kind of person to work, live, or study at CMM. The unity of vision and purpose that Sister Barbara inherited when she first governed in the economic "boom times" of the late 1950s and 1960s no longer exists. Nevertheless, the actors see their collective past—processes and decisions—in dramatically different ways. What follows are specific examples of different ways of seeing the past of College of Mother Mary.

History and Change

The actors at CMM had various modes in which they spoke about their past. At All-College Day, to start the year off, Sister Vera addressed the entire college community about the changes that needed to take place. She equated these changes as part of a journey that was entirely in keeping with the history and tradition of CMM. She stated:

> Forward movement is part of our history and our tradition. If we go back to the women who founded this college, the Sisters of Mother Mary who landed in California with 25¢ in their purse [we find] these women were women who were willing to take risks and they moved forward because they took risks ... Later, the Sisters who founded the college moved to Rosewood. That was a very painful, indeed, a deathlike movement. But out of that death came the life at Rosewood. Again, willing to take a risk, willing to move. And even closer to our time, the movement into coeducation. This movement again meant relinquishing something dear— women's education which had been a part of our history and our tradition... And again, the college moved forward into the unknown.

The President spoke of the proposed changes as a continuation of CMM's history and tradition. Change implied that certain parts of the college—such as coeducation—had to be dropped or altered in order to confront the present. At ceremonial occasions such as All-College Day speakers made common reference to the poverty in which CMM began. From Sister Vera's viewpoint lack of fiscal resources meant the college had to take risks, and consequently the changes she mandated were in keeping with the history of CMM. The Sisters arrived "with 25 cents in their purse," and thus, "these women were women who were willing to take risks."

In conversations with Sister Barbara, however, she stated that her administration sought to minimize risk, and she implied that the financial undertaking of the move to Rosewood was not satisfactory. "The Sisters had bad advice, you know, and ever since that move we have had problems with the financial side of the college. Money has always been a problem for us. I never built a building until I had all the money for it. That may have been conservative, I know, but I wasn't going to take a foolish chance."

When older faculty members and members of the Board of Trustees spoke of Sister Barbara's reign, they consistently mentioned how she never built anything unless she had money for it. One trustee said, "She was very prudent. She didn't spend money before she had it, and that is good philosophy. She's not a gambler." A faculty member sought to defuse the present fiscal crisis by referring to the past in a way different from Sister Vera: "We've always operated on a shoestring. That 25 cents story and all that. That's the way Catholic colleges are."

We have, then, different interpretations of the fiscal traditions of CMM. The President equated the proposed changes to be another risk in line with CMM's history of taking risks due to financial exigencies. The previous President pointed out that she had no desire for risks; in fact, she accepted the fiscal implications of CMM, but rejected risk-taking. Change, for her, did not mean moving "forward into the unknown," for she had paid for everything prior to moving into the future. Faculty members either pointed to the penurious regime of Sister Barbara, or the consistency with which CMM faced financial impoverishment to defuse the idea of present crisis.

The Curriculum

Sister Vera continued her speech by talking about the educational heritage of the college:

The founder of our congregation, a very fine, down to earth peasant woman ... when she was setting up her educational program for children after the French Revolution said ... "teach them what they need to know for life." So simple. But so complex. The Sisters of Mother Mary have consistently allied themselves with the educational mission of the Church. In the last six years they have recommitted themselves ... to the liberating action of the gospel and to the fostering of peace and justice in our world.

Sister Vera's mention of the founder of the Order also relayed a message about the changing curricular structure of CMM. "Teach them what they need to know for life" was a changing concept wherein the curriculum of the college needed to keep pace with the times. CMM has become a liberal arts college where 50 percent of the undergraduates major in business; the strongest program in the college is the MBA. The encroachment of business into a liberal arts college has been a source of constant controversy. As one professor said, "I'm not a Catholic, but I don't mind what the mission is here. That's not the problem. But business is not an academic discipline. It's the tail wagging the dog. Why don't we just call ourselves a vocational school?"

The point for the liberal arts faculty was that business was not a liberal art. The traditional liberal arts at CMM—music, art, drama—constantly felt threatened by the strength of the business department and the fiscal weakness of their own programs. For example, the music department chair noted, "The first college was known as a conservatory. The outward image of the college has always been musically oriented. Performances exist here and in the community, yet we continue to have a very small budget. Our instruments are terrible." The newly appointed divisional chair for fine arts made a similar point at an Executive Committee meeting: "My most important question is how you see fine arts at this school. Mother Mary has a strong history of fine arts. We see it as professional training. I think how you people feel about this very much affects what I can do. If I'm taking over a division where sometime it may be convenient and expedient to move out of this then ..."

Again, the President used the founder's words from the past to justify needed changes for the 1980s. The faculty viewed that same past as a mandate for the liberal arts to retain control of the curricula. Another way of viewing Sister Vera's comments about the founder is through a discussion of historical ceremonies and traditions.

Ceremonies and Traditions

The use of references from the founder of the college links the institution and the President to the Catholic tradition. No institutional histories exist that do not use the Sisters of Mother Mary as the frame of reference. When one speaks about CMM's past, no one mentions a college president other than Sister Barbara Therese. That is, when one speaks of a 120-year-old institution one expects to find reference to various college presidents. At CMM, however, when people make reference to the historical past they refer to the founder of the Order, who had nothing to do with the establishment of CMM. When people speak of the founding of the college or the move to Rosewood, they speak about the collective Sisters—"If we go back to the women who founded this college."

Pictures of the founder of the Order can be found in many classrooms, and one of the dormitories has her name. It is not uncommon to hear reference to her at ceremonial occasions. At a stormy Faculty Senate meeting in March, the Faculty Senate had asked the President to address them concerning their grievances with the administration. "This is not the first tight spot I've been in," said the President at the meeting. "When I get into these situations and begin to feel very depressed and angry I take much solace and courage from our foundress's words to a young Sister who had come to her with many problems. She said, 'Better mistakes, than paralysis.' Maybe I've made mistakes, but we're not paralyzed—and if we are, we're through." As Sister Vera spoke, one could hear another Sister in the back of the room echo the founder's words. The founder's statement had called people to action, and in times such as the crisis-ridden present the administration might well have made mistakes, but mistakes were better than "paralysis," which implied institutional death.

Historical dates, events, traditions, with a few exceptions, did not play an important role at CMM. The year that the college went coeducational, for example, ranged in people's memories from 1964 to 1971; the actual date was 1969. During the year the administration incorporated Founder's Day with Honors Day, and when the event approached in springtime, they changed the date so they had more time to plan for the event. The President planned to be out of town during the day on a fund-raising trip. The actual ceremony turned out to be not an historical event, but rather a recruitment device for prospective students, which Dr. O'Connell had initiated. Inaugural Teas, Homecoming, special dances—the Diamond Ball—still occurred but received little participation from the principal actors of the institution.

However, when the college chose a new letterhead, they incorporated the founding date into the logo because, as Tim Leary observed, "It says something about the college." Once during a directors' meeting, the newly appointed admissions director, Dave Falconieri, lobbied for a football team and spoke of the history of CMM, "since it started in 1874." An administrator intimately involved with the college shook her head in opposition to the idea and said later, "He's new. He doesn't understand the way the college works, how things get done. He doesn't even know when we began. It undercuts his position and there's less reason to agree with him."

During lunch at All-College Day, two faculty members noted that the business department chair, Louie Canova, had not attended the meeting. "That's Louie's problem," one of them observed humorously. "He doesn't understand this place. You don't miss ceremonies for the college. They don't like it." When asked what events they meant, they referred to the Christmas party, graduation, and All-College events such as the present one.

The impression one gets from listening to and observing the actors is that individuals speak of their history in terms of people instead of dates or events. Few traditions exist that are highly ritualized events that occur at specific points in time; rather, localized customs and interactions come about not from specified rules and laws but through a communicative process determined chiefly by oral means. Rather than point to specific traditions, or the school colors, or mascots, people spoke of the past in terms of individuals.

From this perspective, process comes to play a critical role in the achievement of end results. Individuals are aware change has occurred—the college going coeducational—but how people achieved that goal, individual and collective feelings about themselves in that process, impact future plans. During the course of the year how CMM made decisions under Sister Barbara's reign became increasingly important with regard to present decisions. Faculty anger came about because the Academic Vice President's plans did not go through committee but were done by administrative fiat. The faculty handbook became something of a bible insofar as there were written procedures about how to make decisions at CMM. Many faculty expressed what Sue Ann Simmer said one day after an angry meeting with O'Connell, "We have established policies, and they're rewriting the handbook. That's not how things are done here. They can work with us, or ignore us. If they continue to ignore the policies we've established there can be nothing but trouble."

In one sense what transforms leaden presidential statements—"the college is you"—into an embraceable ideology is the individual's ability to articulate the mission of the college within an interpretive framework that accommodates different constituencies' visions of history. This chapter has discussed the conflict both in the present, and between the past and present, as mediated by the actors' creation of their past.

Part II

Actors and Their Roles

Introduction

The drama unfolds so that the actors enact scenes that form a composite picture of the world of College of Mother Mary. The portrait of any people during the entirety of a season has inveterate signals that the play uncovers as it wends its way toward conclusion. The conclusion, however, is not in the sense of a resolution to the dilemmas presented, but rather the stopping place where we gather together the disparate strands of these scenes within the framework outlined in Chapter I. I present a drama wherein individuals exist as subjects and as objects. Thus, we look at ways that people become subjects as well as at the forces by which they are objectified.

A chronological listing of the rush of events that occurred throughout the year does not do justice to the tenor, problems, and crises that beset College of Mother Mary. This part demonstrates that while some groups—the Executive Committee and faculty, for example—concerned themselves intensively with particular issues, other groups did not partake of the decision-making problems and process. While groups such as the faculty took on new roles, other groups continued to act and operate in ways consistent with the way they always acted.

As mentioned in Chapter II, identifiable groups such as the Executive Committee and middle managers are a new phenomenon for CMM. The flurry of change during the last decade has compartmentalized individuals within specified clusters. This is not to say that informal networks and unspecified roles for individuals do not continue to exist; a large degree of informality still operates. Nevertheless, identifiable groups do appear, and, to a large extent, individuals increasingly relate to the college through the roles they play. A senior faculty member, Jake Barnes, stated at the beginning of the school year, "I'm a friend of Vera's, and I love this place, and I'd hate to see these problems degenerate into a we-they kind of thing, but if it comes to that, I'd identify totally with the faculty. My loyalty would have to go there. It's how I see myself. It's my identity." A staff member echoed that feeling when she spoke about her relation to the college. "I really like this place. I do. There's a split, though, between faculty and staff. Some faculty feel like, 'I'm the one who's paid to think, and you're the one to work.' So I'm a staff person, and it's very clear what I can do, and what I can't."

Leadership is culturally defined by people's views of power. The ascribed power of the role "president" allows Sister Vera to be oftentimes center stage for the drama. Although she does not play center stage for all of the actions depicted, she is quite often close to the action, maneuvering about constituencies as they conduct their business. Chapter III investigates groups who played major parts in the year's conflict—faculty, midmanagement, Executive Committee, and Board of Trustees. Chapter IV discusses those groups which carried out their daily existence as the conflict occurred, but who did not centrally concern themselves with the crises—the Sisters of Mother Mary, alumni, students, and staff.

A caveat exists. The variegating forms of influence different groups have upon one another and the system do not imply that power resides within particular enclaves. In other words because one cluster receives more attention than another does not mean that a particular group exists as powerful, and another does not. To return to a concept from Chapter I, the investigation notes that over time all groups and individuals within an organization exercise and are subjected to mechanisms of power. One need only to study the late 1960s to see how students played a critical role in the internal functions and decisions of the college, yet in 1984 the student voice was relatively mute. Thus, one needs to be aware of the arbitrariness of the chapter headings and that the groups within these headings can change over time.

The stage is set; we approach the play with the knowledge of CMM's history and a theoretical framework that allows us to view leadership from different angles. The President walks through the scenes as they change over time, and as different constituencies hold center stage. As a theater in the round, the actions enable us to piece together identifiable patterns and structured elements of the ongoing drama.

Chapter III

Primary Groups

MIDMANAGEMENT

The drama begins with a midmanagement meeting that took place in early December between the Facilities Manager, Tom Brady, and the President. The President has weekly meetings with three people in the institution—Patrick O'Connell, the Academic Vice President; Dan Grant, the Director of Finance; and Tom Brady. Sister Vera talks frequently with the AVP, whose office is next door to hers. Their weekly meetings on Monday mornings are more a continuation of discussions they have been having informally throughout the week than an agenda-like formal meeting. O'Connell always has a written agenda for Sister Vera, and Sister Vera often has points she wishes to bring up. The meetings do not meet closure in the sense that O'Connell might return later that day, or the next, with additional information. A meeting in October ended with Sister Vera saying, "Tomorrow we have Executive Committee. Do we have anything? Oh yes. We have to set the priorities for Administrative Council. Could you think about it and let's get back together this afternoon." At a meeting in March O'Connell wanted to know about the advisability of hiring a consultant. Sister Vera stated, "He doesn't sound like he knows what to do. Let me talk with Tim, and see what he thinks. I'll let you know in a bit."

Meetings with O'Connell are friendly, and Sister Vera drifts into the meetings after conversation about any number of topics—family, what they did that weekend, politics, how they feel. The meetings often begin with Sister Vera saying, "So, how are you doing?" O'Connell's answer has been either a hurried "fine" or a longer response that has lasted up to 15 minutes in length.

By contrast, meetings with Tom Brady take place on Thursdays at nine o'clock in the morning in her office and are formal occasions. For this particular meeting Sister Vera arrived at the office at 8:45. As customary, Tom arrived punctually at nine. He sat down, pulled out his handwritten agenda, and Sister Vera said, "Hi, why don't you go through your list, and then I'll tell you—" not finishing the statement as she came around from behind her desk and sat in the other cushioned chair in front of her desk. She held her pink-framed glasses in her right hand with one of the edges pursed on her lips. Her eyes remained on Tom as she spoke, "Let's see, there's no hot water in Belchamp, but we're working on it." He brought up the minor crises of the week, and as he did so, Sister Vera nodded her head, and said, through her eyeglasses, "yeah, yeah, uh-huh, ok." When Tom announced that the blackout curtains for Melton Hall had arrived, I remembered my conversation with Sue Ann Simmer, an English professor at CMM for 27 years. In late September Sue Ann was furious that they had no curtains for Melton Hall in order to show movies. She wanted the curtains in a week's time, and now, 10 weeks later, they had arrived.

When Tom finished with his list Sister Vera said, "I have another request. We're getting that new furniture in the dining hall, and we'd like your help on it. You can do it after the fourth, when you're done with installing the computers." There was a slight pause, and as Sister Vera stared impassively at Tom he said, "I'm not sure the computers can be installed by the fourth." Sister Vera mentioned that he had better talk with the Academic Vice President because, "the computer training will begin on the fourth and that room had better be ready." "I've already talked with Patrick," said Tom, "and I can't do anything until they move Admissions out of that room. My hands are tied." The President cut him off and said, "I understand that. I've had a few things on my mind, you know. I'll get to it when I can. I'm spending the entire day down in Belchamp." She never took her eyes off of him as she spoke; a five-second silence ensued, and he said, "OK" and got up to leave. As he exited Sister Vera also stood up and said to his back as he walked out, "Thank-you for being there the other night. I appreciate your being there." The back of his head bobbed up and down, and the meeting ended. Two minutes later Sister Vera headed down to Belchamp. The meeting had lasted 11 minutes.

I met Tom later that afternoon near the current Admissions Office and future Computer Center. I smiled and said, "How's it going?" He motioned with both arms open, pointing toward the admissions/computer room. "Does she treat everybody like she treats me?" he asked. "What do you mean?" I ventured. "Well, it's like I'm talking to a brick wall. I never know what she's thinking, where she's coming from. Decisions don't get made, they don't get discussed, or they are simply made without talking to anyone. She always wants something yesterday and if I point a problem out to her, it's like it's my fault." We talked about the work that needed to be done, and we laughed that he would have to spend his New Year's Eve working in the room to meet the deadline.

This meeting was characteristic of meetings between Tom and Sister Vera. They were brief, no conversation occurred outside of the business at hand, and the two of them were at loggerheads as to how best to proceed about a particular problem. On this occasion the problem was installing computers in a room that currently held the six-member admissions staff. They had been slated to move to Belchamp, but Sister Vera's preoccupation with another problem had made it impossible for her to decide who would go where in the new offices in Belchamp Hall.

Two nights before the meeting between Tom and Sister Vera there had been the climax to a two-month-long struggle to have the city rescind its half million dollar tax assessment of the college for storm drainage. The college had spent $15,000 on legal advice, and plans had been made to fight an assessment that CMM considered exorbitant. The President spent enormous time and energy in fighting this project, and it had been emotionally draining. The college already had grave financial problems and to be burdened with a tax pushed the institution even closer to a fiscal Armageddon. What the college had not anticipated was the depth of feeling and resentment on the part of the Rosewood citizenry against the assessment. Each property owner had been assessed an amount to pay, and by the time of the public hearing 2800 people amassed to fight the measure. Although CMM and the townspeople were on the same side, no formal alliance existed between them. Each group heard about what the other was doing by word-of-mouth and because some of the staff members at CMM lived in Rosewood and were active in the citizen groups fighting the measure. At the City Council meeting, the President and her legal advisors never had to say a word. The City Council, humbled by the opposition to the measure, unanimously voted to rescind the tax, thereby saving the college $500,000.

Nevertheless, the President had been through a difficult time with this problem, and her comment to Tom reflects her edginess that she had not done something she should have done. Later in the year, in conversation with someone about her job, she said, "People never remember the good you accomplish. Hassles and crisis. That's all this job is. Hassles and crisis." To my knowledge, no one told her she did a good job in fighting the tax assessment, yet many people complained about the slowness in relocating to Belchamp. The President, Tom, and others involved with the move assumed that it was the President's task to assign rooms for the different offices in Belchamp. Room assignments meant tagging old furniture, moving boxes, and determining what articles should be saved and what should be thrown out. After their meeting the President spent the morning hard at work in Belchamp.

When Tom left the room that morning Sister Vera thanked him for showing up at the meeting, and this, too, was fairly regular. Support, to Sister Vera, was when people attended particular meetings or functions, and it was something to be acknowledged either in a quick handwritten note, a memo, or a formal announcement at a meeting, or verbally as she had with Tom that morning.

One final point concerns the statement made about the curtains for Melton Hall, for the comment had consequences for Professor Simmer's attitude toward the administration. The professor, a favorite of the previous President who continues to work extraordinarily hard on behalf of the college, had written and spoken with Sister Vera about getting the curtains. When they did not arrive she grew exasperated, not because they were not there but because of the seeming indifference of the President. "This would never have happened in the old days," was Sue Ann's feeling. Such comparisons of style between the previous President and Sister Vera were commonplace.

The Admissions Office eventually relocated to spacious quarters in Belchamp. "This is what we need," related the Admissions Director, Dave Falconieri, "when prospective students come here.

Now they'll get a positive image of the college, as opposed to that cubicle we used to have." The newly appointed Admissions Director had countless ideas about how to attract students to CMM, but he was at a loss about how to get his ideas transformed into concrete plans. "What about a chess club? A track team. Football. Why can't we have a beer license for the Inn? We've got to make this place more exciting, but people just want to continue life as usual."

One morning I accompanied the Admissions Director on visits to local high schools. At one school no one showed up to be interviewed by CMM, and at the other school a reticent young woman arrived at the interview room and announced she wanted to enroll at CMM. As Dave talked with the young woman I queried other students in the room concerning the possibility of going to College of Mother Mary. "It's too close to home, " said one, "I want to get away from my folks." Another student added, "It's too expensive. I'm gonna go to a state school. Besides, it's so small." The lone young man in the room just laughed and said, "I'm not going to some Catholic girls' school." On the drive back to the college Falconieri reflected on their comments and acknowledged the problem. "Mother Mary's been coed for 15 years, but we keep getting comments like that—that we're a girls' school. Tuition's a problem, but the main thing is we don't have a sellable image. Who are we? If we have to keep relying on foreign students and girls like the one we got today, we're doomed." Image, for the Admissions Director, meant concentrating on domestic students of the traditional age group, yet the reality was that the administration wanted to reach out to previously untapped audiences—weekend students, or off-campus areas where educational programs did not exist.

During the course of the year Falconieri and his staff became increasingly dismayed at the static nature of the change process at CMM. Where others cautioned moderation, Falconieri in particular wanted speedy change. Falconieri and his staff reflected an esprit de corps that was both welcome and cheerful. The age diversity of the group—from 21 to over 60—promoted a family-like tenor to the staff, yet they still worked busily at recruiting students. As with most departments at the college, individuals within the department liked one another and worked well together.

One day the entire staff went out for lunch together and invited me to tag along. As I entered the office toward noon two people said jokingly, "He's here. We can go now." Another individual came out of her office and said to Falconieri, "Hey big guy, let's get going." As we headed out the door the oldest member of the staff called to Dave and said, "Don't forget your coat. It's cold outside." We proceeded to the restaurant and before we sat down I asked one individual how it was going. The person said, "It's ok. All these guys are nice. It worries me sometimes that we don't get any leadership from O'Connell. We never see Vera. I hope Dave speaks effectively in those meetings." We then sat down and proceeded to have a humorous luncheon conversation about many of the personalities at CMM.

The luncheon engagement illustrates that staff and administrators are generally on a first-name basis with one another, and staff members use terms of endearment such as "big guy" for administrators. Individuals socialize with one another quite often, but discussion often revolves around life at the college. People expect direction from top administrators and often feel they do not get it. Staff members look to their middle manager—in this instance, Falconieri—to represent their ideas and concerns, which they had communicated to their director. Informality, friendly bantering, and social outings produced an inner-group cohesiveness, while at the same time the universe of CMM became polarized.

The Director of Finance, Dan Grant, also had private doubts about the policies of the institution, but in his case the concern was fiscal. For Dan Grant a major stumbling block was that Sister Vera did not see fit to include him within the executive circle. "My salary is the same as theirs," he reasoned, "but they don't want to hear what I've got to say. If the Executive Committee makes decisions around here, and we've got financial problems, doesn't it make sense to have the chief financial officer included in those deliberations?" In good health, and relatively free of stress and tension, Dan Grant's heart attack at the beginning of the school year came as a complete surprise to everyone.

Sister Vera found out about the heart attack the morning Grant was to have his weekly meeting with her. She walked in, greeted her secretary and me, and moved toward her desk. Sally stood up and said, "Sister, there's no easy way to tell you this. Dan's wife called 15 minutes ago, and he had a massive heart attack over the weekend." Sister Vera's face went white, and she immediately went into Tim Leary's office, where O'Connell and Leary proffered possible alternatives and replacements. "I know someone in the city," said Leary. "Maybe the auditor could help us out," added O'Connell. "I just want to see him," said the President. "I don't want to make any decisions until I see him. I've got to go and see him," she said, and headed out the door to the hospital.

College-wide response to Grant's heart attack was quick and dramatic; phone calls, letters, cards, flowers cascaded into the hospital until the hospital administrators asked that they be stopped. When Grant eventually returned he noted the support of Sister Vera and the college:

> You know, that really meant something. I must have gotten a card from everybody here. It sure helped. I was surprised, but I shouldn't have been. The people are really nice here. Vera was especially great. She came to see me an awful lot. Although I disagree with the financial things she does sometimes, I really care for her as a person. As a human being, I don't want her to get hurt. It's a shame what's happening. I really care.

Miraculously, within three months' time, Grant returned to work. Although he had physically recovered, his disposition toward his job had plummeted. In mid-January after a Budget and Finance Committee meeting he stated to me, "You're catching me at a low point now. If they want me to be a puppet, I will. I was really pissed off yesterday. Maybe you caught that. It's just goddamned common sense—to raise tuition only 4 percent is crazy. How are we going to give people raises when the revenue doesn't increase?" He referred to the previous day's Budget and Finance meeting which he chaired. On the advice of the AVP they agreed to a relatively low tuition increase of 4 percent in comparison to a 7 to 8 percent increase at other comparable institutions. As chair of the committee Grant was careful not to press his ideas on the committee, but instead let individuals speak and decide for themselves. The committee consisted of the President, the Vice Presidents, Grant and his aide, two members from the faculty, and one each from staff and administration. In actuality, Sister Vera, Leary, and O'Connell rarely attended the meetings, and during the course of the year reaching a quorum grew increasingly difficult. Out of frustration Grant cancelled one meeting because not enough members showed up on time.

Throughout the year members were well aware of the absence of the President from the committee. At a Faculty Senate meeting in October, for example, one of the faculty members to the committee reported on the work of Budget and Finance by saying, "Because Sister Vera wasn't there, and Dan is sick, we really didn't make much progress. Dr. O'Connell wanted us to go over a worksheet, but we really didn't make progress." His comments pertained to the meeting where the committee made the one significant decision of the year—to raise tuition—yet because the President was not there, he viewed the committee's work as minimal.

Budget and Finance met monthly from 2:30 until 4:00 PM on Mondays. Individuals received agendas and minutes prior to the meeting, and they considered issues such as health care and personnel benefits, and the systemization of charges for units of study. The staff members to the committee spoke less than 5 percent of the time, with the lion's share of talking done by the two faculty members, and, if he showed up, Dr. O'Connell.

The scope, function, and membership of the committee came to a head on April 2 at a meeting scheduled after the previous one had been cancelled due to a lack of attendance. The day after the meeting Grant came up to me in the hall and said, "What did you think of the meeting yesterday?" When I asked him what he meant he smiled and said, "It was a working group. Everybody participated. It was frank. We got things done. We brought secrets out into the open." When I asked him if he knew that Jake Barnes, a faculty member on the committee, was going to bring up the "secret," he said, "Yeah. Jake told me in the hall before the meeting that he wanted to discuss it, and I said, 'fine.' This is a budget meeting, and as long as I am chair people have a right to know."

The meeting began promptly at 2:30 PM. As with every other meeting, Grant and his aide were there ahead of time, to arrange the room, organize papers, and watch the clock. Grant sat at the head of the rectangular table and announced that Sister Vera, Leary, and O'Connell would not be at the meeting. One individual asked, "Is Tim Leary actually on this committee? I've never seen him here." They began a discussion of personnel benefits. Jake Barnes said, "The thing about this committee is that we don't have the knowledge to deal with this information. It's really frustrating." As they continued to discuss a 10-20 percent increase in the benefits, Sister Joan Rinelli, Vice President for Student Affairs, spoke up for a 20 percent increase. "Most of my staff is single, and they could really use the larger increase. They are simply getting killed by taxes." The meeting continued in uncharacteristic fashion; by 3:30 PM each of the members had spoken, and no one had spoken more than 20 percent of the time.

The last half hour of the meeting dealt with Jake Barnes's secret. As he spoke Sister Joan looked down at the table, and Grant stared blankly at Barnes as he said, "Joe Calabrese reported to the Faculty Senate that we finished last year with a half million dollar excess. It's simply unbelievable. People have come to me as a member of this committee to ask me if it's true, and I have to say I know nothing about it. Why? This group represents the community, and it should know about such things. I feel like I am participating in a committee where information is kept hidden from me. To have an extra half million dollars is good news, and I want to know why we weren't allowed to share that good news."

Grant suggested that the auditor come to the next meeting to explain the previous year's budget. Sister Joan reflected later on the revelation. "When Jake started talking my heart started pounding. We should have had the information. What can I say?" Another individual thought aloud that this committee, "can't be too important if we don't get the information." Another member added, "They obviously don't think it's important. The Executive Committee doesn't even attend. And when O'Connell shows up, it's not to participate, it's to tell us what to do." The members continued to vent their feelings about the committee until four o'clock. They unanimously agreed to have the auditor come to the next meeting, and they wanted to continue the discussion about the function and membership of the committee.

The meeting draws attention to several personal and group patterns discovered throughout the year. Dan Grant stayed neutral throughout the meeting; he had gained a reputation for fairness by actions such as suggesting that they bring in the auditor. A month later he willingly talked with the Faculty Senate about how the money had been spent. Sister Joan's comment about her staff was also typical in that she frequently spoke up for those people who worked for her. Although she was a member of the Executive Committee, most people did not consider her "them." One individual, for example, stated, "The Executive Committee doesn't even attend," although Sister Joan had been at every meeting but one. The frankness with which members talked related to the atmosphere of frustration individuals felt with the Executive Committee. Finally, the secret half million dollar excess caused anger not because the money had been misspent, but because the information had been kept hidden.

The President found out about the excess income on October 4, one day before the year's first Board of Trustees meeting, and immediately prior to an Executive Committee meeting. Sister Vera walked quickly into her office where Tim Leary and Patrick O'Connell waited for her. Sister Joan Rinelli was on vacation in Europe. Speaking quickly, Sister Vera informed them of the money and said, "I'm being real frank with you. I'm going to have a severe credibility problem." Leary offered alternatives about how to spend the money and seemed relatively unconcerned that they reported excess income; if there was a deficit, then he felt there was cause for concern. Sister Vera interrupted him as he expressed his thoughts and said, "Look, I'm not worried with what we can do with this income. I'm worried that people will see this and wonder how people will feel who didn't get a big raise and then see that we ended with a half million dollar surplus. I can't deal with how to spend this today. I need to know how to communicate it." They talked about possible ways to present the information to the Board of Trustees, and toward the end of the meeting Sister Vera said, "I'm sorry if I overreacted." Tim casually responded, "It's just a problem you deal with—" Sister Vera reacted heatedly: "Look, Tim, I know it's a problem you deal with, but six hours before a meeting I was just handed this, and if it gets out, it will really hit at my credibility." One-half year later, Sister Vera's comment had come true. The administration had communicated the need for massive change because of a fiscal crisis. The report that the college had finished the year with a half million dollar excess struck at the heart of that assertion.

This section demonstrates themes and patterns which we will see recur. Except with her closest informants, meetings with the President were formal occurrences wherein the role of "president" constituted the importance of the meetings, rather than the individual who filled the role. That is, the President's absence at Budget and Finance signaled that no significant decisions occurred even though the committee voted to raise tuition. The actors' conception of the roles of the Executive Committee and their absence from Budget and Finance meant top administrators did not care about the committee.

At the same time, perceptions of the individuals who filled roles looked not at formalized structures, but rather toward an informal process of communication. As with the Admissions Department, most groups existed not as executive or subordinate, but rather as friends or family. A member of the Executive Committee—Sister Joan—retained her individuality even though she sat on the committee. Actors received formalized support from the President—letters or formal statements of thanks—yet they did not garner the individualized attention that they had become accustomed to from the previous President.

BOARD OF TRUSTEES

The Board of Trustees meets four times a year for a two-hour meeting and lunch. Subcommittees such as finance, revenue, land-use, and academic affairs meet at other times to provide information and advice to the trustees and the President. This section provides two examples of board work concerning issues previously discussed. The Executive Task Force will lend an additional explanation of how the "secret" half million became public knowledge. The discussion will then return to one of the major issues of the fall—the tax assessment by the city of Rosewood. We begin with a general overview.

Board members are divided almost evenly between lay and Sisters, yet at the meetings the Sisters account for less than 20 percent of the speaking. The Chair of the Board—the chief executive officer of a major company—chairs the meeting with written notes by Tim Leary guiding his presentation. Sister Vera begins the meeting with an oral summary of the events and actions of the college, and the information she provides is met with support both publicly at the meeting and in private. One member offered this analysis of the President's style with the Board: "There has been an ongoing effort since Vera became President for the Board to become better and better. The Board composition is excellent. It's very professional. She gives us adequate information and we really have to do our homework now." Another trustee concurred: "She's so diplomatic. She brings us up to date and she's a wonder for having learned so much in such a short time. It's a rough job being President."

The Board did not concern themselves with the day-to-day operation of the college; they remained informed primarily through their committee work and the reports of the President. At the spring meeting Sister Vera informed them of the conflict on campus by saying at the end of her report, "I would be remiss if I did not mention that the faculty are concerned. They were able to put into writing a six-page summary of what is causing them great concern. … They feel some processes were not observed. We are engaged in an ongoing dialogue. Again I would be remiss if I did not alert the Board to this. There is a great deal of tension. We are not heading toward disaster, but it needs to be considered due to the high tension here." The chair responded by saying that change causes anxiety, and that he and the Board offered their support and cooperation. His statement was indicative of the way they operated; the Board supported Sister Vera's action and had some sense of the problems that currently beset the college.

The consequences of the information about the surplus income were not entirely understood by the trustees. As businessmen, a surplus at the end of the year is not harmful news, but something that warrants applause. Consequently, the chair of the Finance Committee announced at the opening of the year, "While I don't have the audit report with me due to Dan Grant's illness, I can report that we will have several hundred thousand dollars over our expenditures from last year." Some members of the Board smiled, and others nodded their heads in affirmation. One individual said, "We must be doing something right if we're coming in ahead of the game."

Sister Vera had communicated the news to no other individuals than the Executive Committee and Board. In reality only two individuals could have uncovered this information. To discover the excess income demanded a proficient reading of the audit report which remained in the President's office. No one asked for the report except one faculty member on the Executive Task Force.

During the spring of the previous year the President decided to create an Executive Task Force concerned with salary schedules and alternative sources of funding. The committee consisted of two board members, two faculty members chosen by the faculty, and two administrators chosen by the administrative staff. The Task Force met for the first time on November 14 at nine o'clock. Sister Vera arrived at the conference room early to check to see if everything was set up the way she wanted. The faculty walked in separately, as did the members of the Executive Committee and the Board. The two administrators walked in together. Sister Vera asked everyone to get assembled, "so we can get out of here," she said humorously. She sat at the head of the table for this meeting, informed everyone about the storm drainage assessment, and then introduced everyone to one another. She mentioned that one Board member, Tim Thompson, would not be at the meeting because he was sick. Faculty expectations for this committee were high, demonstrated by one professor's comment about Thompson, "If Thompson's on the committee that will mean it has muscle. They'll really get something done."

Sister Vera outlined what they needed to do by saying, "Everyone expects the President to have all the answers. I don't. I need help. I don't feel helpless, but I am at the same time asking for help." She said she wanted a report by the end of February; any information they wanted she would give them. After a few minutes of discussion about the nature of the work, Sister Vera concluded her portion of the meeting. "Well, if there aren't any questions then I will leave you to your work. Please feel free to ask me for anything you need." She stood up and exited with her Executive Committee following behind her.

An awkward 10-second silence ensued, and then one of the faculty members said, "I think Mr. Sanger [the other board member] should be the chair of this committee." Both administrators immediately concurred, and Mr. Sanger affably said, "Well, I would only accpet it in a very, very, conditional sense. This has to be a team effort." The other faculty member, Joe Calabrese, had a different idea. "That's funny," he said. "I was going to say either you Jane [the administrator] or you Roy [the professor] should become chair because you know the most about the institution." "Oh no," said Roy, "the chair should definitely be a board member." Well, maybe Tim Thompson could be chair," said Sanger. "He and I are both close friends. Why don't I go give him a call." He stood up and went to look for a phone.

When the Board member left the four settled comfortably in with one another and confided thoughts. Roy told Joe, "For this committee to have any credibility it would have to have a board person as chair. They don't listen to us, Joe. We're here to help the board make some decisions. We have no power. The Faculty Senate is a joke." Joe grew visibly angry upon hearing this and responded, "I should resign right now if you're telling me that I'm just here to suck up to the board. Do you really believe that?" "Yes, I do," said Jane. "We can still change things, but we have to let the board know. The Executive Committee doesn't listen to us." Mr. Sanger returned and said, "Tim says he'll accept." They spent the next hour discussing problems of the college and set a date for the next meeting.

As the year progressed it seemed as if the members of the Task Force shared information, but were unsure of their essential purpose. They had interpreted Sister Vera's directive—to design alternate sources of revenue—in the broadest possible sense. One day in the Executive Committee Leary mentioned in passing, "I don't know if you're aware of it, but the Task Force is gathering information from all over the place. It's not just budgetary." Later in the year another individual reported, "That group is going to make a recommendation about advising." Sister Vera expressesd mild surprise that a group she thought had worked on land revenue and salary scales had gotten involved in the advising process at CMM.

This committee was unique for the college—a small group of people elected from each representative's constituency to talk about budgetary policy. At the same time, as seen with Budget and Finance, the committee had a problem endemic to committees at CMM—it was unsure of its task. Although guidelines, agendas, timelines, minutes, could be drawn up, the members constantly grappled with deciding what issues most centrally concerned them, rather than solving a particular problem. In a year of organizational change, an increased difficulty in accomplishing that change concerned committees' inability to understand the processes whereby they could reach their stated goals.

In January Joe Calabrese asked for and received the audit of the college. As he poured over the document he realized the college had finished the year in the black. At the Faculty In-Service on March 12 Calabrese announced the information to the faculty. He concluded his report to the faculty by saying, "We should put the idea of a crisis behind us. The college is not in financial crisis.

In fact, we're doing better financially than we were three years ago." This information produced a new wave of anger, resentment, and mistrust.

The Task Force went "out of business" in May with its final report. The major recommendations from the group were to hire a consultant and a Director of Planning so that orderly, planned change could occur. In many respects trustee work with this group was more extensive than on any other committee of the Board of Trustees. Trustees, however, also had individual roles that they performed for the college. The next example returns to a discussion of the tax assessment by Rosewood, and the work of one trustee—Jim Yoshihira.

The tax assessment arose during the first week of November. The Catholic high school in Rosewood heard about the issue from a neighbor. Sister Vera had CMM's lawyer check it out, and when it appeared the college might have to pay a large tax she immediately called a meeting of a law firm friendly to the college, the Executive Committee, the CMM lawyer, and Mr. Yoshihira, the youngest member of the Board of Trustees, who was a lawyer for a prominent law firm. Sister Vera indicated that Yoshihira was one of her favorites on the board when I asked her which trustees should be interviewed. She immediately referred to Yoshihira by saying, "He's a really good guy, and he works real hard for us."

They contacted one another frequently throughout the storm drainage crisis. Yoshihira provided the President not only valuable advice as to possible options, but he also lent the proceedings a sense of humor which helped relieve the tension. One morning in late November he called her from his city office. They had a 10-minute conversation and she laughed at his comments; it was the only time I observed her laughing all that week. "Yes, Jim, that's what I'm considering all right," said Sister Vera, "wouldn't I love to abdicate ... you want to come down and take over? The job is yours."

The first meeting about what to do to fight the tax assessment took place on the morning of November 12. Mr. Yoshihira arrived at Sister Vera's office as she was about to head to the conference room. Clad with a notebook and pen, she headed out the door and looked up and saw him. She smiled, then said, "Oh good, you came," and gave his arm a tight squeeze. They walked over to the room talking with each other and the other participants drifted slowly into the meeting. They sat down with Sister Vera in the middle of a rectangular table, and Yoshihira at one end.

Sister Vera said, "Maybe I can give you a little background about this." She relayed the history of how they found out about the assessment and ended a five-minute monologue by saying,

> I don't know if it is appropriate for me to say this. I'm going to say it anyway—the sum is staggering to us. I don't know how we'll pay it, but I want to walk a fine line. I don't want to isolate these people. We live here. I don't want relations between the city and college to be antagonistic. I can be extremely simplistic about this. We are operating in a state of urgency. We need this by December 6, and we need to enter a written protest. How much are we to benefit from the storm drainage pipes. We're not being flooded. These are simplistic questions I know, but what can we do?

At this point, Yoshihira provided information that he had collected on behalf of the college concerning tax assessments, and how to go about fighting the problem. "I share with our President here maintaining a public profile, but a half million dollars is worth a fight. I'd like to explore the litigation potential. I'd like to tell you all what I've found out from a few phone calls." He told them of his information and the question then arose concerning the possibility of an informal bargaining session being undertaken between the city and the college. The lawyer downplayed the possibility: "If six months ago you'd found out from the mayor, perhaps you'd had him over to watch a football game, and over beer and peanuts he'd told you about the assessment, maybe then, early on in the game, you could have had your portion of the assessment reduced because you're not like a business. But it's too late to do that now, I'm afraid."

The meeting continued for two hours and they finally agreed to investigate the possibility of filing a written protest. During the ensuing month the President, Executive Committee, Mr. Yoshihira, and the law firm met approximately half a dozen times in order to determine their line of attack with the city. By the time of the open hearing on December 6, they had filed a written protest, and the litigation potential that Mr. Yoshihira had spoken about had been used. The defeat of the measure by the City Council, however, came not because of CMM's efforts, but because of the city's homeowners.

Although relations between Rosewood and CMM are not bad, the relationship between both groups has always been one of indifference. The lawyer had suggested that a friendly meeting between the President and mayor might have prevented the problem, but no such friendly relations existed. In fact, I once asked Sister Vera who I should talk with in the city about the college. "The only two people I know," she said, "are Jim Eliot and Sam Black, on the City Council. They're friends of the college because they went here. But I really don't know anyone else." When an alumnus of CMM spoke about the town, she said, "We don't use the city. Rosewood doesn't even know we're alive. They think we're a secluded girls' college and don't have anything to do with us. It's really a dead city." Relations, then, between the city and the college were proper, but not friendly. The President learned of city news not through informal city channels such as Rotary lunches or the Kiwanis, but through formal written notification.

Prior to a discussion of the faculty and the Executive Committee, a brief review of the actors, issues, and problems would be helpful. The tax assessment followed closely on the heels of Dan Grant's heart attack. While he was sick, Sister Vera found out and reported to the Board of Trustees that the college finished the previous fiscal year with excess income. The rest of the campus did not learn about the excess until March. Ongoing problems continued throughout the year. Personnel needed to move into Belchamp Hall, and a computer program was in the process of being implemented. Admissions was unsure how to articulate the mission of the college; the Finance Director questioned the fiscal policies, and the Facilities Manager felt his voice went unheard. Trustee involvement came from trustee meetings, subcommittees, and individual work. As none of these problems existed in isolation, a description of the faculty returns to some of these issues and develops new information. Thus, we now meet some new actors and observe different scenes, yet many of the issues remain the same.

FACULTY

The drama continues with faculty affairs and concerns; the vehicle for discussion will be the Faculty Senate. Over 80 percent of the faculty hold doctorates, and 42 percent of the faculty have tenure.

Salaries range from $17,000 to $30,000, and while work at CMM is often an individual's principal income, in order to survive many individuals have second jobs, or the individual's spouse also works.

Faculty representation was on every major committee of the school except the Executive Committee. Although no faculty members sat on the Board of Trustees as representatives, there were Sisters of Mother Mary who were Board members and faculty. Either the administration appointed the faculty to the committee, or the faculty held elections among themselves to see who would sit on the committees. Throughout the year no one ever mentioned that appointed faculty members were weaker or less vocal than elected officials, yet one did occasionally hear the faculty voice a desire to have only elected members on the committees. One faculty member observed, "It's not a big deal, but it might become one. I think maybe all faculty representation should be by election and not appointment by the President."

The crisis, conflict, and problems that occurred throughout the year breathed new life into a six-year-old organization previously ignored by many faculty—the Faculty Senate. Prior to 1983/84 the Senate often had fewer than eight members in attendance. The major functions of the Senate had been to recommend salaries and benefits to the administration and to elect faculty members to the committees. From the start of the current year, however, attendance averaged 35 members at monthly meetings concerned with the present problems of the college.

Faculty personalities stood out, and while it could be arguably stated that the chair of the Senate, Dan Blue-Smith, was the coalescing force for the faculty, by no means was there a single voice who spoke for the professoriate. All segments of the faculty worked against many of the perceived actions and processes of the administration. Sue Ann Simmer was perhaps the most dramatic example of a concerned faculty member against the proposed changes. As a senior faculty member of 27 years, individuals often deferred to her in order to listen to her historical voice. "O'Connell has made Honors Day a recruiting device for Admissions. Are we supposed to go to it?" queried a young faculty member at a Senate meeting. Sue Ann replied, "That's not the way it used to be, the way it's supposed to be. Faculty have always been involved with Honors Day. It was an All-College Day, and everyone got involved, especially faculty. The work, direction, and activity always came from the dean's office. He [O'Connell] doesn't understand what it means to us."

Initially, Simmer had little use for the Faculty Senate. She told me at the beginning of the year, "I have refused to take an office in it. It lacks an historical perspective. It tends to be a grievance committee over salary. Look, we've spent all our nonrestricted funds. That ought to condition our demands. For those of us who see this as a career, we can't say what's in it for us. We have to seek the welfare of the college over the welfare of the faculty." At the beginning of the year other faculty noted their respect for Simmer, but also that she was a "company woman" who was not entirely faculty. Their comments related to what Simmer had said to me; she would not support demands for salary increases at the expense of the college. By springtime, however, at the Faculty In-Service, she had come full circle. The Faculty Senate had become the forum for concerned opposition to the actions of the administration; Sue Ann attended every meeting and allied herself fully with the faculty. At the In-Service she joked about her transformation. "This has certainly been an atypical year. I've become active in the Faculty Senate, which is quite different, and I find myself constantly fighting the policies of the administration."

Throughout the year Sue Ann Simmer was a key informant who freely voiced her opinion about the actions of the administration. As the year began her main objection was over the abundance of administrative positions at the college, and the increasing criticism of the faculty. Over coffee and danish in her campus apartment one morning, Sue Ann said, "There is now a superstructure in place. We are too heavy with an Executive Committee and an administrative staff that is sheer proliferation. We have added additional people, and of course, salaries have increased." As the conversation progressed she turned her attention to Sister Vera's inaccessiblity, and criticism of the faculty:

> You don't have to have dinner with everybody, but casual contact, conversation, is a necessity. You've got to make yourself visible, and Vera does not do that. With Barbara Therese the door was always open. Walking by in the hall you could see if Sister Barbara was in her office and just pop in. With Vera she has moved her desk, and you really don't feel like popping in. She's not accessible. We also get the feeling that retention, the

problems of the school, are all our fault. I really don't like placing the blame on people because of a preconceived idea.

Patterns developed out of that conversation which occurred throughout the year. Simmer made her judgment about Sister Vera in part by comparing her to the previous President. Accessibility was an important attribute mentioned as a presidential necessity. Particular groups received blame for the problems that beset the college. It was also in this conversation that the curtains for Melton Hall received mention as something that "would have been taken care of immediately in the past."

As the year progressed Simmer's criticism intensified and shifted toward the administration's handling of change and the adherence to the faculty handbook. People heard her voice in all corners— to the Faculty Senate, in committees, to the Sisters, and to the President and Chancellor. She remained dedicated to teaching her English students; even at the low point of her year, in March, when she felt all was lost, she encouraged other faculty to show up for Honors Day in order to applaud students' work. At the end of one Faculty Senate meeting she stood up and spoke about soon-approaching Honors Day. "It hasn't jelled yet. The AVP won't take responsibility and students are being made to feel responsible for something they don't know how to coordinate. They need our help. They deserve our help. We have to give it some support."

As a body that tried to present a unified faculty voice on the issues, the Senate struggled with a twofold task. First, they had to grapple with the processes and procedures of decision making. Second, they had to implement the curricular and divisional changes which the administration presented to them. That is, because the Senate was young and it had little previous voice in decision making, it was unaccustomed to accomplishing tasks with set procedures and policies. The changes ahead of the Senate members were more difficult because they were unsure how to go about restructuring those changes.

As noted in Chapter II, O'Connell took the faculty completely by surprise with his proposed ideas announced at the beginning of the year. Initially, faculty faced the changes with resigned skepticism. The first Faculty Senate meeting of the year ended not in hostility, but with serious questions for which they hoped to find answers from the AVP. "Does the reorganization save money?" queried one professor. "The AVP premises his plan for curricular reorganization in that we will save money with the reorganization. From where?"

By the middle of October the faculty began to resent the changes O'Connell proposed, and most particularly the way he went about initiating those alterations. The most dramatic example occurred in a Curriculum Committee meeting in which faculty members stood up in anger and walked out of the room. O'Connell twice had angry exchanges with two faculty members; one of them subsequently received his dismissal notice; the other, a Professor Trumble, resigned, in part to protest the direction in which the college was headed.

Two days before Professor Trumble sent her letter of resignation to the AVP she called me to her office and showed me her letter. The letter was succinct, and did not detail why she resigned. She said to me, "You're the first to see it. I don't want people to get demoralized, but I know it's right. I've got three reasons for resigning. I want more time to do research, and the salary is just too low. I've been here five years and I'm still not making 20 thousand. I also don't have any faith in the administration. I had a lot of hope that O'Connell would turn things around, but he seems even worse. He won't listen, and I'm not willing to fight." Trumble had been chair of the English department, very popular with students, and an individual who worked hard on the committees of the college. As we talked, Dan Blue-Smith, chair of the Faculty Senate, happened by and she showed him the letter. "It's really a shame, Bobbi," he said. "I don't want to see you go." The discussion continued in her office for half an hour, and as we sat over coffee on a rainy day, they reflected on the difficulty of defining problems that were essentially communicative.

Problems in communication began immediately at the first Faculty Senate meeting on September 15. Fifty-nine people showed up to hear the address of the AVP at a Senate meeting, whereas traditionally no more than eight individuals attended. O'Connell gave a prophetic address to the faculty wherein he raised three of the major issues to be developed throughout the year. First, in response to a question from the Senate chair about faculty input with regard to college governance, O'Connell stated, "You must realize that you are bound by every word in the handbook once you sign a contract, so you should have some say in what you are binding yourselves to." Second, he linked the rationale for the reorganization to the financial crisis. Joe Calabrese had asked the AVP if CMM was going into bankruptcy, and while O'Connell said no, he also made it clear that the college was "vulnerable to liquidation." Finally, when one individual stated that reorganizations often affect small programs adversely—they get lost in the shuffle—O'Connell tried to allay people's fears and said that he doubted that would happen.

At subsequent meetings the faculty felt positive enough with the AVP's comments to vote that they would cooperate with the change, and that they essentially agreed with the shapes of the divisional structures. There was a modicum of tinkering with the divisions—history became a social science rather than reside in the humanities, for example—but in general they accepted O'Connell's plan. In December, at an upbeat meeting of the Faculty Senate, Sister Vera announced who were to be the chairs of the five divisions. By this time the storm drainage assessment had been defeated, which caused obvious relief in the administration, but the faculty had not concerned themselves about the matter. Their concerns were with the reorganization the had voted for. Now they waited to see who the administration chose for the position of divisional chairs. One could see a visual easing of tension as the holidays approached; not only was there a Christmas break, but CMM had a month-long "Intersession" in January that gave everyone time to reflect on the proposed changes and physically get away from the college. The five divisional chairs, and the newly appointed Dean of the Faculty, were all active faculty members whom the faculty supported. Soon after the announcement, faculty discussions and conversations turned to what one expects to hear at Christmas time—the rush to fill in grades, how they would spend the holidays, and the like.

By February 21 the tension had risen perceptibly higher than it had at any other time. Prior to a Senate meeting, the chair put out a memo which stated: "Considerable concern has developed and been expressed by members of the faculty over the issues of organizational change and communication at the college. In recent weeks I have been contacted by a number of colleagues, junior and senior faculty, who have reported that, in their opinion, we have reached a critical stage. Therefore, the agenda for the next Faculty

Senate meeting will be changed. The single item to be discussed will be communication at the college."

The meeting took place in the Art Gallery amid pictures of struggle and conflict by one local artist. By 12:30 some 30 people had assembled in small groups, talking among one another. When I asked Sue Ann Simmer if I could talk with her sometime in the near future about "what's been happening" she agreed, and said shaking her head resolutely, "It's a shame. There is absolutely no reason for it either. All of this could be resolved, but they just won't listen to us." We agreed to meet later in the week, and I went to the back of the room and sat in an inconspicuous blue chair apart from the others. Joe Calabrese approached, shook my hand, and sat to one side of me. I asked him about "what's going on." He laughed, threw back his head, and said, "How the hell should I know. I just come in, teach my classes, and go home. There's no communication here. That's the way they want it." He did not appear particularly angry, but just stated a fact.

The meeting started promptly, and during the next hour and a half a dozen additional faculty entered, and only one individual left early. The chair proceeded to place the meeting in context by stating he had talked with many faculty who were extremely upset, and that even the students had asked to attend the meeting, and Blue-Smith denied them entrance because he did not want the information to go public. The chair then introduced a member of the music department.

This individual mentioned that he had never spoken at Faculty Senate, and he alluded to the fact that he would rather be playing the faculty a sonata than addressing them, but he felt it imperative to talk. He had prepared a written text that he read nervously to a silent faculty. He likened the college to a family, and to a community. He pointed out that because a child was expensive it did not mean that the parents should abandon the child, yet the administration wanted to abandon master's programs in music and other areas because they were expensive children.

When he finished there was a burst of applause, not so much for what he said, but for the fervor with which he talked. As one professor later mentioned,

You couldn't help but feel moved. Did you see his hands shaking? He's really hurt, but you know, I think those little master's programs should be dismantled. They don't support themselves economically or academically. We've got graduate programs that are essentially graduate students sitting in undergraduate classes. What's too bad is that I wholeheartedly side with him, because O'Connell is being so obnoxious.

A few moments after the music professor finished, a Franciscan professor of theology raised his hand, the chair recognized him, and the priest stood up in his brown robes and firmly walked to the front of the room, where he made this statement:

> We must draw up a bill of particulars, a declaration of independence ... We are not being listened to. We're changing the model of administration in this institution from one of collegiality, and we've moved into a business model in which the high administration can override at will decisions made below. We have completely reversed what this college is built on, and it's a complete disaster. In the Graduate Committee we had voted to keep two programs, and Dr. O'Connell came in and said the programs did not meet the criteria, so we have to rework our decisions. Those programs do meet the criteria. We devised the criteria. We have moved from collegiality to dictatorship. We must protest this action. Now.

He returned to his seat, but he faced a groundswell of support. Two professors related how similar incidents had occurred in the Rank and Tenure Committee where O'Connell had said the handbook was not the "bible" on which to base decisions.

An individual to my left leaned over and whispered, "You can't even tell anymore who's who. Now even the sisters and priests are against Vera." What impressed the faculty that day was the firmness of the Franciscan's words. "The way he spoke really did it," said one individual. "When a man like Damien stands up and says this is wrong, you really listen. In the fall he tried to be a pacifier, but to come full circle and say what he said—Damien is so fair-minded, so just, that if he feels the way he does, then the time has come for action." A senior faculty member, Jake Barnes, moved that they have a three-person committee write a letter of protest to the administration and that a special meeting be called by the Senate to approve the letter. They adopted the motion unanimously, and shortly thereafter, Sue Ann, the Franciscan, and a psychology professor agreed to draft the letter. As the meeting ended and faculty filed out of the room a young teacher came up to me and said, "You should have been here last year. There were no problems, nothing like this. I've never seen such angry meetings."

During the ensuing week the faculty sent a letter to Sister Vera and the Executive Committee. The letter tried to show by concrete examples the problems in communication. Administrative reaction, however, was to rebut the examples point by point. The administration had a meeting with the writers of the document and the Faculty Senate chair. While the meeting had been cordial, it produced no change whatsoever. Both sides had so orchestrated their responses that in the relatively short time—one-half hour—allotted for the meeting nothing more happened than a recital of both sides' views. The administration agreed to meet with the Faculty Senate in order to air administrative response to the six-page document.

The meeting began with a brief statement by the chair, stating how CMM was a community of educators and professionals with years of experience, and that the meeting was not to be a prejudged affair, but rather a meeting of listening to and hearing one another. Blue-Smith introduced Sister Vera who began speaking from a written text. She had the flu, and looked tired and flushed as she spoke. She began:

> It seems to me we're dealing with two things. Obviously we're dealing with perception, emotion, and feeling, It's very clear to me that I'm dealing with anger, resentment, and hurt. I'd like to try to deal with it if I can ... I'd like to take full responsibility for all actions that have happened here. My style is one of delegation. I try to let people do their jobs and I respect them. I have standing appointments with my chief administrative officers. I am the president. Some of my actions may have been perceived as not going through established channels. I believe we're in a state of crisis, and I've tried to communicate that crisis.

She continued speaking for approximately 15 minutes, whereupon the AVP presented his report. His comments focused on primarily one aspect of decision making—the legality of the handbook. He stated that the handbook was binding to the degree that everyone agreed that it was binding. Because decisions had to be made on a daily basis he thought it something of an "existential situation" if one had to rely on a written document that did not answer each problem that came before his desk. That is, O'Connell felt the manifold problems that he encountered each day demanded his swift interpretation and response; to rely on a written document for answers was simply untenable. Finally, as a living community he noted that a written document could not reflect the everchanging nature of the community. He likened the handbook to a moving train that needs painting, and consequently had to have constant changes.

The presentation ended with virtually no questions from the faculty, and the chair thanked them for coming. The Executive Committee filed out behind Sister Vera, and the faculty remained and tried to figure out the next step. A faculty member sitting next to me exhaled deeply and said, "Oh boy." "You've not happy?" I ventured. "How'd you guess," he angrily said. "They didn't hear one word of what we wrote. She talked to us like we were bad little boys and girls. Dealing with anger and hurt? Come off it." The chair expressed a similar view to the group. "It's obvious that we're dealing wtih completely different perceptions of reality. We need time to think about this, and then come back together again."

In addition to the appearance at the Faculty Senate, the administration handed out a letter from Sister Vera and the Executive Committee. The letter began, "The memorandum of March 1 asserts that there is a breakdown in communication ... In the course of narrating these illustrations specific allegations are made accusing college administrators of actions that contravene the 'collegial model of governance' on which the handbook is based."

These meetings highlight several points. Sister Vera responded to faculty concerns—both in writing and orally—not by accepting that a problem existed, but by accepting that faculty were upset. The letter began with an "assertion" that a breakdown in communication existed, rather than the acknowledgement of that breakdown. In her speech she tried to deal with "anger, resentment, and hurt," when the faculty perceived that the problem was entirely different. Sister Vera acknowledged that the normal routes for decision making had not been followed, but she had not followed those routes because of the crisis nature of the moment. As an example of that crisis she pointed out the serious financial shape of CMM. At the time, the faculty accepted a crisis existed, but objected to running roughshod over established guidelines and procedures.

At the beginning of the year the faculty carefully debated the reasons and plans for change, and they worked within a two-point framework laid out by O'Connell at the previously noted Faculty Senate meeting in September: (1) the handbook was valid and the way to order change, and (2) the overriding reason for the change was due to the serious fiscal shape of the college. By March, however, in the eyes of the faculty O'Connell reversed himself on the status of the handbook by implying that one could not guide oneself on a "living document." After the meeting with the Senate, in private with the Senate Chair, Sister Vera acknowledged that problems remained and told Blue-Smith she needed to think about what next to do. The following week Dan Blue-Smith received a letter that he read at the Faculty In-Service in March. The President noted that a problem existed, the handbook was in effect, and invited Dan Blue-Smith to sit in the Executive Committee meetings.

It was at the In-Service in March that Joe Calabrese told the faculty about the previous year's excess income. The issue of the half million dollar surplus so seriously eroded the credibility of the administration that the faculty no longer believed a fiscal crisis existed; the focal point of "crisis" had changed.

After Calabrese's statements roughly a dozen faculty members stood up and made exhortative statements like the following: "If we have a crisis, it's a crisis of leadership. We are the leaders of this institution. We aren't going to get help from the administration so we've got to support ourselves. We are wonderful people." Another professor added: "She [Sister Vera] 'asserts' a problem exists, she doesn't believe us. We have to assume a greater degree of leadership. We're not in crisis, the administration is." There was general agreement, however, that the inclusion of Dan Blue-Smith in the Executive Committee was a positive step if for no other reason than that the faculty would have a voice in the most important committee of the college.

Dan Blue-Smith was a sociology professor who received tenure at the end of 1983/84. In appearance, actions, and beliefs, Blue-Smith stood out among the CMM faculty. I only heard two instructors whose students called them by their first names—Blue-Smith was one of them. Whereas many male faculty members wore suits, or at least semiformal attire, Blue-Smith dressed in pullover sweaters and sandals, had longish hair, and a full beard.

One faculty member jokingly said, "Dan's success is because he's a throwback to the mellow world of the '60s; he calms us all down and that's what we need this year." Another faculty member added, "Dan and I are the furthest left in politics and ideology."

When the faculty elected him chair of the Senate he felt that his main task was to pressure the administration to increase faculty salaries. Almost immediately the other problems of the college forced him to rethink and redefine the role of the Faculty Senate chair, and therefore the role of the Faculty Senate. More than any other individual, Dan broached the gap between faculty and administration throughout the year. At one Faculty Senate meeting a professor stood up and said, "I'd just like to publicly acknowledge how great a job you've done for us. We'd be lost without you," whereupon he received a round of applause. When he interviewed with the Executive Committee for the position of Dean of the Faculty, Sister Vera commended him by saying, "I couldn't be more supportive of you. Your ability to draw people out, to get people motivated, is a tremendous gift."

In part he was able to garner support by communicating to each group a message they wanted to hear. He said to the Faculty Senate, for example, "I think it's a positive step that Vera included me on the Executive Committee. They trust me, and we'll have a voice in there now and know what's going on." To the Executive Committee he said, "The letter you wrote, Vera, was perfect. They didn't hear it when you said the handbook was the guide at the meeting. They just didn't hear it. Your letter was great." The point, of course, was that the faculty had heard Sister Vera, but Dr. O'Connell had spoken after her, throwing the handbook's viability into doubt. Although it came as something of a surprise that the president asked Blue-Smith to sit on the Executive Committtee, it was also a logical move that initially provided a glimmer of hope for the improvement of faculty-administered relations.

EXECUTIVE COMMITTEE

The Executive Committee met weekly in Sister Vera's office on Tuesday mornings at 9:30. Meetings lasted at least an hour and a half, and quite frankly, they scheduled additional meetings for special topics such as accreditation or the storm drainage assessment. In the summer they had no scheduled meetings. Initially, the meetings consisted of the three Vice Presidents and Sister Vera. The President's secretary, Sally, who shared Sister's office, always left the room and shut the door when the meetings began. When I worked out my agreement with the President concerning which meetings I would sit in on during the course of the year, she said, "Of course you're going to want to sit in Executive Committee. That's where a lot happens." Frequently throughout the year Sister Vera said to individuals and at meetings, "The Executive Committee is an extension of myself."

There were no written minutes of the meeting, but at midyear the President decided to publish in the bimonthly campus bulletin a brief listing of items that the Executive Committee discussed. The March 15 *CMM News*, for example, said: "Executive Committee report: Review with Dan Grant the Open Finance Meeting, review of the Admissions recruitment plan. Preliminary discussion regarding commencement preparations." The written communication of the committee's agenda was one attempt to help inform the college community about what got discussed in the closed-door meetings. The attempt, however, was not particularly successful. Upon reading one summary a professor noted, "Do they really expect me to believe that? What gets in the *CMM News* is a sanitized version of what really goes on, I'm sure."

Sister Vera was nominally in charge of the agenda. She either verbally outlined the agenda at the beginning of the meeting or she handed out a short typewritten list. At the first meeting Dan Blue-Smith attended he announced at the outset, "I have something for the committee," and Sister Vera explained the ground rules by which things got discussed. "I usually go around to everybody and ask them before the meeting if they have anything. Sometimes I just ask everybody at the start of the meeting if they've got anything." The meetings were a mixture of information and decision making and frank conversation was the norm. Information concerned any number of items: upcoming festivities such as a play or special student event, brief bits of news from the world of higher education such as who got foundation grants, or news about the admissions picture at CMM.

The start of most meetings saw individuals file in singly and take seats in a semicircle in front of Sister Vera's desk. While people sat haphazardly in the gray cushioned chairs each week, patterns did occur. Tim Leary, Vice President for Development, most often sat on the outside corner nearest the door and furthest away from the group. Sister Joan Rinelli, Vice President for Student Affairs, planted herself and her chair within direct eyesight of the President. Patrick O'Connell usually had one of the outside chairs, and during the course of the meeting his chair moved closer to the President's so that often by the end of the meeting his line of vision was similar to the President's. On occasion, the committee invited someone in to talk with them, and when they did this, Sister Vera went next door to Leary's office and dragged one of his chairs into her room. Before the meeting began she arranged the chairs in front of her desk, and she most often waited at her desk for the officers to arrive. The only reason her secretary interrupted the meeting was if the President received a phone call from an important trustee, in which case she stood up, excused herself and took the call in Leary's office. There were no other interruptions.

Meetings always began with a bit of casual conversation between two individuals that might eventually involve the whole committee. The day after the storm drainage hearing with the city the meeting started in the following manner: As Sister Vera arranged the chairs for the meeting, O'Connell entered and said, "Good morning," in a cheerful voice. Sister Vera responded, "Good morning. Boy, they were something else last night." He took the chair to her right, and she sat in her own chair behind her desk. She shuffled through files on her desk looking for a copy of the protest by the citizens of Rosewood. "I sure wouldn't want to face a mob like that," she said. "Boy, they were organized. There must have been two thousand people who were just screaming at the city council. Just screaming. It was a real circus." Leary entered and listened to her. He stood behind his chosen chair, and with both hands on the chair agreed with Sister Vera. "It was really a lesson in city politics. Those people had the thing so orchestrated I couldn't believe it. We just sat there, and didn't have to say a thing." The euphoria over the defeat of the tax assessment lasted 20 minutes as everyone joined in about the actions of the citizen groups who worked to defeat the measure.

When guests attended the meeting she greeted them and then

explained why the committee wanted to talk with them. In the fall when they interviewed Dan Blue-Smith, she began, "Good morning, Dan. What we would like to do this morning—I guess Patrick has talked with you—is to talk about how you feel about assuming the Dean of the Faculty." She then stated how much she was in support of the idea, and asked him what questions he had for them. When visitors were not present she provided an outline for the entire meeting such as, "All right, we're going to do two things. We're going to go through the accreditation report point by point, and then we'll talk about the division appointments as a top of the head idea." Characteristically, she then added, "Which would you like to begin with, Patrick?" Meetings neither existed by predefined agendas that could not be altered, nor was there a strict time limit within which they had to operate. If they needed more time they added on another meeting. The advice and suggestions of members of the Executive Committee had equal, if not more, weight than Sister Vera's ideas.

Although there were no time limits put on discussion, the meetings did not meander meaninglessly toward a conclusion; the President moved toward closure of a particular topic and on to another one when she felt that they had exhausted discussion. "Well, I would just like to thank-you very much for coming in to talk with us," Sister Vera said to Dan at the conclusion of his interview. "Unless someone else has a question, or you have anything else you'd like to say to us, I don't see why we should keep you here. We're just going to talk about some budgetary matters." This comment came approximately one hour after they began talking and it was Sister Vera's initiative which summed up one agenda topic and moved them to the next topic. She allowed the interviewee and the Vice Presidents the leeway to ask any lingering questions. After Blue-Smith left, the President returned to the agenda and said, "I don't want to keep everybody too much longer, but could we talk for a minute about the different tuition rates in day and evening division?"

Sister Vera and the other members also pointed out future agenda items throughout the meeting for which they needed to plan. "Ok, one of the things we need to think about—and I don't mean today—is what to do with that building at the foot of the hill. Something's going to have to be done, and we need to think about it." Meetings were informational exchanges where they either made tentative plans with one another for the future, or one of them informed the others about a particular group's plans.

During the course of the year the meetings took on a distinct atmosphere, with the actors increasingly playing the same parts over and over again. At every meeting he attended, the Academic Vice President was the executive officer who spoke most often. Timothy Leary struck one of three poses—or all three—at these meetings. First, his humor was always evident, and most particularly so when Sister Vera was worried. Sister Joan noted in November, "I get tired of his jokes, but he says them to relieve the tension a little. Vera can get so upset, and we just don't know what to do." One example of his humor was when they invited the Admissions Director to talk with them, and he showed up in a blue blazer. Coincidentally, both O'Connell and Leary also wore blazers. Seeing the men in blazers, Leary said to me so that everyone heard it, "Look Bill, if you want to be an administrator, you've got to get a blazer. That's the first sign of an administrator. And a blue one."

The second pose Leary struck was when they discussed issues that did not concern him; he sat quietly and impatiently waiting for the meeting to end. This pose provided a ritualistic form of interchange for the committee. Everyone was well aware of Leary's dislike of meetings, and if he seemed anxious for the meeting to be finished he might receive a comment from Sister Vera like the following: "Timothy! We're not finished. Now just calm down. He has an appointment in Sacramento, and you know how he just loves meetings. We'll be done in a minute."

Finally, Leary was the harshest and most blunt critic of the faculty. As the year progressed and little progress had been made he went off on what one observer labeled, "one of Tim's little tirades." Said Leary, "I'm tired of being carped at because I sit on this committee. If they don't wake up soon and realize that we're all in this together then there just won't be a college around for them to teach in. If there's anything I can't stand it's self-righteous indignation, and that's them. When are they going to wake up?" Leary served the President and saw the issues from an administrative standpoint. The bantering and criticism the faculty gave Sister Vera incensed him, and it was at these meetings that he "let off steam" and, in so doing, helped create group camaraderie among the Executive Committee.

Among Leary, O'Connell, and Sister Vera a form of "gallows humor" developed, which helped relieve the tension of the problems they faced, as well as point the "guilt" of the problems away from them and toward the faculty. After a long series of personal brushfires with the faculty, O'Connell informed Leary at the Committee in April, "Your time hasn't come yet, Tim. The President and I have had a long talk and we recognize that you're the problem. You need to go to Hollywood and talk with Michael Jackson to get money. You're not doing your job, and you're next in line to take the heat." The three of them laughed, and Sister Joan looked down at her papers.

The we-they attitude delineating different groups existed as much in the Executive Committee as it did anywhere on campus. The Executive Committee had pointed out a series of problems to the college and they expected answers to those problems. The problems had different persons' names attached to them so that the blame for the problem concretely resided in factions on the campus. Retention was a major problem that the committee hoped the faculty would handle. As the committee considered ways to combat attrition they discussed possible forms student advising should take. Leary stated, "Look, if we hired a staff for a student advising center and it failed, then whose fault is it? Who would we have to blame? Retention is the faculty's concern." The point of his comment was that they had identified a problem—retention—and they had a definite idea who could solve the problem. The Executive Committee could try other avenues, but then Leary was unsure who they could "blame" if the efforts failed.

While Leary, O'Connell, and Sister Vera have been discussed elsewhere and in this section, another individual, Sister Joan Rinelli, Vice President for Student Affairs, has not entered centrally into the examples given. Sister Joan played a unique role both for the college and the Executive Committee. A shy woman with a quick mind, she has been at the college since 1967, and has served primarily in two capacities—in the Business Office and in her current position. Under the previous reign Student Affairs had not fared so well; the President often turned down budget requests, and staffing was at a minimum. When Sister Vera came into office the student affairs section of the college grew so that by 1984 Sister Joan had a staff of 120.

Sister Joan's actions in Executive Committee were in keeping with how she dealt with people in general. She was quick to bring vocal support for her staff, yet extremely reticent in confronting either O'Connell or Sister Vera about policies with which she did not agree. We have seen how in the Budget and Finance Committee meeting she spoke up for her support staff in order to give them increased benefits. She was quietly popular with virtually every group on campus. One of her staff noted how, "we'd walk if she ever quit," implying they worked at the college because of Rinelli, and not because of income or general love of the institution. During the course of the year faculty frequently conferred with her on an individual basis, and one professor said one day, "Isn't it crazy. I can talk practically, honestly, without fear to Joan, but she's without power. The guy we should be able to talk to is unapproachable, and Vera, well, you know ..." Sister Joan was also the only executive administrator who gave informal attention to students. It was not uncommon to see students chatting in her office, or to observe her having lunch or a coke in the cafeteria with a student.

Her work with students gave her cause for worry about the Executive Committee. Initially, when Sister Vera created the committee, Sister Joan was a quietly unwilling participant. She saw the group becoming what many people perceived it to be— an elitist committee that made decisions in secret. As she noted to me, "I personally don't like it. I support Vera, but that title— Vice President—just sticks in my throat. That's why I initially opposed the move to Belchamp. It will be a little cluster of isolated people down there, and I don't want to be isolated from the group I serve—the students. I'm here to help students, and some official title—well, it makes me uncomfortable." Nevertheless she acceded to Sister Vera's request and took the title of Vice President and plans to move to Belchamp when Sister Vera says it is time to leave.

During the course of the year she became increasingly isolated from the Executive Committee. Anyone who had an opinion about the executive group looked on it as triangular—consisting of the President, O'Connell, and Tim Leary. At the meetings Sister Joan spoke the least, and took part neither in the black humor nor the search for who was to blame about a particular issue. She struck a typical pose the day Dan Blue-Smith arrived for his first meeting. Shortly before the meeting I bumped into her outside of Sister Vera's office and I said, "It's meeting time, huh?" "Are they in there yet?" she queried, not wanting to be sitting with Sister Vera alone having to fill time before the others arrived. Leary and O'Connell soon entered and she followed them, taking the middle chair. Leary asked her how her case of posion oak was and she replied that she was getting better. Although she had had the rash for two weeks and it was bad enough for her to get cortisone shots, O'Connell had not noticed it. Patrick and Sister Joan chattted about how one gets poison oak, and as the meeting began she put on her half glasses and began to read the brief agenda. She crossed her arms, and looked at the information as the others spoke. For one hour she said nothing as the others discussed faculty problems and development funds. The black humor O'Connell used for Leary elicited neither a smile nor a laugh from Sister Joan.

In one respect she sat in the most difficult seat in the administration. She recognized and acknowledged faculty and staff concerns about the manner in which decisions had been made, but at the same time she had to support those decisions. She was increasingly caught in the middle. And because she was willing to listen, she had to bear the brunt of staff and faculty anger over the policies that guided the administration. Because people felt comfortable and safe talking with her, they let their feelings be known—unlike how they acted with the President or Academic Vice President. At the same time that she tried to explain the administration's rationale for certain actions, she privately was in agreement with many of the faculty concerns. "Maybe I'm the fly in the ointment and it's time for me to go. Vera and Patrick won't listen to their [faculty] problems. They have legitimate concerns. We're moving too fast and we have to get our own house in order," she confided to me.

Another way of exploring the roles, functions, and structure of the Executive Committee is to offer an example of a full meeting to inform the reader how it is they go about their work. The example given concerns the Tuesday morning meeting of May 8. As the time for the meeting approached Sister Vera arranged the chairs in the room, and brought in an extra chair from Leary's office for Dan Grant. O'Connell was in the room prior to 9:30 talking with the President about salary increases for the faculty. Leary looked in the office and saw that the meeting was not set to begin, so he retreated to his office for a quick phone call. Sister Joan stood in the hall watching the door and talking with the registrar. At 9:35 Blue-Smith hurried down the hall and entered the office. Leary, and then Sister Joan, followed him. The secretary gathered up her materials and shut the door as everyone sat down in front of Sister's desk.

Because they were going to talk about the budget this morning, Sister Vera invited Dan Grant to the meeting, and he sat closest to the exit. Leary sat next to him, and pushed his chair furthest away from the desk. O'Connell sat closest to Sister Vera's right, with Sister Joan and Blue-Smith in the middle. Sister Vera began, "I'm sorry for not getting this typed up, but I didn't have a chance to tell Sally to get it done. Anyway, we're going to talk about student employment, and the budget, which is why I invited Dan here today."

The meeting initially revolved around how to systematize the bookkeeping of student financial aid. Some administrators had not gone through the personnel office when they hired students, which resulted in a handful of students being paid twice for doing the same work, or students worked 60 hours a week and received 20 hours of overtime which cost the college income. Sister Vera responded at one point, "How do you solve that? I guess my feeling is that it's Hildegard's [the personnel director] responsibility, so she should send out a notice saying the Executive Committee has discussed the matter and heretofore all students must come to her office if they want a job. Put the notice in the student newspaper. Let them know that way." Leary added, "Gee, some gal's working one job and getting paid twice? I'd like to talk with her. I should get her in development ... have her talk with my daughter." Sister Joan added that students could work hard if they had the right direction, but frequently they didn't have adequate supervision. Sister Vera agreed, saying, "You're right. The problem is not with the students. The problem is with the directors." She then added, "Well, it seems to me that it's a workable solution. Now the other thing I want to do is to go over the 1984/85 budget."

Patterns previously discussed have recurred. Sister Vera outlined the agenda for the meeting and concluded discussion on the first topic. Leary's humor was evident, as well as Sister Joan's support for students. Sister Vera saw the problem as people-oriented, and the solution came about through written communication in a campuswide publication. Sister Joan did not initiate entrance into the meeting, and Leary did his own work until the meeting was set to begin. Seating arrangements were normal; O'Connell sat in one of the outside chairs near the President, and Leary sat furthest from the group. Uncharacteristically, O'Connell said very little. By the meeting's end only Sister Joan had spoken less than he.

Dan Grant handed out printed sheets of the revised budget which he and Sister Vera had worked on the previous weekend. The last budget information they received contained a $600,000 difference between expected income and expenditures. Even with this difference they had been optimistic. For example, all year they had planned for an additional 20 percent increase in incoming students, and then they projected 40 additional students to decrease the deficit. No one was certain—especially the Admissions Director—from where the 40 students would come. "We'll be lucky to get the 20 percent increase. There's no way we'll get 40 students above that," said Dave Falconieri.

They deferred hiring a few additional faculty, and they demanded level funding from all program directors. Nevertheless, with the attrition rate soaring and no new sources of income generated, they faced a $600,000 deficit. Half of this deficit was due to a 6 percent salary increase for all personnel.

They had balanced the revised budget by increasing income figures. They increased gifts by $100,000; miscellaneous income by $125,000; graduate student income by $30,000; they "plugged" other line items higher than originally planned, and they used the remaining unrestricted funds from the endowment. In this way, they could present a balanced budget to the Board of Trustees at their meeting the next week. Leary was the first to question what Sister Vera and Dan had done:

Leary: Look, we're discussing the goddamn budget here. We've got to think about what we're doing. I hate to say it, but you've got to think about not giving raises. We're selling the college's future to balance the budget. It will catch up with us.

Blue-Smith: We can generate much greater enthusiasm if we give an increase. I've talked with faculty and they're really willing to work. They say they'll get behind working on retention.

Grant: This is the only way we can present a balanced budget without cutting people. We're buying time.

Leary: I thought people would be behind us this year and look what's happened. When the hell will the faculty get moving. It always comes back to the peasant idea that there's a conspiracy somewhere. That we're hiding money. They've got to realize that there is no money left, and they had better get working on it or—

Blue-Smith: People just aren't aware of what a budget is. They see us building a $100,000 bridge to Belchamp and think it should be used for salaries instead.

Leary: Oh hell, look we—

Sister Vera: Look, anybody who wants to take the budget and make some suggestions is free to do so. We've had open finance meetings for people, but it's quite clear to me that that's not the way to go. The option is to present a deficit budget.

This interchange highlights several familiar patterns. Sister Joan did not speak. For the previous three years Leary had spoken for deferring salary raises, and, again, the culprits were an intransigent faculty. Blue-Smith made it appear that the faculty faced the future with "enthusiasm" when in reality he meant that not giving salary increases engendered revolution on the part of an already low-paid staff. Grant provided a neutral, public, comment about presenting a balanced budget. In private he said, "That's all Vera's idea. I'll support her publicly, but that's not what I'd do. We should think about cutting positions now, not next year." For her part, Sister Vera had thought formal meetings such as the open revenue forum brought everything into the open, yet the year's actions had made it clear: "That's not the way to go."

A vote on the budget in the Executive Committee was never taken. The discussion ended with Sister Vera saying, "Okay, if it's agreeable with you, Dan [Grant] and I will go over it again. If you have any questions or comments come back to me." The individuals began to stand as if the meeting had ended when O'Connell said, "I have one major item for the agenda." Grant stood up and said, "I'm leaving now."

O'Connell then reported on the action of the Rank and Tenure Committee the previous day. Sister Vera had sent the Committee—composed solely of faculty—a letter informing them that the "Administrators and Faculty Handbook" would be divided so that both groups had handbooks. The letter began, "During the past three and a half years I have been aware of the overlap and occasional confusion caused by the combined handbook for faculty and administrators. In order to alleviate some of the complication I propose to separate the two and design an Administrative Handbook." Sister Vera's intention was simply to inform the group that she planned to create an administrative handbook; she had no intention of interfering with the faculty handbook. The faculty, however, saw the issue in a different light:

O'Connell: I couldn't believe what happened. They were incredibly angry, said it was a *fait accompli,* that it was just another example of administration informing people rather than talking with them first. I can't deal with that level of paranoia. I felt terribly deflated last night. I feel terribly tired after all we have done. You want to end the year on a good note and then they come at us with raving paranoia—

Blue-Smith: I think you're right about the paranoia level—

Leary: So now they want to control the administrators too ...

Sister Vera: This just blows my mind. I had no intention—

O'Connell: Their feeling was it was one more example of the president not consulting with people. I'm left feeling that I can't open my mouth without people seeing me in an adversarial role. First of all, I feel the president has a right, period. She has a legal right to change the handbook. They've got to let go, for God's sake.

Blue-Smith: I think we should just take that on as a lobbying project. I'll go talk with them and find out what's what.

Later that morning I met Sue Ann Simmer on her way back from an English class. We talked a bit about the previous weekend's Diamond Ball and then she said, "You haven't heard the latest. Let me tell you what they tried yesterday." She then related the contents of the letter and how everyone on the Rank and Tenure Committee was upset. I told her I did not understand exactly why the faculty wanted to hold on to the administrative handbook. Her answer is integral to the discussion about the groups that make up CMM. "It's just another division. They want to create differences, separate groups. A lot of people are in both groups, too. We want to be together on this, and they're removing themselves." Later that week I spoke with two other members of the Rank and Tenure Committee who concurred with Simmer's statement.

A few final points remain about this issue. Grant left the room when the issue came up, which emphasized that he was only a guest at the meeting. Sister Joan remained quiet. O'Connell felt depressed that people saw him in an adversarial role, yet his next comment was "adversarial." "The president has a right, period." At the same time, no one worked harder at implementing change than O'Connell and his cause for depression was his perception of the faculty's unwillingness to accept his proposals.

Sister Vera had shown him the letter to Rank and Tenure as a rough draft; he had changed one key word. She initially had ended the letter, saying, "Since the revision of the handbook has traditionally been the prerogative of the Rank and Tenure Committee, I am requesting your confirmation of this plan." He changed "confirmation" to "cooperation." The difference is subtle, but important. Simmer had mentioned, "What do they want us to do? It's just something handed down. We certainly didn't vote on this change. They just told us." Faculty, then, saw unintended actions of O'Connell and Sister Vera as trying to create separate worlds wherein the faculty had no input.

This section of the chapter on the faculty and the Executive Committee highlights the segmentation of the college community that took place throughout the year. While issues such as the legality of the handbook, curricular change, and the surplus income held the attention of the groups, underlying all of these issues was how the groups communicated among themselves and with one another. This section has seen how the faculty presented a united front so that differences such as tenured-untenured; lay-religious; humanities-business; or young-old, did not matter. We have heard a business professor, a priest, a senior faculty member, and a young untenured professor all speak against the perceived actions of the administration. The Executive Committee had differences among themselves in that Sister Joan quietly disagreed with many of their views, and Blue-Smith tried to temper the hostility the committee felt for the faculty. Finally, the level of trust and cooperation among the different groups reached a point where even the most unintended of actions—the separation of administrative and faculty handbooks—produced fierce opposition.

Other groups now wait to be examined. These enclaves did not occupy center stage as much as those groups just mentioned. Nevertheless, for a more complete understanding of the College of Mother Mary we must explore the secondary worlds of the college.

Chapter IV

Secondary Groups

SISTERS OF MOTHER MARY

The Sisters of Mother Mary are one enclave that transcends a definable group such as faculty or midmanagers. Even though their numbers are minute in comparison to the total college population, one finds Sisters in all strata of the college. Nine Sisters sit on the Board of Trustees. Sister Vera and Sister Joan are executive administrators. Sister Barbara Therese is Chancellor. Five Sisters are midmanagers who occupy the offices of Dean of Education, Director of Special Programs, Library Director, Director of Institutional Research, and Assistant Director of Development. The catalogue lists a dozen Sisters who are either emeritus or occasionally teach a course; six Sisters are professors in the departments of the college.

No easy generalizations can be made regarding the Sisters' ideological orientation and outlook on life, education, and the philosophy of the college. It is nevertheless necessary to consider this group in relation to the changes and conflict that occurred during the course of the year. In her address to the Faculty Senate Sister Vera included the Sisters of Mother Mary as one key group to whom she is accountable. "The perception that I am autocratic brings me to my third point, and that is the decision-making apparatus of the President. I'd like to explain to you that I am not only accountable to you, but also the Board, and the Sisters of Mother Mary." Individuals noted her inclusion of the Sisters as a group to whom she must answer, and some people concluded that if changes were to be made, such as the President's removal from office, the decision ultimately resided with the Sisters, and not the Board of Trustees. The feeling of one individual was, "The Board doesn't know what's going on here, the Sisters do. They're not going to let this place die." Another individual mentioned the need for the provincial head of the Sisters to become informed of the problems, "and perhaps step in and tell Vera what to do."

Even though the Sisters' numbers were small, their power as holders of the historical traditions of the college was vast. In the spring one professor began preliminary discussions with a small number of faculty about a radical restructuring of the curricula. When I asked him with whom he was working he mentioned five individuals, two of whom were Sisters. "I'm really glad they've agreed to be on it," he said. "You know how important their support will be if I want to get anything accomplished." At the elections for Faculty Senate officers for the coming year, a professor noted that a Sister had nominated a relatively young professor for the office of Vice President. The professor said, "It surprised me that she'd nominate Bob. It's significant that she'd do that." In the fall, appointments for divisional chairs consumed much of the time of the Executive Committee. By late November they had chosen five of the six positions and none of them were Sisters. Leary raised the question, "Don't we cause problems by not naming a Sister to one of these? I think Randy would be the best of all candidates, but politically it would be best to choose [Sister] Evelyn." They discussed the issue for half an hour and ultimately chose Sister Evelyn.

While public criticism by the Sisters of the administration was relatively mute, private comments about the administration were the fiercest encountered. Of the active teaching faculty, all Sisters taught in the humanities-social sciences and their views of the college were grounded in the humanism of a liberating education. As the Sisters of Mother Mary worldwide had called for a rededication to the issues of peace and social justice, a curriculum that moved the college away from humanistic issues and toward business training was antithetical to how the Sisters viewed the college. One Sister spoke of her hopes for the college: "I want us to become a superb liberal arts college for the 21st century. If we go for business I want to see us as a humanistic business department. What are the values a business needs for the 21st century?

That's how we should build the curriculum, and you don't come to us unless you are interested in that humanistic ethic. If we did that there would be a real culture here ... but that's very different than what we're doing now. Now we're churning out people for industry-type jobs."

Sister Vera received credit for attracting younger nuns to the college, whereas the average age of Sisters continued to rise during the reign of Sister Barbara. Sisters active in the functions of the school ranged in age from 32 to 75. As one might expect, the ideological/political scope of these individuals ranged from nuns who actively supported and worked with such groups as the farm workers and battered women, to women who fit more easily into the mold of religiosity of what many continue to think Sisters "are supposed to do." As the population of the Sisters dramatically changed, so had their habitats. Whereas Belchamp Hall was once the residence not only for the Sisters of CMM, but for the entire province, 15 Sisters now live in the new residence on campus and other women have a variety of living styles either with a handful of other Sisters, or by themselves.

While many different living arrangements exist for the Sisters, not everyone agrees about which styles are the "correct" way for a Sister of Mother Mary to live. Sister Vera, for example, initially resided in Belchamp when she became President, but soon moved off-campus to her own apartment. Many people noted her living alone as a further example of her deviating from the norm of what Sisters should do with regard to living in community. Further, living arrangements were also an issue as the province revised its charter and had to contend with the more conservative precepts of Rome concerning how religious women should live their lives. Finally, although most Sisters have not worn habits for over 15 years, it is necessary to point out that these women dress like any professional woman living and working in the 1980s, if not a bit more conservatively. The Sisters who lived and worked at CMM were not readily identifiable from other women who worked at the college.

A criticism one consistently heard about the Sisters as faculty and administrators was that they had an unrealistic vision of the salary lay people needed to survive. The feeling among faculty and staff was that because the Sisters did not officially live on the salary accorded them, salary increases and fringe benefits were relatively unimportant. Exceptions to the rule existed. As mentioned, Sister Joan was one of the most vigilant individuals to look out for her staff's benefits. Sister Vera entered office with the expressed desire to raise salaries and benefits.

In sum, I reiterate the contemporary worldview in which most Sisters live and act. The most common misperception outsiders had about the college was that Sisters lived in a cloistered world removed from present-day concerns and actions. While it is true one can still find examples of Sisters who live and act the way they did 30 years ago, it is far more common to find women who are active theologians concerned with spiritual issues and social justice. The Sisters existed not as impediments to change, but as agents fomenting change in bringing about a humanistic, liberating education. We see, then, how one group both preserved the history and mission of the college and, at the same time, welcomed change for the future.

ALUMNI

The alumni office consisted of one director, who reported to Tim Leary, and her two part-time secretaries. Prior to Sister Vera's reign, the Director of Alumni reported directly to the President, and the Alumni Director never has adjusted comfortably to the President's inaccessibility. "I used to talk with Sister Barbara daily," said Molly Dish, "now I'm lucky if the President even says hello to me in the hallway." The proposed relocation of the Alumni Office to the third floor of Belchamp Hall furthered her dismay about the status of the alumni at CMM. "We need to be where the action is, on the first floor," said Dish. "Why is she sticking us up on the third floor? Don't you think that says something about how the college treats its alums?"

The Alumni Office saw their efforts as part of development. Whereas Leary sought wealthy donors, the Alumni Office courted individuals who gave smaller amounts to the college. The vehicles for raising those funds were activities such as Homecoming, a formal dinner dance, raffles, and house shows. Mailings went out to all alumni four times a year, and the President had a letter written for those functions either by Leary or Dish, or Sister Vera wrote it herself. The President always proofread any letters sent out in her name. Phoneathons occurred twice a year to solicit funds for the college via telephone. The raffle of a car, which was a gift from one of the alumni, netted CMM $40,000.

An alumni newsletter came out four times a year that gave brief bits of CMM news—"Gymnasium Plans Underway"—or profiled pillars of the institution such as Dr. Simmer or Sister Barbara. The main task of the newsletter was to list the donors of the college. There were neither regional alumni chapters nor chapters in areas where CMM traditionally recruited sizable blocs of its students, such as Hawaii or Samoa. Upon her return from her first trip to Hawaii, Sister Vera opened an Executive Committee meeting by saying, "Could I give you a little report about Hawaii? We must plan a very large reception for that area. We have all those contacts and we've just lost them." Leary expressed surprise that nothing had been done in the islands and agreed, "We should establish a club over there or something."

The point about the lack of a club in Hawaii accentuates what the Alumni Director said, "I can do what I want to do, nobody bothers me. But really, I like someone telling me that I'm doing OK. I never really get any directions, just reaction to my own ideas." Virtually all of the work of the Alumni Office came from its director, and she followed the patterns she had developed with the previous president. Island clubs or regional chapters were untested ideas which she hesitated inaugurating, in favor of spending more of her time working on familiar, "successful" events such as the formal dinner dance.

There was an Alumni Board that met four times a year on a weeknight. Two weeks in advance of the meeting Molly Dish sent out written agendas. Dish noted that in recent years people asked to get on the Board, whereas 10 years ago she had to "beg people to sit on the Board." The Alumni Director saw the coordination of the Board as one of her primary activities, and an example from one meeting portrays how the Director and President operate at the meetings.

The meeting began at eight o'clock in the evening in the "Pines," a small meeting room off of the swimming pool at CMM. Coffee and cookies had been arranged by 7:45, and people drifted in one by one. Two of the three men on the committee arrived together and sat next to one another on the couch. A third male, the treasurer, entered alone, and he immediately sat down next to the other men. The Director sat next to the alumni president and greeted everyone as they entered. At two minutes to eight Sister Vera entered, walked immediately to the Alumni Director, and informed her that she had little to report to the group. Sister Vera sat alone on the couch and looked at no one. I remembered my initial meeting with Molly, who said, "Vera gives us an official report. Her biggest asset is that she appeals to people's intelligence. But we need much more than that. People want to be touched by a person, the President. They want to be aware that the President cares about them. Instead, Sister enters and sits by herself. She does give a good report." In the ensuing 10 minutes before the meeting began two people came up to Sister Vera and greeted her.

By 8:10 PM, 18 people had assembled and the Director motioned for the alumni president to begin the meeting. The alumni president asked Sister Vera to give a brief prayer where everyone bowed their heads and listened. Sister Vera's report lasted about 10 minutes where she gave a brief overview of the college, the building projects, and the institution of the new computer center. After her address the group worked through its agenda with reports from individuals who headed up committees such as the "Diamond Ball" or "Homecoming." The treasurer's report was a one-sentence statement that stated how much money they had. Two individuals mentioned how lucky the board was to have men on it, and, specifically, how fortunate they were that a man was the treasurer.

The composition of the alumni group was cause for concern in that they wanted to appear well balanced and to appeal to all segments of the college. By observing the group one easily saw different constituencies represented—men, women, older "traditional" CMM women, and younger women who experienced CMM as a coed college. One group absent from the committee were international alumni, who currently compose one-third of the student body.

Most of the discussion centerd around the plans for the Diamond Ball in April. The plans were for a costume party set in the California Gold Rush period with two faculty members portraying Mr. and Mrs. Belchamp. Sue Ann Simmer was to play the role of Mrs. Belchamp and a Spanish professor would play William Belchamp at the start of the gala supper.

As the meeting ended Sister Vera stood up and exited, bidding good-bye to a few people. Later the next week she talked with her friend, the drama professor, Jake Barnes, about the plans for the Diamond Ball. "You know the Ball is coming up. I was at my favorite group's meeting the other night and they went on and on about costumes and I just wondered if they expect me to dress up that way." Sister Vera's unhappiness with the group was that it did not do enough and portrayed only a certain angle of the college. The drama professor said he would take care of everything and that she would not have to dress up. Nevertheless, Sister Vera wore a costume, and, as one alumni observed, "It was perfect. She really fit in well. I know it's silly to have to wear costumes, but that's what the alums want."

Needless to say, discussions about dinner dances, costumes and homecoming do not indicate a world that centrally concerns itself with decision making at the college. At the same time alumni are one group that provide income, publicity, and moral support to an institution. The alumni distance from the crisis at the college indicates how one group can see its life as successful—the Diamond Ball was quite popular—while other groups are in tremendous conflict. As we have seen with the Sisters of Mother Mary, the alumni can also reside in two other worlds. Initially they are students, and when they graduate, some of them will work in positions at the college.

STUDENTS

The student body played a relatively passive role in the activities of the college with regard to administration, curriculum, and management of student affairs. Student participation in the committees of the college was minimal and students neither voiced opinions in committees nor attended committees such as Curriculum or Administrative Council until well into the middle of the year. Although the college had changed dramatically its posture toward student restrictions, CMM still differed quite considerably from other local colleges. To portray CMM as a religious-affiliated institution where students are kept under strict observation and guidance is not at all true, yet CMM students have requirements that remind one of the earlier days of parietals.

The college did not allow alcohol at the one "Inn" on campus, but students could drink privately in their rooms. As with many student dorm rooms, one could see beer or wine bottles sitting in windows, but no one served alcohol at student functions. Anyone caught smoking marijuana was brought before a tribunal, which could sanction the student with a fine. The residence coordinator had weekly meetings with his resident assistants who reported to him about any student problems—emotional, social, or otherwise—they had encountered during the week. In turn, the residence coordinator reported this information to the Dean of Students who then reported to Sister Joan. Thus, awareness of student problems traversed the entire student affairs staff.

A highly visible, round-the-clock security group patrolled the campus, and people still mentioned how safe the CMM campus was in comparison to other institutions. Students sat at the front desks of the dormitories until midnight to check on who entered the dorms. One notes this information with the awareness that CMM is not in an urban setting where outsiders frequently come and go.

What was visibly striking about students at CMM was their absence. That is, on beautiful, warm California days, or Friday afternoons, one expects to see students lounging on lawns, perhaps playing with a frisbee, or drinking a beer or two with a friend. I never noticed this kind of activity at the college. One spring day I interviewed a student in front of the library where there was a large expanse of lawn. A lone student lay sunning herself. The interviewee commented, "She's one of the eight. I transferred here so it seems strange, but I can tell you who's out here and gets sun, or fools around. There are only about eight students who do it. Who knows where all the students are?" Another day I walked around the campus with a student who observed, "You know, this isn't really our campus. I'm not sure what I mean exactly, but when I was at State there were places that kind of felt like 'this is ours.' At Mother Mary I kind of feel like I'm staying at somebody's estate. It's nice and everything, but it's kinda different." Another reason for students' absence came from the Dean of Students. She said that many students had to work to survive, and consequently many students found jobs off-campus and could not afford the luxury to lie in the sun and get a tan.

Interviews with students shed a different light on the activities at the college. Individuals jokingly admitted that alcohol, drugs, and cohabitation existed just like at other colleges, but the administration was not aware of it. "You want to party? Check out the apartments some Saturday night. Now those guys know how to party, let me tell you. Sure you can get drugs around here. Nothing heavy, but sometimes they [the administration] act like smokin' a joint is some big deal. Well it isn't, and we just do what we want anyway. You just got to be cool about it." Several students cited the cultural mix of the student body as something that was difficult to get used to, but ultimately was rewarding.

One male senior played the role of student whom everyone cited as the "model" student. A male pianist with a 1960s look—beard, longish hair, and blue jeans—he had served in official capacities— president of the honor society, student representative to various committees, and resident assistant. At times individuals mentioned him by first name and everyone was aware of who they meant. At the In-Service as Dan Blue-Smith concluded the morning portion of the agenda he stated, "Marty will be playing for us at lunch, so we can eat and listen to his tunes." At another time, when the faculty worried about Honors Day, Sue Ann Simmer and another faculty member had the following exchange:

Simmer: Nothing has been planned for this by the Academic Vice President. He's left it up to students, and they don't know what to do.

Prof.: Can't Marty advertise the day? Can't he work with the others?

Simmer: Marty's got his senior recital. We can't bother him with this. He should practice.

Prof.: You're right. We shouldn't bother Marty. His recital means a lot.

Students represented a group with whom every other group at CMM interacted, yet students did not play a vocal role in the crisis at the college. They were minimally aware of the problems between the faculty and administration, but not to the point that it affected their ideas about the institution. One student said, "I'm aware that the faculty are mad at the administration, they get low salaries and stuff. I hope nothing big happens." Months after Sister Vera and Dr. O'Connell fired a professor three students made an appointment to talk with her. In a 20-minute session with the President they told her how much they liked the professor, and what a positive influence he had with all of his students. One of the young women began, "We're not here to start trouble. We saw Dr. Beckett's letter of resignation. We just really like the way he teaches. He's a classic."

Each of the three women hesitantly spoke to Sister Vera, and Sister listened to them with her arms on her desk, her hands crossed. She nodded affirmatively as they spoke and when they finished she said, "I think your points are really very valid. I think he's an excellent teacher. Practically all of his students get into graduate school. I remember telling him that at the senior banquet last year. I do appreciate the fact that you came to me, but I didn't have any alternative. The decision was Dr. Beckett's. I'm sorry he's not going to be here, but we have procedures and processes that we must follow."

The students listened to Sister Vera and did not disagree with her. She asked them about their career plans and when they finished Sister Vera got up, thanked them for coming, and gave each of them a little hug. The President's interaction with students was minimal, and this was the only meeting I observed where students questioned a decision by the President. In fact, it appeared that many students were not aware of the President. At a small "teach-in," for example, one student acted as the moderator who introduced the speakers. Sister Vera was one of the speakers, and when she entered she went to the front of the room. The moderator went over to a teacher and said, "When Sister Vera comes in, could you point her out to me. I mean, I don't want to introduce the wrong person." Clearly, he not only had not spoken with the President, but he did not even know her.

Consequently, students played a passive role with regard to the conflict at CMM. Student life had restrictions tighter than at other colleges, but that life by no means resembled a fundamentalist institution. At the same time that restrictions existed, students found their way around those laws. Student voice existed minimally on paper, and on a rare occasion students spoke with the president about a concern. Otherwise, only a handful of students such as Marty played a noticeable role in the other worlds of the college. Marty was the kind of student whom people mentioned casually to demonstrate that they knew students and were not completely in the dark concerning student affairs.

STAFF

Upon graduation some students worked at the college in staff positions or, eventually, in midmanagement positions. The kinds of staff positions students filled were as admissions counselors, secretaries, or departmental clerks. Support staff was the most transient group in the school, yet some individuals stood out and worked at the college for quite specific reasons. One secretary commented, "Why did I come here? I like the values, the religious values of the college. I found out about the job through the bulletin at church, and my husband and I saw it as a way to promote what we believe in. It sure isn't for the money, I'll tell you that. But the money is something, I wouldn't work for nothing. I wanted to grow and give; this job enables me to do that."

The woman's comments represent a microcosm of the staff life. Staff salaries are the lowest in the organization. The entry-level salary for some positions hovers around $10,000. Obviously, people did not come to CMM to make a substantial salary. Some staff like the secretary stayed because of the values of the college. Other people took the job at CMM as they entered or returned to the work force. A woman who worked on the word processor told me, "I need to upgrade my skills and then I'm sure I can make big bucks someplace else, maybe a computer firm or something. I like it here, the people are friendly, but the salary—"

Many people found out about jobs at CMM through avenues such as the church bulletin and word-of-mouth. One older secretary related, "Well, my husband and I owned a pipe shop and when we hit rough times last year Sharon told me of an opening in this office. I thought about it, and it seemed like secure income, so I took it. It's turned out very nice. All these guys are really nice to work for. I miss the pipe shop, though." In the last four years CMM has added a personnel officer, and personnel policies have been instituted. One can anticipate the parochial form of advertising for a job will change in the near future. The most dramatic change to date has come in the area of personnel benefits—the college now pays 85 percent of an individual's health costs, whereas four years ago the college paid five dollars. Unions, or the desire for unions, are not much mentioned by staff members.

As with students, staff voice in decision making is relatively mute, and the voice that does exist has been silent. The staff elected someone to the Budget and Finance Committee, but during the course of the year that individual spoke only eight times. There is little discussion among administrators—except by Dan Blue-Smith—to increase the position of staff members in the decision making of the college.

Staff interaction with the President or her Vice Presidents was minimal. Generally, a staff person's immediate superior—a midmanager—or the Personnel Director dealt with staff concerns and problems. Sister Vera's informal interactions with staff were in stark contrast to those of the previous president, who made it a habit to know everyone's name. The secretary previously mentioned said, "Sister Vera's so different from Barbara Therese. Sister Vera will say hello sometimes, but she doesn't mean it. She withdraws from it. Barbara Therese made a point of coming to me, she knew my name as soon as I started working here. I bet Vera doesn't even know my name." Molly Dish, the Alumni Director, expressed a similar sentiment with regard to her secretaries. "I've got two terrific workers, and they never even get as much as a good morning from Sister. She acts as if they just don't exist, and I feel badly for them. Their salaries are so low, you'd think Sister could at least say hello to cheer them up a little."

Yet staff camaraderie remained high. The President held an end-of-month party at 3:30 PM for the staff. No more than 30 people attended these parties, and one had the uncomfortable feeling of a forced attendance where individuals were unsure how to act. One person said, "Sure I go to them. But they're weird. We all stand around and kind of whisper to one another. It's more fun when just my office gets together, or a couple of friends I've met around here." Office parties did happen, which produced a cohesiveness within particular offices. In Chapter III we saw an example of an Admissions lunch with the entire staff. In the spring, CMM held a festive Hawaiian night on a Saturday that was open to the public. At the crowded gathering one observed at least four different offices that shared a meal and conversation.

Staff were aware of the problems on campus, but like the students, the problems did not overly concern them. I reiterate the rationale for discussing the seemingly "insignificant" worlds of students, alumni, and staff. When discussing decision making, especially in a conflict-ridden time, one can assume that an organization is entirely consumed with conflict and crisis. While the assumption is certainly true with regard to particular worlds, one necessarily needs to understand that other groups can exist as they have in the past, or that their concerns are different from the problems of the moment. Some staff, for example, worried about the low salary; other staff members saw their work as a way to gain the requisite skills so they could get better jobs; other staff worked for the values of the institution. Issues such as who the Executive Committee chose for divisional heads, or how to solve the attrition rate, did not necessarily concern staff personnel. A theater in the round affords us a view not only of the actions that play center stage but also those scenes enacted by less dramatic actors.

This chapter has portrayed the secondary groups of the college, their composition, identity, and how they perceived their daily existence at the College of Mother Mary. We have seen how particular issues provoked anger on the part of particular groups, while other groups remained relatively calm. People conveyed these issues, however, in a variety of manners. The imperative now is to investigate further what Foucault calls the "infinitesimal mechanisms, which each have their own techniques and tactics, and see how these mechanisms have been and continue to be utilized" (1980, p. 99). These mechanisms evolve from the concepts discussed in Chapter I under the generic headings of time, space, and communication. We are now aware of the actors, issues, and groupings of the college. The next chapter unpacks how the actors conveyed these issues to their own constituency and to other constituencies. Thus, we turn to the scripts the actors used to enact their drama and investigate the minutiae of leadership scenes.

Part III

Leadership Scenes and Scripts

.

Introduction

An analysis of space, time, and communication guides the investigation. Language use requires analysis in order to see how codes such as humor, questions, and modals operate to produce perceptions and decisions. The role of president specifies ways of speaking not only marked according to the President's personality, but, also constrained by formal and informal patterns available to the President, these patterns can often be influenced by gender and audience. Further, the President communicates messages not only orally but also by a variety of written methods—memos, letters, articles in college bulletins and newspapers. Through the analysis of discourse we learn how the President communicates messages to the college community. To what extent are her communicative styles and channels consistent with her other behavior patterns?

A study of the interaction of physical space between the President and her subordinates illustrates unspoken attitudes of the actors with one another. We consider where the President spends her day, and how it is spatially constructed. The use of Sister Vera's private and public space offers a dramatic contrast to that of her predecessor. Body language is yet another spatial category which offers insight into the actors' physical interactions.

Time relates to space as we consider the seasonal and ceremonial activities of the college and President. Reference already has been made to activities such as All-College Day, which took on ritualistic overtones of a seasonal celebration. Time focuses events so that the "end-of-the-month" party comes, presumably, because it is the end of the month. Commencement and summer mark the end of one year for a collegiate institution whereas the fiscal year's audit marks the close of a business year, and New Year's Eve may point to an individual's yearly summation. The assumption, of course, is that beginnings and endings exist, and the discussion of time places the college within the specified context wherein the year—and my own experience—began and ended. The discussion reorients the framework in order not to freeze action, so that we view the drama as an ongoing tale with a particular history that helps determine the present.

The chapters that make up this part of the book investigate the scenes and scripts that define the boundaries between what can get said and what cannot and, consequently, what the actors can believe and do and what they cannot. The vehicle for discussion in Chapter V is the script of the monthly meetings of the Administrative Council of the college. As the meetings progress, the chapter weaves together the information with the intent of exposing the underpinnings of the drama. Chapter VI explicates scenes from the daily life of the President in order to understand how the President—and the other actors—used time, space, and communication in their interactions with one another. Finally, Chapter VII discusses the college presidency, and we hear a soliloquy from Sister Vera.

Chapter V

Administrative Council

The Administrative Council met monthly, either on Tuesday or Thursday afternoon, from 12:30 until 2:00. As with every committee, they arranged their meeting times at All-College Day at the start of the year. They planned no meetings for Intersession in January, and their last meeting was at the end of the academic year in May. The task of the Council, as defined in the college handbook, was to "formulate policy for the College, act in all matters dealing with the internal government and administration of the College, give final approval and regular review to all programs initiated by all other groups in the College."

Some of the most active performers on the Committee have already been identified. In addition to Sister Vera and the Executive Committee, the Council consisted of Dave Falconieri, Dan Grant, Dan Blue-Smith, Louie Canova, Tom Brady, and one of the faculty members who resigned at the end of the year. An additional six members from all parts of the college sat on the Council.

As we shall see, the function and role of the Council became increasingly important during the course of the year. Prior to the Council's first meeting the following conversation in Executive Committee ensued:

Sister Vera: I'm thinking about changing the Administrative Council. It seems to me that all it does is, it's a verbal bulletin board. We don't do anything other than listen to people's reports. I guess I feel it should have another role.

O'Connell: The Administrative Council should serve the President as a planning group. That's what those kinds of groups are for—to help the President plan.

Leary: Well, I'll say this. It's a waste of time if we are all going to sit around and listen to one another. Everybody wants some of mother's time (looking at the President) and they'd be better off at their desks doing their jobs.

Sister Vera: As far as I know, it's never taken any action. It just reports.

Sister Joan: (laughing) Oh yes, they did make decisions. BT [the previous President] once asked them to determine tuition and they decided not to increase it. She blew up, had one of her fits, and reversed their decision. Then she created the Budget Committee which reported directly to the President, and the Administrative Council never had another word about finance.

This conversation initiated action based in part on historical fact. The council was the oldest existing committee at the college. On paper, all other committees—except Budget and Finance— reported their actions to the Council, which in turn passed the decisions on to the President and, now, the Executive Committee. To some people, the Council was a socializing agent. The senior faculty member stated, "We've always felt that the Administrative Council was a good introduction to the college to promising young faculty. It gives them a good overview, so that they will eventually be able to take a leadership role here." At their first meeting the President proposed, and received, initial acceptance that the group reform itself as a planning body.

As with most committee meetings at the college, the Administrative Council met most often in the Art Gallery. The members sat around a large rectangular table, with no seat reserved as the chairperson's. Sister Vera chaired the meetings, and her secretary, Sally, took the minutes. The Art Gallery consistently had one-person exhibits that displayed a particular theme. In the winter, as tension at the college grew, people wryly noted the stark, overdrawn pictures of crisis and conflict of one artist. As the brochure for the artist noted: "His drawings present his sense of the difficulty—and the necessity—of coming to grips with the hazardous reality of conflict and confrontation in contemporary society, the complexities and ambiguities inherent in interpersonal relations, and by implication, political situations. They are statements posed in the form of questions: What is going on here? Who are these people? What is their relationship to each other?" In the spring the art department removed that exhibit and replaced it with another exhibition of art deco drawings whose centerpiece was an enclosed casket, with a manikin lying atop it.

Six meetings make up the sections of this chapter. We begin with the October 25 session of the Council. Since their September meeting, individuals had a month to consider the implications of changing the scope of the Committee. Dan Grant was in the hospital recovering from a heart attack. The faculty were skeptical of the proposed changes, but they concerned themselves with how to implement the ideas initiated by Dr. O'Connell at All-College Day. Everyone arrived at the meeting prepared to discuss strategic planning and the role of the Administrative Council.

OCTOBER 25

Sister Vera arrived at 12:33 PM and began with the following comment: "Since I'm probably the last one to arrive, we can start. Are there any additions or corrections to be made to the minutes? (five second silence) Okay, there are four things, three really, that we will talk about. I want to reorder the agenda you've got so first we'll hear from Marty about Honors Day, and then we'll discuss retention and enrollment. Patrick has some information he wants to give us, and then we'll discuss what the priorities of this Council will be. So why don't you begin, Marty?"

Sister Vera's introductory comments to the Council set the stage for discussion. More importantly, her words outline patterns of speech, space, and time seen throughout the year both at the Administrative Council and elsewhere. One notes the linguistic spatial and time-based occurrences in this section as one "infinitesimal mechanism" that points out to the actors who was in charge of the meeting. To break apart her initial comments we see:

"Since I'm probably the last one to arrive ..."

At meetings other than the Executive Committee or a special meeting such as the Executive Task Force, the President never arrived sooner than two minutes prior to the meeting. Although no one ever called roll at meetings, the minutes recorded who was absent or present. Sister Vera also seemed to be intuitively aware of any individual's absence. At the October 25 meeting Louie Canova, the business department chair, was absent; the following day Sister Vera directed her secretary to find out why.

When Sister Vera sat down there were five remaining seats. She chose a seat next to an older nun, Sister Justin. The only consistent seating arrangement observed during the course of the year was that Sister Justin sat next to the President whenever possible. In an interview with Sister Justin she provided a possible rationale: "Vera can get so upset with the faculty comments; they are always asking such difficult questions, in such demanding ways. Sometimes I just want to reach out to her and show my support." On the other hand, O'Connell most often sat alone. If individuals entered after him they chose vacant chairs other than those next to his.

"Are there any additions or corrections to be made to the minutes?"

At every meeting except the Executive Committee a secretary took minutes of the meetings. Occasionally, someone suggested a change or modification; in addition, someone might suggest that a comment not be recorded in the minutes. When Jake Barnes complained about not knowing of the surplus in the Budget and Finance meeting, for example, he began by requesting, "This information should not go into the minutes." The President's office held all committee minutes, and anyone who requested them could see them. Even though the minutes held accounts of actions taken, to my knowledge no one other than myself studied the minutes during the course of the year. Rather than refer to a historical written record for a rationale of why particular programs had begun— Intersession, for example—college members relied on one another's memories, and oral histories of past actions. Chapter II already has referred to the citizens' selective memory, and oral history played an increasingly important part at committee meetings.

"Okay, there are four things, three really, that we will talk about. I want to reorder the agenda you've got so first we'll hear from Marty about Honors Day ..."

At meetings she chaired, the President controlled the agenda and determined what got discussed, and for how long. At all meetings individuals arrived with prior knowledge because the chair had sent out a written agenda via campus mail. Yet the chair determined in what order the issues would be discussed, and the length of time the Committee spent on each item.

Sister Vera reordered the agenda at this meeting so that the Committee first heard from the student, Marty. Even though the student was not a member of the Committee, the President introduced him by first name. The implication is that everyone at the Council already knew the student, and that the President was on a casual first-name basis with him. Having a student address a collegewide Committee about Honors Day differed from the practice of previous years; the previous AVP always had managed what had been a highly ceremonial occasion. Marty reported moving Honors Day to late in the spring, a ceremonial time-change for CMM.

"Then we'll discuss retention and enrollment. Patrick has some information he wants to give us, and then we'll discuss what the priorities of this Council will be."

Again, we see the President in charge of the agenda. Sister Vera combined two points—retention and enrollment—yet referred to only one speaker when the written agenda listed more than O'Connell as a speaker. The President's emphasis that O'Connell would speak points out the esteem in which she held him. O'Connell's "new ideas" and his experience as an Academic Dean on the East Coast were two factors in his favor with the President. She wanted to change the college and move away from the more traditionally minded thinkers at CMM. The first day I met her, for example, she said, "We're a bit too parochial here. Patrick will help us move beyond being a family-run operation and meet the 1980s. He's got the know-how, and is familiar with the larger world of higher education."

"So why don't you begin, Marty?"

The speech patterns of the President included extensive use of questions as directives. One can introduce a speaker in many ways.

"Martin will now begin" is one way for the stage manager to have an actor begin his lines. Another alternative is, "I want you to speak first, Marty." The use of a question for a directive allows the audience and the addressed individual to answer in the negative. That is, Marty could have responded, "I'd rather wait until the end, thanks." The student, however, spoke for four minutes. He entertained questions, and when there were no further questions Sister Vera said, "All right, can we take up the next point on the agenda?"

O'Connell picked up her directive and talked about enrollment patterns and projections, emphasizing a seven-year downward spiral at CMM in order to accentuate the crisis in which he found the college. Jane DeSelm, a graduate of CMM and Dean of Students for the past decade, noted after O'Connell's comments, "We need to understand the reasoning behind the downturn in student enrollment. I'd like to see a study of what accounts for the decline in enrollment over the last seven years." O'Connell immediately followed by saying, "I'm sorry, but I'm really not interested in why it happened. Historical studies of why things happened may be worthwhile for our confreres interested in theory, but we've got a problem to solve. I want to note it, and get on with it."

The discussion continued for another half hour until Sister Vera suggested they move on to the priorities of the Administrative Council. She had prepared a suggestion list concerning priorities the Council might deal with, which had been compiled by the Executive Committee. The list contained such suggestions as, "Recruitment, alternative sources of revenue, academic reorganization, computers." She suggested that the Council prioritize the Executive Committee's suggestions, and add any ideas of their own. Council members proposed two new items. Tom Brady mentioned that "life and safety systems" needed to be installed throughout the campus. Another individual said she wanted the Council to discuss the "mission" of the college. When the Committee voted on its top priority, most members thought that a study of the college's mission was imperative. The group then decided to break into small committees, study particular problems on the list, and at the next meeting report back to the Council.

O'Connell's report and the ensuing discussion are noteworthy on two accounts. First, O'Connell and Sister Vera looked at concrete problems, such as attrition, as items with which the Council should be concerned. To O'Connell and Sister Vera, the mission of the college was not an identifiable problem. Second, most of the members of the Council looked to the past as ways to solve problems for the future. DeSelm suggested a historical study to understand declining enrollments. The overriding concern of the Council members was understanding the mission of the college in light of the context of the 1980s.

DECEMBER 15

The meetings of November and December involved subcommittee reports concerning such issues as enrollment and retention. By December 15 the college had reached a plateau in terms of conflict. The Rosewood tax assessment had been rebuffed, Dan Grant would return to his job full-time in January, and the faculty had been relatively pleased with the divisional appointments made by the President. The President began the meeting by saying, "Maybe we could start now. We're going to discuss revenue sources of the college, and then we'll hear the rest of the reports. Perhaps we could hand out the breakdown for nontuition revenue."

Here the President establishes the agenda, orders the items, and issues an indirect directive using "perhaps" and "maybe" to hedge or mollify a matter-of-fact directive. Such statements allow the audience a degree of negative participation. Sister Vera then spoke about revenue sources and the difficulty of raising nontuition revenue in a small liberal arts college. She spoke for 7 minutes, ending her comments:

Sister Vera: So, it's difficult for us to go to foundations because they are really looking to give their funds to the big rich schools. It's really difficult.

Falconieri: Rather than be a committee of commiseration, we've got to acknowledge that our backs are up against the wall and go out there and raise funds. We can't apologize for who we are.

A Professor: I know some schools that have a capital campaign—

DeSelm: We have a shot-gun approach to fund-raising. We need to raise additional revenue. Of course, it's out there.

Falconieri: Why don't we think about things like a capital campaign? Why are we paying for our computers when other colleges get them free?

O'Connell: The specifics of fund-raising is really not the function of this group. We are a planning group and we need to be visionaries.

Sister Vera: I guess I think we could have 25 different development programs, but if we're not clear as to what we want, I guess I'm wondering, what's the point? I really do believe that.

The discussion continued in this vein for a half hour. We again see the hedge-like quality of Sister Vera's statements such as "I guess," "I think," and the use of the conditional "could." More important to this example, however, is the body language used by Sister Vera as the speakers talked, and the other members' observations of her body language.

As O'Connell spoke the President nodded in agreement, put both elbows on the table, and moved forward in her chair. When Falconieri and the faculty member spoke, however, Sister neither nodded nor had eye contact with the speaker. The discussion continued free-form without the President formally recognizing who was talking, and in what order. After the meeting an administrator new to CMM talked with me about the discussion. "I really got the feeling that development is a holy area that we are not supposed to talk about," she said. I asked her why she said that and she responded, "Did you see Sister's face? She just got really flushed and looked angry."

Four months later I talked with a faculty member and he brought up the problems of the development office and Sister Vera's desire to protect Tim Leary from criticism. "It's like the Administrative Council meeting where Dave kept talking about a capital campaign. I'll tell you everybody on this campus knows how flushed she got, her back arched, and all that. Development is a domain that we are supposed to stay out of." Dave Falconieri, Director of Admissions, learned that he must stay out of development when his immediate superior, Dr. O'Connell, told him that development was not his area and to stay away from it. Thus, months after a meeting, the actors noted spatial, body, and communicative characteristics of the President that constituted ways they learned that some subjects—development, for example— were taboo.

One final point remains with regard to the December meeting. When the subcommittee reports were finished, Sister Vera summed up the meeting. "I wonder if we ought to—this is off the top of my head, I've given it no thought—I would like to see the ideas we've talked about today shared with people. Maybe we could put these ideas in the *CMM News* or something." After people responded in the affirmative, she concluded with the doubly hedged request, "Would it be possible for the group to come back with written recommendations? I guess when we come back we can prioritize them in February. Golly, that seems like such a long time. Have a nice Christmas and a Happy New Year." The avenue for communication was to be a written bulletin. The written word, however, was a formalized process grafted onto a previously informal structure based upon a leader's informal discursive style. Most members of the college community would see only the formal, written result.

FEBRUARY 28

The tension at the college had been rising perceptibly since the faculty returned in early February. Sister Vera began the meeting by displaying the new logo the college adopted and mentioned that she would post the display on her bulletin board the next day. After a few moments of casual conversation she said, "All right, there are a few housekeeping items. I'd like to go back over where we've been and with the help of Patrick, who helped me over this, let me make a suggestion as to where we might go. First let me review." As she reviewed, individuals made comments and suggestions. When she submitted what she wanted to do for the future the following dialogue occurred:

Sister Vera: One of the things I was thinking—and actually Patrick helped me do this, it's not my own—is focus in on what we should look at. I want to winnow the group down as far as priorities. I guess what I want is to focus on where we want to be three years from now. We have made no concerted effort, as far as I know, to think about where we want to be.

Blue-Smith: I like that idea very much.

Sister Vera: One of the things we've got to do is talk one person to another rather than by rumor. I think too much gets talked about by rumor rather than face-to-face.

Blue-Smith: But if it weren't for the informal, nothing would get done.

Sister Vera: I'm wondering if it wouldn't be better to make public in the *CMM News* what's happening. Then we would be information sharers.

O'Connell: We must redouble our efforts, or give this task to an individual. It's February. We've just spent six months deciding what to decide.

DeSelm: I think we really first need to look at who we are, what we can do well, before we break into clusters. We need to set curricular objectives, goals, think about how we can best train our students.

O'Connell: I don't want you to get away with that. I will not do what is in the faculty's court. There is no set direction—we set the direction. We've got to accept that confusion will exist—it's part of planning.

DeSelm: I'm not worried about confusion. I'm worried about who we are—that's confusing to the public, to the staff, to students.

O'Connell: I totally disagree. There are policy making groups that can address that.

DeSelm: I think—

O'Connell: Furthermore,—

DeSelm: Let me finish! Where is that kind of discussion taking place? I think policy has to be based on a common, shared dream.

O'Connell: Look, the shared articulation of what we're doing is an unrealistic goal. The literature just doesn't support what you're saying. Martin Trow calls higher education systems "untidy" and we've got to accept that.

Sister Vera: I think we ought to deal with what this group will do and how it will do it. We've had some discussion today that I think could have been held elsewhere. Let me just ask a question. Do you have ideas, feelings, hopes, about this place? I bet you said yes. My question is, isn't there some way we can order and synthesize all this? It's two o'clock. Our task for next time will be to decide what this group will do. If you have comments or suggestions please get them to me so I can hand them out next time. Thank-you for coming.

The tenor of this meeting reverberated throughout the college. During the course of the year individuals increasingly noted the President's reliance on Dr. O'Connell. Examples of what they meant by reliance occur in the President's two opening comments— "and with the help of Patrick, who helped me over this," and "actually Patrick helped me do this." In addition, arguments such as the one that occurred between O'Connell and DeSelm made people wonder about his tact and clarity as an administrator. The day after the meeting one faculty member said, "I used to think it was me, but I've talked to enough others, and I've seen it enough now. I just don't understand what he's getting at. Why does he get so angry?" Another individual added, "Patrick's way of arguing is dangerous. He wins the battle and loses the war." The comment referred to O'Connell's line of argument. Oftentimes he spoke with reference to a broader scope than many people had. His comment, for example, "The literature just doesn't support what you're saying," was one way of proving what he said, yet the audience had no context for understanding national data.

Blue-Smith followed Sister Vera's comment that too much rumor occurs at the college acknowledging that rumors existed, and that, "if it weren't for the informal nothing would get done." Sister Vera noted his comment by suggesting a formal process for information dispersal—the campus newspaper. She concluded the meeting with the request that comments be sent to her, which again implies a formal means of information gathering. The actors, however, were unaccustomed to such formalized processes, and, as we shall see, they did not entirely believe that the President wanted or would pay attention to their input.

We have seen how Sister Vera controls the agenda, and this example is no exception. She stops the argument between DeSelm and O'Connell, notes the time, and sets the task for the next meeting. Within the agenda itself, however, we see actors who have their own agendas, or are unable to distinguish what the President wants from her own agenda. That is, it was clear to the President what she desired out of the meeting. She wanted people to come away from the meeting with a prioritized list of what the college should be in three years' time, and how the group planned for the college to achieve those goals. The group, however, was unsure how to create goals and how to achieve them. The March 22 meeting exacerbated the problem.

MARCH 22

Prior to the meeting the President sent out a one-page memo regarding the "scope and function of the Council." The letter listed what areas needed to be considered by the Council, such as the size and membership of the Committee. She began, "Since the members of Administrative Council have made it clear that they do not wish this group to assume the function of planning, but rather to operate as it has in the past three years ..." She intended the letter as a blueprint for action, yet the feeling of many members was quite different. "She's mad at us," said one observer. Another person added, "God how I hate going into this meeting. She's angry because we disagreed with Patrick. Mea culpa. Mea culpa." This meeting came when the college faced its most intense stand off between faculty and administration. The President's address to the faculty had occurred, the excess funds had been discovered, and the legality of the handbook had become a central concern. As the meeting began each faculty member walked into the room prominently holding a copy of the handbook so, "if O'Connell tries something we'll be prepared." The tension of the group was perceptibly high. Sister Joan absented herself from the meeting, and said afterward, "I wasn't going to put myself through that again." Ninety percent of the discussion came from Sister Vera, Dr. O'Connell, Dan Blue-Smith, and another faculty member. After the meeting I walked out with two people who each spoke once. One person agreed with the other when she noted, "You just get in trouble raising questions in there on a day like this. We need time to let things cool down. Boy was she ever upset." The meeting began without any conversation. The following discussion characterizes the tenor of the meeting:

Sister Vera: Perhaps I might give a little history. The description in the handbook says the Administrative Council is a policymaking body. I know it's heresy to speak against the handbook, but quite frankly I have a problem. First, the policymaking body for the college is the Board. Second, it has never made policy since I've been here—but that's what the handbook says.

A Professor: Didn't this group review projects from the Curriculum Committee?

Sister Vera: I'm not aware of this Committee ever rejecting anything. Now, that's my personal experience.

An Administrator: I'm just asking a question. Are we asking if we have the authority to change our function, or if we should change—

Sister Vera: I guess if we should change to a planning group, or remain with what the handbook says.

An Administrator: I thought that's where we were in November?

O'Connell: The point is if we are going to take the handbook for fact, then this group must review all policy—everything.

Blue-Smith: Look, the point is we're in a big problem right now. Let's be frank. It's politics, and this Committee serves as a communication vehicle.

O'Connell: But the handbook says it formulates all matters.

Blue-Smith: I really don't want to get caught in semantics. The perception is people are making decisions that affect what I'm doing.

The discussion highlights patterns seen throughout the year. Sister Vera began her talk by providing "a little history." One of the roles she consistently played was college historian. In order to combat what she saw as historical inaccuracies she often verbally communicated the differences between how committees actually operated and how the handbook said they operated. Yet the President's historical view differed from others' perceptions of the past, and thus she only reaffirmed the actors' awareness of one another's differences. The faculty and senior administrators also played a historical role. At one point during this meeting one faculty member said, "Well, we need to ask Robert about how faculty representation got here, and how it's evolved." Robert was the senior faculty member and people often went to him for an oral history of how the college functioned.

Especially at this time, Sister Vera and Dr. O'Connell felt embattled for trying to create change at the college and, hence, make the college viable in the 1980s. Neither individual ever "owned" the crisis in that they perceived the problem as the faculty's resistance to change, whereas the faculty had a completely different view. Sister Vera's comments such as, "I know it's heresy," communicated to her audience that she felt wronged by their accusations. Blue-Smith saw O'Connell playing a semantic game and rebuffed his attempt to interpret the handbook literally—"this group must review all policy."

For the entire meeting the discussion revolved around who had the authority to make policy and how things actually got done.

Toward the end of the meeting, the role of the Board of Trustees and its relationship to the Committee took on significance. The meeting ended with the following comments:

Sister Vera: The accreditation report more than once suggested that the Board get involved.

Blue-Smith: But if they change policy it still comes through here?

Sister Vera: Pardon me?

A Professor: So we then go to the Board with our recommendations?

O'Connell: I guess we were acting with a false presupposition that we have some authority!

Blue-Smith: The perception is that people are making decisions without going through any policymaking committees. All we're trying to do is iron out how policy gets made. There's tremendous tension right now.

Leary: Are you saying the problem is more communication than approval?

Sister Vera: It seems to me that to add planning to a committee that will review every policy in the college is more that it can handle.

Blue-Smith: I think we need a policymaking body, and this Council is it.

Sister Vera: There are a lot of questions about the power of this Committee. I'm not prepared to make any decision, but then, I'm not supposed to make decisions, I guess. I wish for the next meeting that we'd take into consideration our relationship with the governance board and the relationship with other committees. I hesitate to get into the role of the president, but that also needs to get discussed. You know over a year ago I asked this Committee to look at its relationship with the rest of the college, but it didn't think it was important. All right, thank-you for coming.

Sister Vera's rationale for change often came about as she explained why the Board's role had increased: the accreditation team recommended the change. Consequently, the audience frequently heard that the reasons for change were not due to the whim of an administrator, but because an outside, formalized agency demanded the change. Blue-Smith's comments reflect the degree to which college personnel did not fully understand how shared governance works, for at one point in the conversation he suggested that changes in policy by the Board would then go to the Administrative Council. At the same time, his intent was not to work out the legalistic mechanics of decision making, but rather to promulgate a review and communication of policy so they would permeate throughout the college; the Administrative Council was to be the agent for communication.

Sister Vera and O'Connell again disown the problem by comments such as Sister Vera saying, "but then, I'm not supposed to make decisions, I guess." O'Connell guessed, "we were acting with a false presupposition that we have some authority." His statement reflects who he considers to have authority by the use of "we," and the sardonic quality of the statement points out how "they" misunderstood how college governance functions.

Sister Vera's role of historian came about not only to correct misperceptions, but also to remind the college community that she had forewarned them about change. In Chapter III we saw an example in which the President stated, "I tried to communicate how I thought we were in crisis." At the end of the above meeting she relates how she asked people to look into the relationship of the Council and the rest of the college, "but it [the Administrative Council] didn't think it was important." Both comments frame the participants' awareness that the President did not understand their concerns and sought to justify her actions by communicative, spatial, and temporal codes that ultimately placed blame on individuals other than the President and Executive Committee. Although the Committee still discussed its role, the conversation shifted away from a practical everyday solution, to a formal, legalistic decision concerning how the Council must operate vis-à-vis the Board of Trustees.

APRIL 17

Although minor skirmishes continued throughout the remainder of the year, the major brouhahas had passed by the time the Administrative Council met again. The meeting in April continued many of the speech and communicative patterns already discussed, with one major exception. As the Committee discussed what kind of issues could be brought before the Council, Sister Joan Rinelli lent an example from her area:

Sister Joan: Let me give an example. I've been thinking a lot about athletics. I'm getting all kinds of messages. George [the Athletic Director] has an idea of what he'd like, but then Dave [Director of Admissions] also has thoughts. Athletics impacts on development and I'd like to hear Tim's ideas, especially since we're going to build a gym. I don't think there's any overall way we sit down and talk about what to do. Maybe this is the place where we can bring together diverse areas of the college and talk with one another. It's difficult to deal with.

O'Connell: Well, one way to deal with it, Joan, is for you to decide what to do—period. I don't see how that fits with this Committee.

Sister Vera: I think it does Patrick. It seems to fit with Dave's comment about strategic planning. You know, we've grown topsy-turvy. We were all Sisters back then, and we had dinner together every evening, and we all knew what everyone else was doing. We're different and bigger now, and maybe this is the place to discuss ideas like athletics.

O'Connell: Yes, but this group can only talk about it. The Executive Committee has the power to decide. Joan could bring her ideas to the Exec, and then we'd decide.

Sister Vera: Okay, I understand what you're saying, but I must remind you, the Executive Committee has no power. I made it up. There's an assumption that four people sit in my office and make decisions. I make those decisions. There is this thing going around that all the power used to be by the President and Academic Vice President in Belchamp over supper and now it's four people in my office. I have the right to talk with advisors.

Leary: And those advisors have the right to talk with their constituencies.

Sister Vera: Yes. Again, I've said this so many times. One of my fears is that this group will just be an oral bulletin board. I see it as a consummate waste of time. I want frank discussion, and to plan.

Later in the day an individual who attended the meeting walked up to me in the mailroom and said, "Did you catch it? She finally disagreed with O'Connell. He thought the Exec has power. It sure has taken her a long time to disagree." During the next two days two other Council members and one individual who heard about the meeting mentioned how Sister Vera disagreed with Dr. O'Connell. Their observations were generally correct; her two contradictions of what O'Connell said were the first public disagreements the citizens observed. On occasion she disagreed with O'Connell in her meetings with him or in the Executive Committee, but they generally viewed issues with accord.

Sister Vera reminded them twice of historical events. First, she explained how "We've grown topsy-turvy," and, second, she reminded people, "I've said this so many times," when she talked about her desire not to have people merely report to the Council. Sister Vera stated she wanted "frank" discussion, and Leary reiterated that the Vice Presidents needed to solicit comments from their subordinates. Clearly, however, stating a preference for frank conversation did not engender frank conversation, because of the contextualized past in which other formalized communicative patterns contradicted a desire for open dialogue.

Both Leary's and Sister Vera's comments grew out of the Executive Committee meeting that morning, and their discussion of the Administrative Council, and people's inability to talk frankly. Here are their observations:

O'Connell: I'm not comfortable with the idea that I have to report my actions to that Council. Frankly, they have nothing to do with me. I make decisions, and I can't be expected to report back to some body—

Leary: Let me be frank with you. It sounds like the Administrative Council is becoming a Supreme Soviet who run the college. If people have gripes why can't they just hash it out—

O'Connell: It's critical that second-line administrators don't criticize in meetings like that. They don't have the authority to speak against departmental policy, and if they do, it is grounds for insubordination.

Blue-Smith: But you're looking at things from a conflict model of management.

The point of this example is that frank discussion was impossible for administrators who felt what O'Connell privately stated—to publicly disagree was grounds for dismissal. When we return to the fall Council meetings, we observe how questions concerning development—Leary's area—either were stifled or people felt that area "sacred" so that they could not speak. At the April meeting four people absented themselves not because they had prior engagements, but because they did not feel they would be heard. "Why should I go and put myself in for more of O'Connell's wrath," said DeSelm. "It's just not worth it."

We have, then, a Council that struggled all year with its ability—or inability—to have frank, open discussion that could produce strategic planning and change. The context for how individuals approached the meeting, and the idea of free speech, depended as much on what got said at the meeting as what got said prior to, and after, the meeting. Issues such as development and athletics, many people thought, needed to be discussed by a body such as the Council, but the administration did not allow for such a discussion. The administration saw itself as willing to talk and listen but found that people spoke by rumor and gossip rather than head-on discussions with the Executive Committee.

MAY 17

The final meeting of the year for the Council was uncharacteristically short—only one-half hour. Before the meeting a subcommittee of Sister Vera, Blue-Smith, Falconieri, and another administrator tried to iron out the relationship of the Committee to the college. They presented their conclusion at the final meeting. "We decided we needed to do a study over the summer on the legal aspects of our relationship to the Board of Trustees. Phil [the CMM lawyer] and Dan [Blue-Smith] will work over the summer as to what's legal. We must discuss what the bottom line is legally, as well as with customs and tradition." The subcommittee expected questions from the Council, but after only 10 minutes of questions, silence settled over the group. As one silent member said afterward, "I just wanted to get the hell out of there. If they want to decide not to decide let them. I've got better things to do." The meeting was pleasant, no one spoke any angry words, yet the silence had various interpretations. Sister Vera said to O'Connell at their next meeting, "I'm really excited we're going to look at the legal aspects of the Council. The Committee is behind it. It's the way to go." Falconieri said, "I don't understand. The problems don't seem that overwhelming. In fact, I don't see how we even got into studying the legal stuff." Consequently, the Council ended its year with the question it started with at the beginning of the year—what is its purpose, scope, and function.

When no further questions were forthcoming Sister Vera asked if there was any further business. Characteristically, and jokingly, Leary raised his hand and said, "I move we adjourn." Everyone smiled and made motions to leave. Sister Vera said, "I want to express my gratitude for you living through this year. It's really been an experience."

Chapter VI

Daily Life

This chapter provides different scenes throughout the President's day that relate to a leader's uses of time, space, and communication. Scenes from the daily occurrences of the President demonstrate how the President and the other organizational actors used time, space, and communication with one another. The discussion reorients the framework so that we see the drama not only as a series of issues and decisions, but we also view the minutiae of daily life. In so doing, the chapter provides an understanding of how such scenes support or contradict other executive actions and consequently provides additional information about how organizational participants came to understand their reality.

MORNING

Private Space/Public Greetings

Sister Vera invariably arrived at her office by 8:50 AM every day unless events such as All-College Day or a Board meeting were held. In these cases she arrived earlier than 8:45 to check and make sure everything was in order. Normally, however, the President pulled into her packing space immediately adjacent to her office by 8:50. Upon entering the campus one drives up a long winding driveway and ends up in a parking lot for administrators, staff, and faculty adjacent to the administration building and classrooms. The President, however, parked immediately behind her office in a space marked, "Staff parking—do not park." She used a side door for entering and exiting which made it possible for her to come and go without anyone seeing her. Everyone else parked in the lot and reached their destinations by walking through a small quadrangle, or down a long hallway, past the mailroom and numerous faculty offices.

The President spent 70 percent of her time in her office, 15 percent in spheres close to her office, and the remaining time either in meetings, other areas of the college, or off-campus. Sister Barbara Therese, as President, spent part of every day walking through the campus, checking in on people, greeting them, and inquiring about how they were. The marked difference in the use of space provides one possible explanation about why different constituencies did not believe the President cared about their concerns and ideas.

At the start and end of every day Sister Vera's wooden desk was always spotless except for a potted African violet that sat in the upper right hand corner. Sister worked in the same office as her predecessor, and the office remained substantially unchanged. Sister Vera considered remodeling the office but because of the budgetary crunch she held off redecorating. The office was simply decorated with three plants and a painting. One wall was a book shelf that contained books on higher education, such as *Campus in Crisis*, works on Catholicism, and fictional works, such as *A Separate Reality*. The President shared the same office with her secretary, whose desk was immediately in front of the door.

Sister Vera is not a president who sits in public places and greets people, or casually walks through territory alien to her domain. Indeed, the office she currently inhabits, while physically the same as her predecessor's, has been structured differently so that one can no longer see the President when one walks by the door (see Appendix B). Sister Barbara had her desk in sight of the door, whereas Sister Vera's desk is in a hidden corner of the room. To see if the President is with someone or if she is busy, one has two choices. Either the individual can enter the office, peek around the bookshelf and see if the President is busy, or one can walk outside and pass by the President's office. Outside of her office is a mailbox; individuals will sometimes mail a letter to find out what she is doing. If she is not busy, these individuals often enter the office to talk with the President for a brief, unscheduled appointment. Again, the President's use of space demanded that an individual have an explicit, formal need to see the President instead of the President entering the other's domain to find out casually their concerns.

Sister Vera's secretary kept the President's calendar; the President also had a monthly calendar in a leather folder that she took with her when she left the office; otherwise it remained on the right front corner of her desk near the African violet. The secretary penciled in all meetings such as the Board of Trustees or social occasions. Approximately 30 percent of the President's appointments were made the week they occurred. Most often a person stopped by to make an appointment with Sally, and she either made the appointment immediately or offered to get in touch with the person after talking with Sister Vera. Sally and Sister Vera conferred about the calendar at least once a week, and Sally was aware of times Sister wanted to reserve for private work such as reading or preparing for the Board of Trustees meeting. At the start of every day Sally typed a short schedule of Sister Vera's meetings for that day. Oftentimes Sister Vera knew the purpose of an individual's appointment, and at other times she tried to find out why the person wanted to see her. One morning she noted the list and said questioningly, "Joe Calabrese?" Sally responded, "Oh he just wants to talk to you about the Task Force. He said it's not real important."

Time

One day in February frames Sister Vera's regular routine. She arrived at 8:45 and glanced at her appointments for the day. "Does Tim come in today?" she asked Sally. "I'm not sure," responded her secretary. Tim Leary's office was immediately next to the President's, and he had an adjacent door that opened onto the President's office. Frequently throughout the day Sister Vera and Leary conferred with each other in his office behind closed doors. Although Leary was officially a full-time employee, he generally spent no more than 30 hours per week at CMM, and his visibility—or lack of it—received constant mention throughout the year. "You know that guy is never around here," observed one faculty member, "and when he is here he never has time to talk. His purpose is to counsel Vera and that's it." No one was really certain when Leary came and went, except that he was available when Sister Vera needed him for a specific task and to attend meetings such as the Executive Committee.

One remembers the previous chapter's discussion of development as a "sacred" area. In part, this idea came about through administrative use of time insofar as there was no formal process whereby the actors could discuss issues such as development. Leary maintained they could come and talk with him, yet we have seen the actors' reticence about entering a superior's spatial area and disagreeing with him. The previous chapter pointed out the Academic Vice President's demand that subordinates not disagree. Thus, through a variety of temporal, spatial, and communicative actions, subordinate constituencies acknowledged that certain areas were off-limits for discussion.

During the previous week Sister Vera had two regular off-campus appointments. The college belonged to a consortium of collegiate institutions that raised money as a group, and the President or their designates held monthly meetings at the consortium offices in a nearby city. She also attended the local monthly Catholic college Presidents' luncheon which was at one of the Presidents' colleges. The luncheons were casual affairs where leaders of Catholic colleges got together to discuss issues of concern.

In the upcoming week Sister had two regular meetings that took up a large part of her time. First, she had a Board of Trustees meeting. She carefully prepared for these meetings. Two weeks in advance of the meeting she blocked out time with her secretary when she did not want to be disturbed. Prior to the first meeting of the year she told me, "I want you to know I'm probably going to be a basket case these next few days. I view the Board as my immediate superiors and I try to plan what I will say quite carefully." The second meeting was a finance meeting for the Sisters of Mother Mary held at the province house, 30 miles from campus. Other than college work, Sister Vera's main outside tasks related to her Order. She was a member of the financial board for the province, and worked hard on straightening out their finances. Other than her association with the province, her time was kept to herself and her dealings with the college.

Literacy in the President's Office

Soon after she arrived at the college and took note of her meetings, Sister Vera often wrote short remarks on paper printed with the words, "from the desk of Sister Vera." She either placed the note on an individual's desk, or gave them to Sally to hand out. They were usually one- or two-sentence instructions or requests. On yellow-lined paper Sister Vera handwrote letters she wanted her secretary to type. One example was a letter of praise written on college stationery to a new administrator:

> Dear Jane, Please know how much I appreciate all the work you put into the computer fair which was held last week. So much energy, time, and creative effort is needed to make an event like that come off well. You did a remarkable job! Everyone I've spoken to was impressed and stimulated. I'm very glad you're a part of CMM's community. Gratefully, Sister Vera.

Most of the President's positive comments or congratulations came about in this form—a written recognition that someone had done something noteworthy. When contrasted with the highly personalized communicative style of Sister Barbara, the difference is stark.

Other than letters to the college community, Sister Vera wrote roughly four letters a week to outside sources for information or consultation. In addition to passing information on by way of the *CMM News,* there was a presidental bulletin board that provided information to the community. There was no pattern to the information on the bulletin board. Prior to a week's vacation Sister Vera informed the community, "I will be away from October 10 to October 15. During my absence Dr. O'Connell will assume responsibility for college concerns." During her next vacation in the winter no notice appeared. Notification of which individuals had been elected to some committees appeared on the board, and other committee elections did not receive mention. Most often, however, the bulletin board provided information about a CMM member's illness or a death in the family. The bulletin board attracted most attention when Dan Grant had his heart attack and people wanted daily reports.

On occasion, Sister Vera directed her secretary to place phone calls to particular people, but again, no pattern appeared. At times

Sally called a Board member for Sister Vera and at other times Sister Vera placed the call herself. Sometimes Sister Vera called the Admissions Office for street maps of a city she was going to visit; on other occasions she had her secretary do the chore. When her secretary was out of the office and the phone rang, Sister Vera answered the phone, as did her secretary, "This is the President's office."

Informal Encounters

The morning of the Administrative Council meeting in February, Sister Vera had a standing appointment with Dan Grant at 10:30. At 9:00, after a few minutes of notetaking, she walked out into the hall, paused to see if Patrick O'Connell was in his office, and then walked briefly into Sister Joan's office. Sister Vera stayed in that office four minutes, and then returned immediately across the hall into her room. As she walked across the hall a faculty member ambled by and looked at her to see if he could catch her attention. She looked neither up nor down the hall and did not see the professor; the man continued walking down the hall. In part, actors want the individual who inhabits the President's chair to acknowledge them as individuals. Not only had the actors become accustomed to the informal use of time and space with Sister Barbara, they also expected the President—any president— to speak to them as individuals and not merely in a role-related fashion.

Sister Vera sat down at her desk, glanced at her digital clock, and continued waiting. A few minutes after 9:00 Tim Leary walked into his office, briefcase in hand, saying perfunctorily to everyone he saw, "Good morning, good morning." As soon as he arrived, she opened his side door, said "Tim," entered his office, and shut the door.

Ten minutes later she left Leary's office and returned to her own room. During the ensuing hour Sister Vera had 20 unplanned interactions, all but four of these with either O'Connell or Leary. The shortest interchange lasted less than 30 seconds. The longest conversation was when she reentered Leary's office and did not come out for 14 minutes. After she came out of the office and resumed her notetaking, the part-time lawyer for the college entered, walked over to Sister Vera's desk, and said, "Could I get you to sign something for me?" She looked up at him, glasses on, motioned for the piece of paper to sign, and said, "What am I signing?" He sat down in the chair directly in front of her and explained the particulars of a legal document that needed the President's signature.

People who needed to talk with Sister Vera on an unplanned basis struck three different poses. First, an individual stood close to Sister's desk and asked the question, received an answer, and left. Second, a person stood close to one of the chairs in front of her desk with either a hand or perhaps a bent leg on the chair. Third, there were people who slipped into one of the chairs, sitting forward across the desk from the President. Sister never got up unless the individual who entered was an important personage such as a Board member. J. Francis Hanrahan, the oldest member of the Board of Trustees, entered her office later that morning and Sister Vera immediately stood up, greeted him, and then they sat down in the chairs in front of her desk.

As she talked with the lawyer, Leary placed some papers on her desk that concerned the next week's Board meeting. O'Connell walked in the door and said, "Vera I'd like to talk with you if you have a minute." She nodded yes and finished her conversation with the lawyer. As she looked over the papers Leary gave her, Sally placed additional letters on her desk to sign and said, "Should I try to get Mr. Sanger [a Trustee] on the phone now?" Sister Vera said yes; the line was busy, so the President placed a phone call to the chair of the Board. She did not get through but left a message.

As she finished the phone call another individual walked in and complained about the heat in the music department practice rooms. "Patrick and I are working on it," she said. "Tom Brady says it's a problem with the boiler." The professor nodded and marched out of the office. As he left the lawyer returned with the completed copy of the letter and the phone rang.

A group of students laughed loudly in the hallway and raced toward the exit. A Sister who works at the college poked her head in the door and waved, "I'll come by later. I want to ask you something." Sister Vera nodded. Sally put the phone call on hold and said, "Sister, it's Barbara Therese on the phone. She wants to know if you want her to buy a silly card or a nice card for Mr. Carney's birthday tomorrow." The lawyer, Sally, and I laughed at the question, and Sister Vera frowned, saying, "Oh jeez. Let me take it." She answered the phone and said, "Hello Sister. Things are a bit hectic up here. Could you buy whatever you want?" After a brief silence on the phone the conversation turned to the possibility of cable television for the Sisters' residence. Sister Vera continued, "It's not going to be a problem, BT. Everybody can get it. I'm sure we can too. Don't worry, BT. Okay, BT. See you then." We see from this example how a President spends her time not only making significant decisions, but also is encumbered with minute decisions and encounters that populate her day.

Address Forms

The way people addressed one another deserves mention insofar as names helped form a degree of familiarity—and distance. At present, a Sister who enters the Order keeps her own name and generally people refer to someone as "Sister Jane" or "Sister Mary Rose." At no time during the course of the year did I hear anyone refer to a Sister by her last name such as "Sister Regan" or simply "Regan." The use of first names without the title in front occurred regularly. When Sisters talked among themselves, one often heard one another refer to themselves by their first name, or the reference to a third party by first name, such as "Carol and I went to the movies. We saw *Chariots of Fire*. Carol really liked it. Have you seen it yet, Vera?"

Citizens of the college referred to lay people by their first names, or logical nicknames such as "Dave" or "Tim." The only exception to this norm was the Academic Vice President, who was never called "Pat." He was always "Patrick." When Sister Vera began her conversation with her predecessor, she used a distancing technique by saying, "Hello Sister," rather than, "Hello Barbara," or more customarily, "Hello BT." The previous President and Academic Vice President were constantly called by their initials, "BT" and "MT." As a younger Sister explained, "BT is really an endearment. I'd never say it at a formal meeting or something. But it's just a friendly, casual term."

With regard to lay people at the college, only O'Connell uniformly used Sisters' first names in their presence individually, or at meetings, or when their names came up in conversation. When a discussion began about accreditation, for example, O'Connell said, "I've talked with Esther, and I think she will take it on." Esther was an older nun approaching retirement. At the Administrative Council we heard him say, "Well one way for you to deal with it, Joan, is for you to decide what to do." Joan was Sister Joan Rinelli. Third parties who were lay were also mentioned by first name.

The use of titles and names is one way speakers imply familiarity with people endowed with power or people without power recognize the status of powerful others by using titles such as "Sister" or "Dr." The distinctiveness of the college's Catholic tradition allows for a twofold familiarity and distancing technique. The use of last names or titles such as "President Regan" never received mention whereas the more familiar use of first names came into constant play. Presumably if the President and other important people in the organization are to have their first names used—albeit with the title "Sister" in front of the first name—then lay people working with one another will also use their first names when talking with and about other colleagues. Between students and faculty, however, there is a marked status differential, as the use of distancing behavior indicates. With the exception of Dan Blue-Smith and one other instructor, students consistently referred to their teachers as either professor or doctor.

A final point on the use of names is that more often than not people referred to individuals rather than the roles that the individuals filled. "In the Graduate Committee yesterday," noted one professor, "Ellen wanted us to review the function of the Committee." Another way of saying that would be "The graduate dean wanted us to review the function of the Committee," using "graduate dean" rather than "Ellen." Throughout the year all members of the community referred to others by name rather than by role. Again, the exception occurred at formal meetings when the Academic Vice President's name came into use. A faculty member noted at the Faculty Senate, "The Academic Vice President premises his plan that we will save money from the curricular reorganization. From where?"

The Territory of Leadership

Prior to a meeting Sister Vera was to have with Dan Grant, one of the President's closest friends called and asked her to have lunch. "Sure Carol, that's fine. But I've got a meeting at 12:30. So how about if you come up here at 11:30. Okay, fine, see you then, Carol." Sister Vera most often ate lunch off-campus, either with Sister Carol or Tim Leary, or by herself in her office. At times, scheduled luncheon meetings occurred, such as with the Board of Trustees, but only once did I observe the President eating in a "public" place such as the cafeteria, the Inn on campus, or in the quadrangle.

As with any organization, informal meetings and meeting places occurred in a variety of locales. The cafeteria, used by students, staff, and faculty, had no "off-limits" partitions, yet faculty members, the "lunch bunch" more than one observer called them, consistently met in the most private area for lunch or a cup of coffee. A young faculty member once remarked, "You know the lunch bunch is the old guard here, and they really discuss what's going on among themselves. They don't exclude you if you sit with them, but it's pretty clear who sits there, and who doesn't."

The small quadrangle outside of the administrative office was another place where small, private conversations occurred. The mailroom was the most common meeting place. Everyone in the institution except the President had a mailbox in the room and it was not uncommon to meet someone there and either make plans to meet later in the cafeteria or to spend a few moments in the quadrangle. Because the Xerox machine was in the room, and the mailroom was close to faculty and administrative offices, the room constantly had a flow of individuals. Throughout the year I never observed the President either in the mailroom or the quadrangle.

The President's office was the only space anyone recognized as the President's. On occasion I met with Sister Barbara in her "official" office in Belchamp Hall. After initial greetings in the office she shared with her secretary, she led me to a private room she kept closed, without a telephone, so "we won't be disturbed by calls, and we can talk." The President, however, always greeted the public in her office which she shared with her secretary. As already mentioned, individuals entered her office to give her something, or to talk with Sally about a particular item—perhaps a returned memo or a request for an appointment. Invariably, individuals who entered the office looked in the President's direction to see if Sister Vera had observed them. Occasionally someone risked saying a greeting. With certain individuals Sister Vera always noticed their entrance and either initiated a greeting or responded in kind. Most often, however, no response was forthcoming. Clearly demarcated lines of space, public territory, and forms of discourse marked the presidential role.

On March 29 at the Executive Committee, Sister Vera mentioned a note she found upon her return from a short trip to Hawaii:

Sister Vera: It's obvious to me there are still things going on. There was an anonymous letter saying if you just met with people privately you would learn what was going on around here.

Leary: I'll say this about the President. She doesn't like secret, brokered meetings. She didn't deal with us [the Executive Committee] individually. She said, "Let's cut out the intrigue."

Sister Vera: What I do with anonymous letters like that is throw them out in the waste basket.

Blue-Smith: You also said your door is always open.

Sister Vera: Someone also said that walking into this office is totally intimidating.

The President displayed annoyance that someone would leave anonymous notes rather than entering her office and talking with her. At a critical juncture during the year, a faculty subcommittee made the explicit request not to meet in Sister Vera's office because they wanted to meet on neutral turf. Throughout the year individuals noted how people consciously bypassesd the President's and AVP's office on their way to the mailroom or classroom.

As I left the mailroom with an individual one day, for example, and headed across campus, the individual steered me outside the building even though walking by Sister Vera's and O'Connell's office was the shortest route. "I'd rather avoid seeing O'Connell," the individual said. "He's always yelling at me from his desk to come here a minute. It's never just talk. He always tells me something to do."

A faculty member noted, "It used to upset me that Vera would walk by in the hall and not even say hello. I know it's everybody, but I won't walk down there because I always feel as if I did something wrong when I pass her near the office and she won't say hello." Thus, the President and Executive Committee's use of private and public space was an issue for different groups.

Although people's perceptions of how that space should be used differed, all were consciously aware of the space.

MIDMORNING

Gestures

When Dan Grant entered that morning, he said, "Hi, how's it going," to Sister Vera, slipped off his blue blazer, put his sunglasses on her desk, and sat in the chair closest to the door. For planned meetings the President always came from behind her desk to sit next to the person. Grant began to talk about the budget and Sister Vera said, "Oh gosh, I forgot, just a sec." As she said this, she grabbed his left arm lightly, stood up and got some files. During the course of the year I observed Sister Vera touch someone in that manner 32 times. Occasionally she received reciprocal gestures, but only twice did I observe the individual initiate something such as a hug or a peck on the cheek. The first time involved the above-mentioned Board member, who was 77 years old, and in obvious command of respect and deference. When he entered he hugged her, and he kissed her cheek. The other time was when Grant returned from his operation. During the outset of his first meeting back with Sister he gave her a hug, which exemplified their friendly relationship and his thankfulness for her support during his illness. In fact, she most often touched Grant in a brotherly fashion such as just demonstrated. By April, however, I no longer saw these gestures.

Often the President initiated a gesture that went unreciprocated. Once when Sister Vera was in the hall outside of her office talking with someone, the Director of Admissions walked down the hall. "Oh Dave," she called, "could you wait a minute?" He stopped near her and as she wrapped up one conversation she took Dave's hand and held it as a symbol that she would be right with him. Another individual observed the hand-holding and jocularly said, "Wow! Dave and Sister Vera are holding hands." Dave, seeing the humor in the situation but also a bit nonplussed, responded, "Gee, I've never held hands with a president before." Sister Vera said, "Ah! It comes from my working in elementary schools. I always hold the kids' hands."

Seasonal Activities

The meeting with Dan Grant concerned primarily the preparation of the budget, a typical seasonal activity in late winter or early spring. Sister Vera and Grant waited until total enrollments for second semester had been recorded before they built the 1984/85 budget. Seasonal activities are anchored by the calendar year. Most collegiate institutions in the United States begin in August or September and finish in May or early June; College of Mother Mary was no exception. Administrators and staff who worked a 12-month year found the year beginning in August and ending in May. The President announced that her last end-of-month party was April 30 because the school year would be over by the time the next scheduled party took place—even though staff and administrators would be at CMM. The student-run newspaper put out a final issue in May and thanked people for contributing and working on the newspaper. The in-house *CMM News* labeled, "For staff, administrators, and faculty," published on May 24 its final bulletin that said, "This issue is the last Campus *News* until Fall Semester begins. Have a happy summer." Nevertheless, staff, administrators, and the writers of the *News* worked throughout the summer. Seasonal activities are those events tied to a calendar so that the school year looked like the following: All-College Day, Christmas Break, Intersession, Budget Creation, Commencement, and Summer.

Clearly, the calendar year can be modified; it is conceivable that the school year could begin in January and end in September. Christmas cannot be modified, and, indeed, for a Catholic college the Christmas holidays take on a special importance as a time for religious celebration. Intersession is an example of a seasonal activity first created but soon stopped. It was a seasonal activity when CMM created it in the 1970s, yet the President decided to do away with it as of 1985. Work on the budget goes on throughout the year; however, the most intense activity occurs in the early spring months of March and April. Budget preparation occurs early as we saw with the Budget and Finance Committee's fall decision to raise tuition 4 percent. Some individuals want to start the budget process even earlier in the year, yet Sister Vera and Grant believe that the budget needs to be as accurate as possible and they must therefore wait until second semester begins. Sister Vera believes that the budget should be approved by the Board of Trustees prior to the academic year so that the final Board meeting in May is the time when the budget must be finished.

Communicating with Constituents

The meeting about the budget was characteristic of many meetings with Grant in that it was fast paced and ended by eleven o'clock. As he slid back into his jacket and stood up, Sister Vera thanked him for coming. He nodded and said, "See you later at Administrative Council." As he left, nodding good-bye to Sally and myself, Sally took a phone call and said, "Sister is still in a meeting, I think, let me see if she's free." As she put the caller on hold she said, "Sister, it's Mrs. Jason again." Sister Vera frowned and said, "Oh crap. I don't know what to do with her. All right, give it to me." She held the phone in her left hand, stood up, and looked out the window into the small parking area. The caller knew the President and wanted her daughter admitted to the college. After listening to the woman's request, Sister said, "I think you'd probably want to talk with Dave Falconieri in Admissions. I don't handle it on a day-to-day basis. Be sure to tell him you're an alum. Let me transfer you. Thanks for calling." The conversation lasted less than a minute, and as she tried to transfer the call she realized she did not know how to refer calls on the phone system. She faced her secretary and said pleadingly, motioning with the phone, "Sally." Sally stood up, came over to the phone and transferred the call. As Sister sat down she mumbled a thank-you to her secretary and said to one one in particular, "If she thinks I'm gonna get her dumb kid in here, she's crazy." She again stood up, wandered out into the hall, looked into O'Connell's office, and then retreated to her own room.

As she entered she looked out her window and saw one of the basketball team members on crutches. "Oh crumb," she said to herself. "What's the matter with Joey?" A moment later the coach walked by her window and she opened the window and yelled out to him, "Hey George, is Joey going to be hurt for long?" The Athletic Director discussed the student's injury for a bit, and, as they did, Sister Carol arrived for lunch. Sister Vera headed out the door, armed with her purse, and said, "Sally, I'll be back by 12:30. But I've got Administrative Council until two."

She returned to her office briefly at 12:25 to pick up a few papers and then headed by herself to the Art Gallery where the Council met. After the meeting she picked up her papers and walked back to her office directly; as she walked she talked with one of the Council members, said good-bye to him, and entered her office at 2:02.

AFTERNOON

Humor

Sister Vera immediately took off her suit coat, placed it on the back of her chair, and pulled out the guidelines for reaccreditation that recently arrived. She sat straight up, elbows on the table, eyeglasses on, and immersed herself in reading the document. Occasionally she used her pencil to scribble notes in the margins of the paper and pushed the pages ahead with the end of her pencil. A quiet fell on the office for a half hour, and the only noise that one heard was an infrequent cough from the President who then popped a cough mint into her mouth.

She looked up once to her secretary and again asked, "Has Tim gone for the day?" Her secretary looked into his office, returned from the hallway, and said, "I guess so. I don't know. His door is shut and the lights are out. There's a man in the hall talking to Patrick, Sister, that is about twice Patrick's size." Sister Vera, curious, took her glasses off, pushed both hands into her pockets and went down the hallway on an imaginary mission. Seconds later she returned engulfed in good-natured laughter. The picture of the short AVP conferring with a computer software salesman who was at least six feet nine inches tall was funny without even knowing the individual involved.

Shortly thereafter O'Connell entered and said, "Do you have a minute, Vera?" She smiled, came from behind her desk and said, "What's cooking?" He mentioned that he thought he had found a solution to the biology department's mice, and Sister Vera laughingly grimaced. "Don't tell me about it. I just don't want to have them anywhere near where I am." He continued on about the "mouse house" and then switched subjects and mentioned that he had done some thinking about who should head up the accreditation team. "I was thinking," he said, "that we could get

Harry Hayden to lead it." "Will you quit it!" she exclaimed. Harry Hayden was a tenured professor who neither the President nor the AVP considered hard-working. Whenever a difficult task came before them, such as chairing a department or directing the new Weekend College, O'Connell mentioned Hayden with a puckish grin on his face.

Forms of ritual humor punctuated interchanges among the President and Executive Committee. Teasing one another was one way of increasing group solidarity and relieving tension. Leary used humor in the Executive Committee to help the President relax; the President enjoyed teasing Leary about his disdain for meetings and particular people at the institution. O'Connell and Leary often joked about the need for alcoholic beverages in their new offices in Belchamp. Most often, however, one did not see these forms of humor carried over with other, less intimate, associates or at larger meetings such as the Administrative Council.

Informal Decision Making

As Sister Vera and O'Connell discussed who should head up the accreditation team, Leary returned and poked his head in the room. Sister Vera said, "We're just talking about accreditation. Sit down a minute." He remained standing but gave his opinion as they reviewed particular names of faculty and staff members for the committee.

Later in the year Sister Joan would remark:

> I've seen Tim and Patrick in there with Vera, and I know they're discussing things. It's not just chit-chat. I know oftentimes the word "Executive Committee" gets used when we've never discussed it at the meeting. It's at times like those, when they just have an impromptu and then they decide things. I really don't like it. That's just what BT and RT used to do, but they did it down in Belchamp over dinner. Vera's just changed the place.

Again, a spatial comment occurs that explains in part how the actors, even an Executive Committee member, came to believe that the Executive Committee ruled the college and that other committtees' and individuals' ideas were inconsequential.

Messages

Leary had an appointment in the city and he soon left the President's office. O'Connell got up to leave and Sister Vera said, "Have you seen this yet?" She showed him an angry letter from a faculty member regarding the planned use of computers at CMM. "I wish he'd learn how to spell my name," she remarked; he had addressed the letter to "Sister Vera Reagan" instead of "Regan." "Besides," she continued, "this should have gone to you. Why did he send it to me?"

Neither Sister Vera nor O'Connell appeared upset about the letter, yet she later wrote a strong response:

> Your letter raised some issues which are clearly inappropriate, both in substance and in tone ... I need hardly point out that your request to define the future role, if any, of the Advisory Council [on computers] should have been addressed to Dr. O'Connell as Academic Vice President. Matters of curriculum fall under his jurisdiction and yet you neither met with him beforehand, nor subsequently informed him of your letter to me.

The letter concluded, "Your accusations of 'irresponsibility' are totally uncalled for, and I would hope you will be forthcoming with an apology for these tendentious remarks."

Where individuals sent messages were important considerations throughout the year. In every organization one can easily find actors vying for turf; at CMM the organization compounded the problem by an actual confusion concerning where issues were to be brought to get resolved. Two faculty members quit in the fall; one individual sent her letter of resignation to the President, while the other individual sent her letter to the AVP. Dave Falconieri went directly to the Executive Committee with his idea about tuition credits for certain students, and Dan Grant later criticized the Executive Committee for approving the request. "That should have gone through Budget and Finance." When Sue Ann Simmer wanted the curtains for Melton Hall, Sister Vera told her that the registrar was picking out the material. "Could you please tell me why the registrar has anything to do with classroom curtains?" Sue Ann angrily asked. Dan Blue-Smith considered sending a letter to the President when Student Affairs denied the beer license for the Inn on campus. Sister Joan wondered, "Why doesn't he come to me and ask me why I don't want beer served down there instead of making a big thing about it." In short, messages—both written and oral—oftentimes ended up in the hands of people that others thought should not be dealing with the issue.

LATE AFTERNOON

As O'Connell and Sister Vera talked about the faculty member's missent letter, the Purchasing Director, a 68-year-old retired school administrator, walked in and asked a question about the phone system for Belchamp. By 3:30 O'Connell left and Sister Vera returned to her desk. The nun who had come by in the morning returned and stood in the doorway. "Could you come for supper Thursday night, Sister?" asked the nun. "Sure, Sister, that would be fun," said the President, looking up at the nun through the tops of her glasses. "Okay, see you then," said Sister Mary and left less than a minute after entering the room. Shortly after four o'clock the noise in the building fell to a whisper; Sally said good-bye and left. Sister Vera prepared to leave by clearing off her desk so that only the African violet remained. She put on her coat, looked out the window, shut off the lights, and walked out the door to her red car.

Through the use of the foregoing scenes we have observed different uses of time, space, and communication. Temporal scenes demonstrated how the President relied on formalized interchanges with all individuals except her inner circle. Informal encounters occurred frequently in the President's office, but those encounters occurred primarily with Leary and O'Connell. Examples of formalized interactions such as planned meetings showed how they occurred frequently, and that they revolved around preset patterns of interchange.

The private territory of leadership circumscribed the spatial patterns of Sister Vera's presidency. Although individuals occasionally ventured into her office, more often than not the private space of the presidency created a distance between the President and other organizational participants. Gestures of friendship occurred at times between the President and other actors, yet again, they occurred infrequently and appeared less often as the year progressed.

Communication occurred both on verbal and written levels. Examples showed how written notes of praise or anger far outweighed verbal cues by the President. At times decisions occurred quickly and informally through informal communication with her chief lieutenants, but, again, this form of communication occurred primarily with members of the Executive Committee.

Often, the uses of time, space, and communication intersected, such as the example where an individual wrote an anonymous note to the President when she was away on a trip. The writer of the note said that he/she felt intimidated to talk with the President in her office and that the President should be more accessible. The formal mode of communication that discussed spatial patterns at a time when the President was away on a seasonal activity is a good example of how different message units created meaning for the organization.

Organizational conflict came about in large part through the actors' interpretations of the various forms of temporal, spatial, and communicative patterns outlined in this chapter. The actors' perceptions of the minutiae of daily life provide the reader with an understanding of how the reality of the organization was constructed and interpreted. Rather than rely on the assumption that organizational reality exists through environmental determinants or the deeds of a "great man," this chapter has outlined how referents of power such as time, space, and communication give rise to individual and organizational meaning.

Chapter VII

The Presidency

This chapter details the structure of the college presidency in general and specifies how Sister Vera fits within the presidential role. The first section reviews the common conceptions of the role and functions of the college president, presidential careers, and the nomination process for the presidency. The second section provides insight into how Sister Vera views her role at College of Mother Mary, her rationale for assuming the presidency, and her perspective on the problems that beset CMM during the year under study. The data for the second section come from six structured interviews with Sister Vera in the 1983/84 year; the first during the first week of October 1983 and the final interview in mid-July 1984. Though she had no predictive vision of the problems and conflicts at CMM during 1983/84, her response and outlook on the presidency remained quite consistent.

THE COLLEGE PRESIDENCY

Chapter I summarizes theories concerning presidential power and importance. March and Cohen's use of an organized anarchy model of college administration points to the relative impotence of college presidents. From their viewpoint individuals who reside in the presidency carry out functionary tasks prescribed by the role of the office; the anarchic nature of the institution circumscribes presidential power so that it is almost negligible. Because American institutions of higher education have unclear goals, a misunderstood technology, and fluid participation, Cohen and March portray the college president as an individual who drives a car out of control on an icy freeway.

An earlier view of college leadership describes the college president as the person in whose shadow the institution exists. A college president is capable of effecting change in the institution by the ability to develop creative ideas, to articulate to constituencies those plans, and to implement an agenda by the effective use of presidential power and prerogative. Although the view of a powerful president comes primarily from earlier periods of American higher education, authors still maintain the need for a reassertion of presidential power and authority:

> In spite of some changes in the presidential role that came about during the 1960s, such as the evolution of faculty senates and admission of students into deliberative and sometimes decision making roles, presidents ... still represent the most powerful constituency of the institution. They still are chiefly responsible for securing necessary funding, personifying and representing the institution, and resolving those conflicts that inevitably appear in an organization (Mayhew 1980, p. 75).

In short, the way to survive the difficult times ahead is by the reassumption of presidential authority.

The kinds of individuals who have been chosen as college presidents over the last century have been remarkably consistent, yet the office has changed over time. That is, when theorists spoke of the administration of colleges and universities at the turn of the century, they referred primarily to the trustees of the college, the president, and perhaps a "head professor." The president of the 1980s has an array of subordinates ranging from the provost or academic vice president to legal advisors, deans of students, registrars, and the like.

Initially, ministers, priests, or other influential men in the community became college presidents. Over time, theorists developed a model which specified a "regular" path to the college presidency. "Senior positions in academic administration have long been the almost exclusive province of those who served a substantial time in academe," writes Socolow, "moving from one rung of the ladder to the next—most often from professor to chairman to dean to vice-president to president" (Socolow 1978, p. 42). Thus, a presidential "career ladder" resembles the following: faculty—department chair—academic dean—provost—president. Intuitively, the metaphorical ladder makes sense insofar as the individual who becomes president will have experienced the institution from the ground level up and will presumably have the vision and experience for a composite view of the institution.

In a recent study of the presidential career trajectory, however, Kathryn Moore and others noted:

> The normative presidential career trajectory is accurate only to the extent that permutations and variations among its elements are incorporated. As a strictly defined, hierarchical, linear model it does not reflect the actual experience of a national sample. It is most accurate in describing the principal entry portal to the college presidency—faculty experience—and in identifying four other positions that commonly appear within the trajectory, of which the provost position seems the most potent for predicting a subsequent move to president (1983, p. 513).

At the time of Moore's investigation, over 80 percent of college presidents studied had been a faculty member at one time, although they may not have had subsequent experience as a dean or department chair.

Cohen and March have pointed out the haphazard nature of the presidential selection process when compared with the business world. It is not uncommon in business, for example, to find chief executive officers who have been groomed for the position through a vice-presidential role in which the individual and the Board become acquainted with one another, and the individual "learns the ropes." Individuals in businesses also may express the desire to become the president of a company by moving through the ranks to be in position for an ultimate position of authority and power.

A similar process, either by the individual or the organization, generally does not take place in collegiate America. Current practice in higher education is a Board-initiated search for the candidates with the proper credentials. The search may not be for an individual who wants to be president, or someone who has followed the model outlined above. At times institutions seek a fiscal manager, and at other times the president needs the proper academic credentials, or a high enough profile to project the college's image to politicians for political support or to foundations for financial support. Although it is true that some search committees seek an "insider" rather than someone who has no feel for the institution, the opposite can also be found as a priority for search committees. Nevertheless, it is rare that an institution anoints an individual for the position so that he or she can wait for the present president to retire and eventually assume the presidency. Knapp argues this position by stating, "Anticipating recruitment for adminitrative posts has had little acceptance. Rare indeed is the university or college ready to fill an administrative vacancy without a prolonged, expensive, often frantic search.... The academic stance on administrative recruitment, both among faculty and current administrators, is still catch-as-catch-can" (Knapp 1969, p. 58).

Even though search processes vary from institution to institution, and there are no concrete criteria for the selection of a president, a composite picture of a college president does emerge from the literature. As one might expect, the "average" college president is a white male in his forties who has had prior experience in academe, most likely as a faculty member. The individual's tenure as a college president will last roughly five years, and then he will move on to become director of a foundation or business, or possibly return to the professoriate. Exceptions to the rule exist; College of Mother Mary is one notable exception.

One problem that occurs when we seek to typify the colleges is the multitude of institutions that fit under the umbrella of higher education. Small, liberal arts, religious institutions have always had a place in the fabric of collegiate America. The major expansion for these kinds of institutions, however, took place in the 1950s and 1960s. One observer has noted, "Between 1950 and 1960, Catholic women's colleges sprang up like dandelions after a spring shower. By actual account, fifty-six or almost four foundations per year began.... Between the mid-1950s and 1960s 139 Catholic collegiate institutions began" (Reiss 1982, p. 93).

As we have seen, College of Mother Mary always has had as its president a Sister of Mother Mary; more than any other prerequisite the individual had to be a Catholic woman who was a Sister. This pattern can be found elsewhere as well. Jencks and Riesman note: "Church colleges tend to hire members of their own faith, professional schools hired members of the profession, upper-class colleges often hired independently wealthy faculty, and even colleges for women and for Negroes often came to depend mainly on women and Negroes" (1977, p. 6). Thus, CMM was one type of institution that often had Catholic women as its leaders.

In 1956 CMM chose its longest reigning president, Sister Barbara Therese. Her selection came about without a formal search committee or application(s) for the position. As Sister Barbara said, "I was told to go to—it wasn't a choice—that I had been chosen to be president." Previous presidents doubled as the provincial superior; the separation of the two offices points to the Sisters' idea that the office of president had become a full-time task.

The historian for the province remembers how Sister Barbara was chosen, and the qualities the province looked for in the new college president. "She had a certain drive, and also a very good sense of public relations. And for the building up of the new college, that would be extremely interesting. Sister Barbara knew how to make friends ... I used to be impressed by the people that she knew ... She just had a way of reaching out to people and bringing them in." Sister Barbara came from a wealthy family of a nearby city; throughout her career her connections with the wealthy in the city aided the college in its fund-raising efforts. Virtually everyone who knows BT acknowledges her "very good sense of public relations." We have, then, an institution in the 1950s that sought an individual who could help transform the college from a small two-year junior college into a four-year institution. The qualities sought for the presidency were connections with influential citizens, and a personality that would attract people to the college. Although no search process took place, the nomination of Sister Barbara differed from previous presidents in that she was not province superior.

When Sister Barbara announced her retirement, however, the Board of Trustees—and not the provincial superior—had the task of selecting College of Mother Mary's new president. A faculty member on the Search Committee remembered the process: "Vera's search was the most democratic thing that ever happened in this school. Students, faculty, the Board, everybody got involved in the process. It was apparent that major changes were coming because of her view of shared decision making. That's why we liked her. The committee structure had grown so slowly here, and we saw, at least we thought then, that Vera was a process person." Initially, no one nominated anyone or applied for the position. Eventually, the Search Committee either nominated individuals themselves, or another Sister nominated someone. The Committee presented the Board with three choices, and the trustees chose Sister Vera after much discussion. "She was an inside bet from the start," remembers J. Francis Hanrahan. "If I was to characterize who we wanted it was someone who had sound administrative experience and would keep the college afloat." Again, the prerequisite for president was to be a Sister of Mother Mary. Additional qualities such as administrative experience, a doctorate, interest in process, were also important. What impressed the Search Committee was Sister Vera's administrative experience as a principal and administrator for the province, her dedication to shared governance, and her responses during the interviews.

Another Search Committee member reflected, "I literally had people coming up in the halls telling me to nominate Vera, to select her. She was a popular candidate." The drawbacks to Sister Vera's selection as president were threefold. First, she admitted that her experience with finance and accounting was minimal. Second, she did not have a doctorate. The third factor concerned her "moodiness." One individual said what was often mentioned, "We all wondered about her moods but figured it never interfered with her doing her job before. No one ever guessed that her moods would come into play the way they have this year." As previously mentioned some Sisters objected to the personal style of Sister Vera, but this objection did not appear to concern the Search Committee. After extended debate the Board of Trustees chose Sister Vera Regan as President of College of Mother Mary.

INTERVIEWS WITH THE PRESIDENT

During the course of the year the interviews with the President revolved around five topics outlined below. The method for this section will be to pose the questions asked, and then hear Sister Vera's response. Because the interviews took place over a nine-month period, questions and responses have been grafted onto one another to present as coherent a picture as possible. Background information provides the initial introduction to Sister Vera.

Vera Regan grew up in a major city near Rosewood; the last interview I held with her was the day before her fifty-sixth birthday on July 12. She comes from an Irish-Italian family, whose mother worked at CMM. She has two sisters, and two brothers who entered the priesthood. "I never thought about joining the Sisters," she said one day. "I wanted to go to San Diego State like my friends. Then a priest said to me one day that I had better think about joining the Sisters. So I did. How can you say why you did something? You just do it. I was a totally nonreflective child."

After attending CMM as a student she received a BA and performed various tasks for the Sisters, such as teaching. If one sees gradations among levels of a religious community, then one can say Sister Vera rose fairly rapidly through the ranks of Sisters of Mother Mary. In 1960 she attended Stanford University for a master's degree in English. She describes it as one of the major events of her life. "It was my first real non-Catholic experience— doing D.H. Lawrence, James Joyce, all that wonderful stuff. I suddenly realized that there were terribly good human beings out there who had nothing to do with the Catholic Church."

Her hobbies are sewing, furniture refinishing, attending the ballet and opera, and reading. Her reading interests vary from historical novels, to Dorothy Sayers, to Shakespeare. She is an avid football fan and follows a professional sports team quite closely. She tries not to take her work home with her and would rather stay late—"until five or six"—than get into the habit of working at home. She lives by herself in a nearby community and drives to work.

The interview follows.

Woman/Sister

Could you speak about how you see yourself as a woman and a Sister in the context of the 1980s and the college presidency?

I don't know where to start. Let me take one of your points and go with that. I started to be reflective in the early 1960s, and it was connected with my becoming postulant director. This sounds real corny, but the triggering of it was the opening up of the Church, the Vatican Council. I started giving talks about religious life. I went to the Province House and for five years I had 20 to 35 eighteen-year-olds who wanted to be Sisters. They didn't even know what it was to be human. So I first thought you had to know what it was to be human, then a Catholic, then a Sister. As I thought about it, though, I revamped my classes so that we had to consider what it was to be a human being, and then a woman. I said that if they couldn't see themselves as married then they couldn't be a Sister. That caused a scandal, of course. I remember that I thought these kids should not be dressed up like that, in those black dresses. It was romantic as hell for them, walking around like that, swinging their rosary beads. They had no idea what it meant to be a woman, much less a Sister.

You see, one of the simplest ways to lead this life is to deny what being a woman means—I'm being very judgmental and I shouldn't be. Back then we had limited interaction with men, we didn't have families to raise, the vow of chastity, and the isolation. It became clear to me that until we had an understanding of those things we would be second-class citizens.

Would I do it over again? Probably not. Do I regret doing it? Not at all. It's terrible to have to regret something. I wouldn't do it over again because I think that there are a lot more jobs open to me now than there were back then. When I look back I recall my years with the postulants as difficult, but wonderful. To watch those young women grow, it is, was, joyful.

But you see, I don't like the idea that Sisters have a pipeline to God, that we should get special treatment, have doors open for us and that stuff because we're Sisters. I'm no better than anyone else, and we have to realize that we need to treat all people equally, and perhaps some people need special treatment not because of their role, but because of their human needs at the moment. That means that our old conceptions of what it means to be a Sister are changing. The definitions have to change. Sharing the same bathroom with somebody is not what community is about. In our Order we tended to find visionaries and expected them to lead us through things. I saw this happening to me, and I didn't want it. When people look upon you as having the answers you either burn out or you get a strange sense of integrity that you can change the world—and you can't.

An individual chooses to belong to this group, which doesn't mean you do everything the group does, but there is some vision, some belief that you share. You make a public statement of belonging to this group. For us, it's a belief that somehow or other we are a redeemed world. What we're all about is to somehow help move the world in the direction of Jesus—that we have a desire for the world to be peaceful, just, honest, and caring. We've got to realize that we are no better than anyone else.

Nomination to CMM

Why did you apply for this job? What was the nomination process like?

I knew I was leaving where I had been—in charge of that school. I had several offers of positions, superintendencies, things like that. When BT announced her resignation it had crossed my mind and I wasn't really sure about it. Actually I was really thinking about it when some people here invited me out to dinner. In the course of supper I heard about all the bad feelings at the college, all the things that were wrong, all the injustices. At the end of the supper I knew one thing, and I told them, it was not the way I wanted to spend my life. So I decided to forget applying.

I didn't know it at the time but no one else applied either. At some point, about four to six weeks later someone—a friend—on the Search Committee called and asked if I would consider being nominated. I thought about it and finally I reluctantly said that I'd allow to have my name put in. I will say that I almost enjoyed the interviews here. I was a little nervous, of course, I guess one would be. But it didn't throw me. I learned more about the college, and had the chance to think about it. I wanted to change things.

One of the things that was uppermost in my mind was that I wanted the image of the college to be changed. I didn't want to be associated with an [old-style] president, and a college that looked like a 1930s high school. I didn't want the Sisters of the province to avoid the place because it was so out of touch. I wanted to raise salaries because they were too low. The Academic Dean. Curriculum. I knew it needed work, but I didn't know what.

I guess there were other things I wanted to change, too. I didn't realize how difficuilt it would be to change things. I never had that problem before, to lead people. I have a gut reaction that I don't think I'm suited to the institution. I think I'm a poor match. I'm too thin-skinned, but I said that before I became President. They can't say I didn't warn them. I also think people had a pretty good deal here, and knew it.

Life at CMM

What keeps you here? What are those things which you enjoy, and what you'd like to be remembered for?

It's when I see the divisions taking shape, or the freshman courses beginning to go that I get jazzed about things. I enjoy talking about the college, what I'd like it to be. I really don't know what kinds of things I enjoy. It's difficult to say. I know this job is a big hassle, and it's not enjoyable. It would be selfish of me to resign, though. When BT resigned it cost the people here a lot—emotionally, psychologically, spiritually. The search for a successor, the uncertainty, the big question as to what would happen. BT had been here for such a long time that it would be really selfish to put them through that again. It's a matter of enduring for a couple more years. I know I'm not staying here for 24, that's for sure.

And what to be remembered for? I don't know. I know what I will be remembered for—for creating hell and firing lots of people. But I don't know what I want to be remembered for, I really haven't thought about it.

College Leadership

When you think about leading a college what comes to mind? What does a college president need, and specifically, what does someone need to be president at CMM? How does leading CMM differ from other organizations, schools, you have been in charge of?

I don't know. I don't know what the answer is. Maybe I am less able to communicate now than before, but let me give you an example. My experience before here has been [that] I've been able to communicate to people what my vision was. They were able to buy into it, and go with it. That doesn't seem to be at all possible here. When I worked at the elementary school we had crossreading across grades. It seemed to me really wise that we just did open grading throughout the whole school. I got the idea, I was able to communicate it, and everybody just went bugs over it—families, teachers. It wasn't difficult to get that going there.

That's impossible here. Part of it, I guess, has to do with size. We're much bigger. The ruts had been established here, too. Maybe

I've become less able to deal with differences of opinion. I don't know.

A college president today needs a detailed grasp of finances. I don't regret the fact I spent the first two years having to learn about accounting principles, but I do think whoever gets into it has to have a clear grasp of financial principles. I mean down to the very basic things. I guess another thing you have to be careful about is that your expectations are not too high, which is a terrible thing to say. I'm torn between saying I know the institution and don't know anything about the institution. I don't know which is better. I knew—at least I thought I knew—this place.

[She laughs.] Develop a thick skin. As for here, I think that I have no real background in academics. I've been on the fringe of the world of the faculty, but I don't have a real academic background. I think that's necessary, and if you look at my background that's one of the weak points. Finance was a weak point, but I think I took care of that. I don't have a doctorate. I think a Ph.D. and coming from the academic world are real important. I think there's a certain lack of credibility.

But you know, it's funny, the thought just went through my mind, if I were going to do it all over again, I think I wouldn't do it any different. That's a stupid thing to say, but it shows my inherent masochism.

The Past Year

Talk about this year, and your hopes for the college in the future.

I'd like to think that the worst is over. People I hope will know next year that they can't throw temper tantrums and have everything go the way they'd like it to go. There is a certain amount of determination and direction and we will move ahead. I also think that we—we being the Executive Committee—have to go in with the sense that we have to try to remember that every vague idea that goes through our consciousness gets communicated. Whenever Patrick and I talk now we always think, say, "Well, let's be sure to put that in the *[CMM] News*." I don't know if that's going to work, or continue, but at least we're aware of it.

I'd like to see us really start to deal with curriculum. It's not just rearranging numbers. It's creating something exciting. I hope we get some money, individual donors. I'd like us to begin to be proud of the college. It just seems that there are so many exciting things we could go with, but they have to be seen as a possibility rather than an obstacle. I'd like to see us as a community of scholars, that one group of people just doesn't show another. I'd like us to live the values we say we stand for. See, all of this is intangible, it's not a clear plan. I don't know what to do about that.

With regard to this year, I have to say I don't spend a lot of time thinking about the past. I probably would have been more forceful about not having certain people stay around here. I'd like to see people who disagree use the forums we have. I mean, if you disagree about curriculum or other kinds of issues, I'd like to see those kinds of groups used more practically, not theoretically.

Individuals disagree, too, and I'd like to see them come and talk with the individual rather than go behind someone's back and talk. I find that really, really difficult. If we just faced each other ... it's not very easy, I know. But we have to screw our courage to the sticking point and confront one another.

Look, people have a certain perception as to who I am, simply because I'm the President. I don't experience myself, I don't see myself as a powerful person, at all. I don't know. There are people who told me they wouldn't walk into this office. I find that strange. I don't know what's so forbidding about it. It's like I don't think of myself as the President, I don't even try to refer to that. Like, when my food card expires and the dining hall won't give me any food. They just won't give it to me. I mean, I could stand there and say, "I am the President." But I don't. I mean, so what. That's embarrassing.

I guess I don't see people as functions very much. I think of people as persons and when I have problems with people I go and talk with them. Here there are a series of rumors that exist, and it turns into a witch-hunt. Small places like this often place the blame at one person's doorstep. This past year it's become more than one witch—a coven—with the Executive Committee. One rumor had it that Patrick was getting a kickback from the computers and that's why we did it. He was getting a kickback under the table. There's a series of things like that.

So much went on this year. There were the rumors, the witch-hunt, then there was Dan's heart attack, there was the surplus, the tax assessment, there were a whole series of things going along with that and all these things were known to everybody, so it is real difficult to separate things out. As I said, I try not to mull things over. I constantly try to tell myself that there's nothing I can do about it, so worrying won't help. Continuously going over and over things doesn't do any good. What I want now is for the worst to be over with and for us to move ahead.

ANALYSIS

The opening section of this chapter contrasted opinions of the role and function of the college presidency. One view sees the president as the individual responsible for the articulation and financial management of the institution. The other view sees presidential power circumscribed by countervailing factors that seriously limit presidential prerogative. The search process for the presidency revealed that generally "heir-apparents" or individuals who plan to be president do not exist. The "presidential career trajectory" served as a model for how someone rises from the ranks to the top position, yet Moore's research demonstrated the oversimplification of the linear model. The main factor gleaned from the data is that most often a president has been at one time or another a faculty member.

The discussion of the presidency at College of Mother Mary provided similarities to and differences from the national data. The president at CMM had to be a Catholic sister, and hence a woman. The search process for Sister Vera was "the most democratic thing that ever happened in this school," so that no heir-apparent existed. Sister Vera had no long-term goal to be president and, at one point, "decided to forget applying." She had experience as a dean of students at CMM in the 1960s, but had never been a faculty member, and thought that, combined with her lack of a doctorate, "there was a certain lack of credibility." In addition, she saw the need for a president to have "a detailed grasp of finances," which pointed to the president as the fiscal manager of the college.

Sister Vera saw one of her problems during this past year as an inability to articulate her ideas about the college: "Maybe I am less able to communicate now ... My experience before here has been [that] I've been able to communicate to people what my vision was." At the same time, she spoke about the hemmed-in actions of the presidency with regard to the previous year. "There were the rumors, the witch-hunt, Dan's heart attack, the surplus, the tax assessment, a whole series of things, so it is real difficult to separate things out."

The interviews provide additional data in support of patterns outlined in the previous chapter and insight into how the President viewed the crisis of the previous year. Hedgelike statements such as, "I guess I don't see people as functions very much" indicate the compromising nature of her comments. Twice she used "we" to speak of the Executive Committee, but followed each statement by an example concerning only the Academic Vice President. "I also think that we—we being the Executive Committee—have to try to remember that every vague idea that goes through our consciousness gets communicated. You know, like whenever Patrick and I talk ..." She concluded the example about O'Connell with the need for communication; communication meant the written word. "Whenever Patrick and I talk now we always think, say, 'Well, let's be sure to put that in the [CMM] News.'"

Sister Vera expressed mystification that her office space was alien to certain people so that they would not come and talk with her. "I find that strange. I don't know what's so forbidding about it." She did not see entering the President's office as "forbidding" because she does not see herself as "the President." She provided the example of her expired food card and her having to wait her turn as evidence that she was just like everyone else. "It's like, I don't think of myself as the President. I don't even try to refer to that," she concluded.

Her view of herself as a person and not a role is consistent with other statements made about the changing nature of the sisterhood. She noted that her Order "tended to find visionaries and expected them to lead" and she saw this happening to herself. We saw in Chapter II how individuals looked on the founders of the Order as visionaries so that her statement gains historical credibility. She opted out of the visionary role in part because, "you get a strange sense of integrity that you can change the world—and you can't." Again, we see the circumscribed nature of a president who does not believe that one should have, "expectations [that] are too high." She admits she does not "spend a lot of time thinking about the past," or "what to be remembered for," in part, because of the intangibility of leadership. Sister Barbara, however, supplied quite tangible examples for which she wanted to be remembered. "I helped keep the college afloat. I'm only one person, but we were able to increase the student body. Our friends and public increased. Modern buildings were built. And the faculty, students, and staff kept that special spirit of CMM."

Although Sister Vera admitted to not enjoying her job—"hassles and crisis, that's all it is"—she reflects the selfless nature of the Sisters as her rationale for her continuation. "It would be selfish of me to resign, though. When BT resigned it cost the people here a lot." Her statements relate to her view that Sisters need to be seen—and see themselves—as human beings, as women, and "perhaps some people need special treatment not because of their role, but because of their human needs at the moment." One can assume that in part Sister Vera remains President of College of Mother Mary because the people of CMM need special treatment due to their particular human needs.

Part IV

Interpreting Leadership

Introduction

Part IV weaves together the information from the previous chapters with the intention of exposing the underpinnings that made it possible for the actors to speak their lines and for the scenes to occur. Chapter VIII discusses time, space, and communication in order to determine how these three coordinates affect the actions discussed in Parts II and III. The disparate threads mentioned in previous chapters—humor, private space, informal decisions, for example—receive systematic attention in the three sections that make up Chapter VIII.

Each coordinate provides additional understanding about how organizational participants arrived at an understanding of organizational reality. To reiterate, rather than rely on issues or situations, this analysis has viewed leadership as a social construction that people develop out of the actions and occurrences of everyday life. Through the explication of temporal, spatial, and communicative patterns, the reader gains insight into how each coordinate fosters organizational meaning about leadership.

The section on time relates to how the President used time, and the different contexts within which the actions took place. The discussion on space revolves around the domains of public and private spheres of interaction. Public space refers to areas considered by the participants to be community areas such as common meeting places. Private space connotes areas that people commonly assume to be the domain of a particular individual or group of individuals. An individual's office is one example of private space. The analysis of the President's communicative styles and forms considers written discourse first, then oral means of communication.

Once the specifics of time, space, and communication have been delineated, I turn in the final chapter to a summation of the study. Chapter IX returns to the framework originally discussed and points out how the study of leadership at College of Mother Mary incorporated the framework of Foucault, by way of ethnography. I return to the initial problems raised in previous studies of leadership and explore how this study worked to alleviate those problems. Finally, I suggest possible avenues to explore in future work concerning leadership in higher education.

Chapter VIII

The Context of Time, Space, and Communication

TIME

Formality/Informality

Individuals conversed with the President by making an appointment to see her, attending a meeting and airing ideas, or going to her office for an unplanned discussion. Dan Grant's weekly appointments, the Administrative Council meetings, and the lawyer's brief interchanges with Sister Vera are examples of the formal use of time. The President reserved the informal use of time for her inner circle. Sister Vera spent almost no time in casual conversation in public places. We observed the dramatic contrast with her predecessor when they both entered the administration building one day and Sister Vera walked immediately into her office whereas BT spent her time conversing with people about parties, weekend plans, and interior decoration of an office. Sister Vera did have a high degree of informality— 20 unplanned interchanges in one hour—yet she spent most of her informal time with a specified set of individuals—Leary, O'Connell, and, to a certain extent, Blue-Smith and Sister Joan.

Past Events; Future Plans

The tenor and discussion of issues at the Administrative Council clearly reflected the degree of tension evident at CMM beyond the confines of a particular meeting. At the March meeting, Sister Vera prefaced her comment about changing the function of the Council by saying, "I know it's heresy to speak against the handbook." Her idea that it was "heresy" came not from anything anyone said at the meeting, but from the actions in a previous meeting of another group—the Faculty Senate. Further, the observed actions during a presidential day pointed out how the previous week's time had been spent off-campus. One of her conversations with Leary, for example, concerned the consortium's efforts to raise funds for the college.

Future plans came into play for current activities. Part of Sister Vera's day had been spent reading and underlining what the college needed to do for the upcoming accreditation report. She tried to talk with trustees in preparation for the next week's meeting. Part of every Administrative Council meeting, and the entire last meeting, contained discussions of what the Council would do in the future.

The private use of time is also important. An intensely private woman, Sister Vera also had a life beyond the confines of the role of President and Sister. A week after Dan Grant had his heart attack in the fall, her young nephew with whom she was especially close, badly injured himself in a fall. During the following weeks much of her time was spent visiting not only Grant but also her nephew. Sister Vera's widowed mother grew increasingly infirm throughout the year. Each of these private examples demonstrates that Sister Vera—and presumably any individual—arrived at meetings and worked throughout the day not only within the context of the college, but also within private circumstances that might well have impacted upon her view of daily activity.

Seasonal and Ceremonial Time

Administrative Council meetings "began" in September and "ended" in May. Seasonal activity on the budget began in February and ended by the final trustees meeting in May. Indeed, when I initially asked an administrator in March 1983 about the possibility of conducting research at CMM, she responded, "This is the wrong time to ask her [Sister Vera] questions like that. We're in the midst of the budget right now, and everybody's real nervous. Wait for a couple of months, and ask when it is all over with."

Commencement, obviously, comes at the end of the school term and occurs in May. Functions and activities take place throughout commencement week, which marks a sizable segment of the community leaving the college. Commencement includes the final year-end activities of the faculty, most of whom will not return to CMM until All-College Day in August. The summer months, during which CMM offers classes and staff and administrators work, are nonetheless a slow time for all segments of the community. It is the time when most people take at least part of their vacation. Administrators dress more casually, and the pace of the college slows down.

Naturally, some of these seasonal activities engender ceremonial functions such as the Christmas Social or graduation. Other institutional ceremonies occur, however, independent of the larger seasonal time frame. Founder's Day, Honors Day, and Awards Day are examples of functions that could occur at anytime throughout the year, and, indeed, they did. Founder's Day, for example, traditionally happens in the fall, but Dr. O'Connell combined it with Honors Day in the springtime.

Ceremonial occasions, whether dependent upon the season or not, were once obligatory. At the Baccalaureate Mass, where only a dozen faculty showed up to parade inside, one professor later commented, "That was one thing where MT really rode herd. You practically had to have a note from your mother explaining why you would be absent." Patrick O'Connell, however, did not place the same emphasis on these ceremonies as the AVP in the previous administration. Honors Day was not so much a time when the normal workings of the college ceased, but rather was a recruiting tool on behalf of the admissions office. O'Connell gave no released time. As Sister Barbara related to me prior to the occasion, "It's chintzy, if you ask me. We used to really celebrate it and everything. Now nothing has been done. I think I'll stay home and watch television." That evening incoming freshmen and parents listened to honors students discuss the merits of a liberal arts education. The function, held in Belchamp, had two platters of cookies and one vat of juice, augmented by a lone flower from an administrator's desk to dress up the ceremony.

The point of this analysis is that many of the demarcated time periods of the year occur not by individual or presidential action, but rather in accordance with a larger sphere of activity in higher education. Yet ceremonies that might help create an esprit de corps, however important to one group of people, can pass quite rapidly without major upheaval. Individual tinkering with the system occurs—such as the creation and abolition of Intersession—but generally the tempo, tenor, and speed with which the college acts are in large part determined not by a lone individual or a collection of top administrators, but by the predetermined start and end of the school year.

The President has particular activities both within and outside of the college that she must fulfill no matter who resides in the role. A president must attend not only Board of Trustees meetings and ceremonial occasions such as Founder's Day, but also celebratory events such as Homecoming, or student-run theater productions. Beyond the college, the President—not a surrogate—must attend professional meetings, luncheons with other local Catholic college presidents, and trips to foundations in search of financial support. As a Sister of Mother Mary, Sister Vera had obligations to the provincewide community as well as to specific committees of this group.

One additional note concerns the range of activities and types of decisions with which the President concerned herself. On the one hand the college President considered how to create a planning council that could develop a plan of action for the next five years. At another point during her "day" she began to consider how to allocate a $5 million budget. On the other hand she had to contend with someone buying a "funny card or happy card" for another's birthday. The President had to find curtains for Melton Hall and deal with an alumnus who wanted her daughter admitted to the college. Clearly, presidential time includes mundane demands. The President is not merely an individual who is "philosopher-king," unencumbered by the minute activities and decisions such as those that populated Sister Vera's terrain.

SPACE

Public Space

Sister Vera's absence from the mailroom, cafeteria, and quadrangle—public information centers where individuals discussed the events of the college—forced members of the college community to go to the President's office to see Sister Vera. Anonymous notes sometimes told Sister to meet with people on their own turf, and at other times Blue-Smith and the Executive Committee mentioned her open-door policy. At a critical meeting of the Faculty Senate, a subcommittee delegated to talk with the President asked to meet not in her office, but on neutral ground.

Although the President hoped to move the main administrative offices down to Belchamp Hall during the course of the year, the extensive renovations required to meet building codes delayed the move until the spring of 1985. At public functions throughout the year Sister Vera noted her alarm that people might see the move as a movement of the administration away from, specifically, the faculty, and, in general, the whole college community.

At All-College Day, when she relayed the information that the administration would move to Belchamp, she said, "This can't be seen as distancing from you. I am speaking very personally now, but I don't want our move to be considered a movement away from you. We'll just be in Belchamp." During her address to the Faculty Senate in the spring, she noted, "Don't think because we are moving to Belchamp we won't see one another. We're moving the mailroom down there. There will be a faculty lounge ..." The President's statement implies that she worried some people might see Belchamp Hall as an administrative unit divorced from college. Dan Grant and Dave Falconieri, however, already had spent a year in Belchamp; no one ever spoke about feeling isolated from them. On the other hand, Dan Blue-Smith intended to take an office in Belchamp as Dean of the Faculty. One indivdiual noted, "See, he's become one of them. He sits on that committee and now he's going to work in that ivory tower."

Private Space

Private space has been mentioned with regard to professional gestures, seating, and physical movements. Personal space, as with body language, incorporates matters of dress and personal style. Sister Vera was a pleasant looking woman who appeared much younger than her age of 56. Her style of dress received constant attention. Three individuals who had been acquainted with the presidential search process admitted that Sister Vera's manner of dress received mention from the Sisters on the Board. Because she wore white stockings, or earrings, or spiked high heels, some individuals thought her attire inappropriate for a college president and a Sister. Though her dress was no different from that of an executive business woman in the 1980s, people constantly noted what she wore. At an alumni meeting, for example, Molly Dish related later how, "One of the girls really thinks Sister Vera dresses too fancy. She always watches what Sister has on."

Gestures such as touching an arm or holding a hand were private spatial movements that signified both support of an individual as well as the signification of who was in charge. Movement from behind her desk to one of the cushioned chairs in her office signaled to visitors that the President would not distance herself from them in her private space. Finally, as mentioned, most of Sister Vera's time was spent in private spaces.

COMMUNICATION

Written Discourse

Most written correspondence from the President's office went to internal members of the college. External letters primarily were informative or sought fiscal support either from individuals or foundations. Correspondence external to the college in the President's name came from either Tim Leary, the Alumni Office, or the President. In all cases the President reviewed the information prior to its being mailed.

Internal correspondence to the President oftentimes had problems of audience definition. People were unsure about to whom their correspondence should be sent and the President redirected letters in order that the appropriate party receive and answer the information. The use of writing by the President at CMM can be grouped in seven functionally defined categories. Each of these categories outlines how literacy operates at CMM. In order to understand how each category functions, it is necessary to consider the method used to communicate the message.

Informational. At the Administrative Council Sister Vera suggested that the *CMM News* (the biweekly in-house publication) publish the Council's plans for the future. The President also made use of the *News* in the winter for listing what the Executive Committee talked about "behind closed doors," so that the citizens would not see the meeting as secretive.

On occasion the President sent a letter addressed "Dear Colleague" to the community or to a specified subgroup such as the faculty. These letters provided information about the state of the college in general, or a particular problem. The President wrote a "Dear Colleague" letter to inform the citizenry that she used the unrestricted funds in the endowment to balance the budget, and that such an action demanded drastic action. The use of information in this written mode provided a dramatic contrast to Sister Vera's predecessor.

News-related. The presidential bulletin board provided local "news" from the President to the college community. These items are such activities as the President's vacation, the new logo for the college, or a serious illness in a member's family. When Dan Grant had a heart attack, the college received daily updates via the bulletin board. Again, the break from the past by using the written word rather than verbal communication displayed a dramatic difference in the way individuals perceived a leader should communicate.

Historical. Historical records such as minutes of meetings and the faculty handbook took on an increasingly important role throughout the year because different groups talked about how other groups did not follow what had been written—or that the college had never observed what had been written. The administration, for example, noted written inconsistencies in the records as a rationale for change. The faculty charged that administrative plans contravened what was in the handbook.

Written minutes of meetings resided in the President's office. Even though no one made use of, or read, the minutes after they had been discussed at the meeting, individuals took care to avoid having certain topics printed in the minutes. At the Budget and Finance meeting, Jake Barnes's question about the surplus income came about only after he requested that the discussion not be noted in the minutes of the meeting.

Ceremonial. The President used written correspondence to congratulate and seek the support of an individual or a particular group. Christmas letters or end-of-year letters thanked the community for their support. One letter ended, "Please accept my gratitude for all you do for College of Mother Mary. I hope that your summer will give you an opportunity for rest and renewal."

When a young woman won a track meet, Sister Vera sent her a letter as a ceremonial sign of support and congratulation: "We're proud of you! Please know our good wishes go with you." Administrators or faculty who worked hard on behalf of the college also received congratulatory letters. The ceremonial function pertains to an event that has occurred that is of great personal and emotional significance to the college. Prior to Sister Vera, the college had made extensive use of oral ceremonies to congratulate members of the college community. Consistent with her communicative style, the use of writing as a ceremonial tool nonetheless created dissonance with previously established leadership patterns.

Confirmational. Sister Vera used written letters, memos, or other written documents to confirm a previous action. When the faculty accused the administration of manufacturing a crisis, the President noted how the written WASC report cited aspects of the college that needed change. Further, she wrote a letter explaining how she previously sent an informational letter to the college community outlining the serious fiscal crisis with which the college found itself.

When the faculty sent her a six-page list of grievances, she responded to them by letter and speech. Her letter sought to confirm the decisions and actions she and O'Connell had taken. After the President and Academic Vice President addressed the Faculty Senate and many people thought the Academic Vice President said the handbook was no longer in effect, she sent Dan Blue-Smith a letter. It began, "Dear Colleague, Please be assured we still intend to work with you in the spirit of collegiality and support. I want to reaffirm that the handbook is still in effect." Thus, the President sought to confirm in writing previous actions or to set the record straight.

Sanction. Another way to "set the record straight" was by sanction. When a professor sent a strongly worded letter concerning the administration's proposed computer projects, the President wrote to the individual and demanded an apology. When another faculty member resigned from all committee work at CMM, Sister Vera sent him a letter "accepting his resignation" for the next year. When a member of the education department did not inform the President or the AVP about an upcoming accreditation visit, the President wrote: "I would have appreciated discussing this with you before all plans were formulated. I am sure that there are budgetary commitments that are entailed and have not been planned. I would like to discuss the evaluation with you as soon as possible."

We see, then, that the use of writing came about not only as an information vehicle for communication, but also as an artifact whereby members talked about a particular problem, such as the legality of the handbook. Each writing use set up particular concepts of leadership for the college community that oftentimes conflicted with the culture of the organization. From the Administrative Council, daily life and the investigation of groups at the college, we saw different oral techniques employed by the President as she spoke her lines. The next section outlines the functions that different types of speech assumed.

Oral Discourse

Agenda. The President controlled the agenda at meetings, cut off discussion, and directed who was to speak and when. We saw this at the Administrative Council when she said, "There are four things, three really, that we will talk about ... First we'll hear from Marty." By controlling the agenda, the President verbally implied she held power and authority.

History. The use of oral history as a means for settling disputes and reminding people what the past "really" was took on a twofold meaning. First, the President used history to inform the audience about how meetings previously functioned. Second, she used history to remind people that the topic under discussion was not a new discussion, but something she previously discussed with the audience.

Address Forms. Because the President and other actors were Sisters, a dual quality existed with regard to nomenclature. No one used the more formal terms of address such as "President Regan." At the same time, the use of "Vera," at meetings or individually, implied a friendship, and a power relationship, that may not have existed for others.

Ownership of Problem. As the year progressed one senses from the administrative statements that the problem—and the resolution—resided with the faculty. O'Connell's statement, "I guess we were acting with a false presupposition that we have some authority," and Leary saying, "It sounds like the Administrative Council is becoming a Supreme Soviet who runs the college," are examples of administrative belief that the problem lies in someone else's court.

Deference. Sister Vera often gave the impression that others helped her make decisions, and that she deferred her own decisions until others counseled her. "One of the things I was thinking— and actually Patrick helped me do this—it's not my own." The use of deference in oral statements created the sense in the college community that leadership and power resided not with the President, but with the AVP.

Hedges. A common linguistic occurrence resulted from the President modifying declamatory or imperative comments by the use of "hedging" statements such as the following: "I guess what I want is to focus on where we want to be three years from now." Again, hedging comments helped create the sense that the leader did not have a clear vision of what she wanted.

Reemphasized Hedge. This statement is similar to the above-mentioned hedge, yet the individual tries to reemphasize what she desires. The President stated, "I guess I think too much gets talked about by rumor rather than face-to-face. I really do believe that."

Embedded Imperatives. These statements are declaratives as well as questions that allow the listener to respond in the affirmative or negative, rather than the speaker stating a command: "I'm wondering if it wouldn't be better to make public in the *CMM*

News what's happening." Thus, rather than rely on presidential command, "Put it in the *CMM News*," the President allowed respondents a degree of authority normally ceded to the leader.

Humor. Group camaraderie among the Executive Committee came about in part through the use of humor. Ritualized interchanges pointed out the friendship O'Connell, Leary, and Sister Vera had for one another: "Tim's problem is that he hasn't gone down to Hollywood and gotten money from Michael Jackson," O'Connell laughed one day.

Small Talk. Intrinsic to the use of this device is with whom the speaker "talks small." Top administrators reserved informal conversation for themselves; faculty and staff rarely had casual conversation or shared humorous interchanges with the Executive Committee.

Apologize. The speaker admits a mistake or that problems exist due to the speaker's action. In the following statement at the first meeting of the Executive Task Force, Sister Vera used a variation of the "reemphasized hedge" that implies helplessness: "I called you together because I need help. The President is supposed to have all the answers, and I don't. I'm not saying I feel helpless, but I really do need help." The President's apology imparted to the audience that she was not really in command.

Overstatement. The speaker conveys an apology for restating an idea, and reemphasizing what he/she believes. In the Executive Committee Sister Vera stated during the discussion of who should be chosen for divisional chairpersons, "I'm sure you're getting tired of my saying this—I've said it a hundred times—but we must choose good administrators, not good teachers, for these positions."

In-group Language. When one refers to the "WASC accreditation report" or the need to build up the "FTE count," a form of private language occurs that provides discursive power to the speaker. When speakers refer to individuals rather than by title—"Ellen suggested we talk about the function of the committee"—we assume the audience knows who Ellen is and why she has the authority to tell us what to do.

Safe Topics. One way of claiming common ground is to seek ways in which it is possible for the speaker and audience to agree. Safe topics for the college involved reports about the water tax assessment because the issues concerned the college and the citizens of Rosewood against the City Council. Throughout the year Sister Vera raised the topic in public community.

Point-of-View Distancing. Comparable to a hedge, the speaker expresses a point of view, but distances herself from total commitment to the statement. Sister Vera, for example, said, "I wonder if we ought to—this is off the top of my head, I've given it no thought—I would like to see the ideas we've talked about today shared with people." By trying to distance herself from her own idea the leader would lose no power if the ideas were rejected out of hand. At the same time, when the leader distances herself from her own ideas she negates her own implied power.

Greetings. Because the President shared her office with her secretary it became the prerogative of Sister Vera whom she greeted and invited to sit and talk, and whom she merely acknowledged. To O'Connell she said, "Hi, what's cooking?" To another individual she returned a greeting by saying "Hello," and she ignored another individual's initial opening. By not greeting everyone, the leader created a distinct communication difference from her predecessor and communicated to the general populace a formality of leadership.

Metaphors. Metaphors are literally incorrect and allow for different interpretations. The President used one principal metaphor throughout the year. At her All-College Day address, she said,

> I'd like to say that I am not particularly satisfied to use the term "state of the college." The reason for that is because I think "state" connotes a kind of static situation. I would prefer, ... to refer to the journey of the college. We are talking about a journey because we are indeed traveling in a specific direction.

Pronouns. How people used pronouns is one way of ascertaining with whom they identified. Blue-Smith, a faculty member and new member of the Executive Committee stated, "People [faculty] don't follow it because they are not used to it or something." O'Connell stated, "Joan could bring her ideas to the Exec, and then we'd decide," which implies that the "we"—the decision makers—are the Executive Committee. Earlier in the meeting Sister Joan said, "Maybe this is the place where we can bring together diverse areas of the college and talk with one another." The "we" in this situation is the entire college.

Through the analysis of time, space, and communication we have seen different modes by which the actors expressed the way they felt about one another and the activities of the college. The foregoing analysis does not intend to provide the reader with a simplified list of do's and don't's for leaders. To isolate a particular variable—how one uses pronouns, for example—and to contend that one must see a particular form to achieve a particular result belies the thesis of this work. In part, the actors at College of Mother Mary arrived at their impressions when they entered someone else's terrain, communicated verbally or otherwise with another actor, or spent moments with one group of people and not another.

The significance of the analysis relies on the integration of the minutiae of everyday life in order to comprehend how these mechanisms fit together to form the complexity of a strategic situation. It is only when we analyze data within a constantly transformable matrix that we can comprehend why the actors felt the way they did. If organizational reality is socially constructed, then we necessarily need to deconstruct the situations that compose that reality to find the reference points of power. This chapter has outlined how the actors' use of temporal, spatial, and discursive practices both imposed and maintained the social construction of College of Mother Mary's objective reality. The web of leadership, then, comes out of this social construction. What remains is to tie the data from this chapter and the other chapters to the framework developed in Chapter I.

Chapter IX

Conclusion

During the course of the study the reader may well have asked how presidential parking or with whom the President shakes hands aids our understanding of leadership. It is at this point that we return to Clifford Geertz's analysis of the symbolics of power. Geertz submits that leaders

> justify their existence and order their actions in terms of a collection of stories, ceremonies, insignia, formalities, and appurtenances that they have either inherited or, in more revolutionary situations, invented. It is these— crowns and coronations, limousines and conferences—that mark the center as center and give what goes in there its aura of being not merely important but in some odd fashion connected with the way the world is built (1983, p. 124).

Consequently, this study has outlined the "stories, ceremonies, insignia ..." whereby leadership can be understood. This summative chapter connects "the way the world is built" with our understanding of leadership.

The study began with a criticism of previous research because of the lack of a historical context, the ambiguity of the term "leadership," and the limitation of measures and values used to study leadership. We return to a discussion of each of these topics to demonstrate how ethnography incorporated each issue.

CONTEXTUALIZING LEADERSHIP

Historical Context

We have seen how the avoidance of a historical discussion can alter understanding of present practices. The form, style, and use of space, time, and discourse by Sister Barbara Therese influenced the way the actors at CMM viewed the presidency and, hence, Sister Vera's leadership. Sister Barbara used the entire campus as her domain and walked throughout offices and public places in order to have casual interchanges with the citizens. People viewed her office as a room in which they were welcome to enter, and informal conversation was routine. To contrast Sister Vera's style of administration with that of BT is to see differences. Informality under Sister Vera was at a minimum, having been reduced from scenes throughout the campus to contexts primarily within the President's domain. The President maintained informal conversation with her top administrators, but otherwise individuals talked with the President at formal gatherings about formal topics.

The context of leadership in the 1980s reflects a different period than that in which BT governed. The 1950s and 1960s were periods of expansion and growth, while the 1980s force administrators to deal with problems such as decline and fiscal entrenchment. When Sister Barbara took office, the administrative structure at CMM was relatively small, whereas Sister Vera governs with three vice presidents, three deans, and a multitude of directors of programs such as Campus Activities, Religious Life, International Students, and Finance. The Board of Trustees has grown from a body primarily ruled by Sisters of Mother Mary to one whose main spokespeople are influential businessmen.

As a city, Rosewood, too, has expanded along with the college. Prior to Sister Vera's administration it was possible to ignore the city and to develop programs or build buildings with minimal outside interference. At present the college takes into careful consideration the needs of the city in order to develop programs that might bolster enrollment. The tax assessment by the city demonstrates the increased influence of Rosewood in the affairs of the college.

As the college and community grew, so did the diversity of the faculty, staff, administration, and students. Sister Barbara initially governed a preponderence of Sisters and lay Catholics, and the student body were young American Catholic women who majored in the arts. By the time Sister Vera took office a third of the student body were international students, a third of the college were adults, and 40 percent were non-Catholic. The college was coed, there were graduate programs, and half of the students majored in business.

As the personnel, size, and times changed, the traditions and ceremonies of CMM were modified. Ritualized events for young women who announced their marriage engagements have long passed by the wayside. Formalized dress such as habits for Sisters and long dresses for students ceased in the post-Ecumenical Council days of the 1960s. Obligatory faculty attendance at All-College functions like Commencement no longer take on the unconscious necessity to appear. Ceremonial occasions such as Founder's Day did not occur during the current year but rather fit into Honors Day as a recruitment tool for the Admissions Office. There is, then, a different historical context within which the leader of the institution operates in 1984 as opposed to the previous administration.

We have seen the uses of history in explaining actors' variegated perceptions of leadership. Yet this analysis avoids causal interpretations of events as well as the use of history merely to describe. As with Foucault, this work's definition of history refers to the arrangement of an organization's knowledge, which involves notions of time:

> If in this analysis [we] suspend a causal analysis ... it is in order to discover the domain of existence and functioning of a discursive practice. In other words, the ... description of discourses is deployed in the dimension of a general history; it seeks to discover that whole domain of institutions, economic processes and social relations on which a discursive formation can be articulated ... What it wishes to uncover is the particular level in which history can give place to definite types of discourse, which have their own type of historicity and which are related to a whole set of various historicities" (1972, pp. 163-164).

This interpretation differs from past work in that previous theories conceived of leadership as either time-free or deterministic. The absence of historical understanding oriented theory toward interactionist or interpersonal assumptions of how leadership operates in a synchronic system. If a distinctiveness, an identity, exists as an objective structure for an organization, the framework for understanding such a structure must necessarily include a history concerned with time. The pursuit of a project within this framework, then, is neither to discover abstract laws that exist across time nor to define ahistorical dimensions of leadership.

Again, a cultural interpretation of leadership is not "an experimental science in search of law, but an interpretive one in search of meaning" (Geertz 1973, p. 5). The study of organizational culture from an anthropological framework offers a fuller interpretation of leadership than a study that is either situation specific or individually oriented. Organizational culture incorporates previous theoretical propositions into its analysis so that we take into account, for example, the individual who resides in the president's chair, but we extend the analysis across time.

From this angle we incorporate the actors' perception of past histories as a product of the organization's reality. Throughout this study we have seen examples of different actors' perceptions of past events. Actors influenced decisions by attempting to alter present events in light of previous perceptions, setting the record straight, and having the ability to perceive of similar events differently because of a different historical context. "That's not the way it used to be, the way it's supposed to be," said Sue Ann one day in response to how the Administrative Council functioned. In order to determine present actions speakers relied on oral history to inform them of the "correct" way committees operated.

The faculty perceived that all new programs came about by committee action. When the administration tried to create a new program such as Weekend College without committee approval, the faculty objected. Sister Vera responded, "The procedures followed for the exploration of the Santa Barbara Program are the same as those followed when CMM piloted a business program with the National Guard in Sacramento in 1981. That program was subsequently discontinued because it was neither financially nor academically viable. That program went through no committee action." Thus, administrative decision making based itself in part on the rejection of false perceptions rather than utilizing those perceptions as part of administrative style. That is, one variation that can be attempted when people's perception of an event is inaccurate is to incorporate that perception into one's decision making. To analyze decision making, one must include the organization's history. Consequently, the study of "great men" or anarchic organizations without reference to history loses sight of a key variable used in decision making: historical perceptions and the actors' knowledge of historical data and information.

We have further seen how actors believed decisions had been made in Belchamp over supper by the previous administration, and how individuals had had to bargain for their contracts. Sister Vera consistently spoke of her desire "not to make decisions after five o'clock outside of the office," so that no one received special favors. In the introduction, however, we observed how Sue Ann Simmer had "bargained" for her future contract by requesting that her teaching load be relieved. Dan Blue-Smith noted, "You know we're not supposed to have paid department chairs next year, but almost on an ad hoc basis they've bargained individually." Another actor likened the Executive Committee's closed door meetings to BT and MT's decision-making style over supper in Belchamp. Sister Joan noted how Leary, O'Connell, and Sister Vera met informally to decide issues in the name of the Executive Committee.

The point is not that an individual repeats specified patterns as one approaches a decision, or that anyone sees him or herself repeating acts construed as improper; rather, actors' perceptions of the past and their response to those perceptions in part determine the paths taken and account for present practices and present reality. From the vantage point of history, a conception of leadership arises in opposition to previous ambiguities.

Competing Theories

As mentioned, previous theories have used the word "leadership" to describe quite different values, traits, concepts. Writers such as James MacGregor Burns spoke of leadership as the ability of an individual to head an organization, social movement, or idea to produce change. Theorists like Fiedler, however, compartmentalize a particular quality of a leader, such as the ability of an individual to have "friendly" relations with a subordinate.

Most recently, studies of educational leadership have gone in one of two directions. The assumption that educational organizations

are loosely coupled systems with low levels of work interdepend-
ence has brought forth conceptual approaches that reflect an
individual's orientation toward different subordinates. This
approach concerns itself with how a leader can improve the
performance of subordinates. Again, the assumption of works of
this kind—situational leadership theory and behavioral
management, for example—is that leadership can have an
important bearing on the behavior of individuals and, hence, on
the life of an institution.

The second direction of recent work on leadership is a movement
away from Cohen and March's model of an "organized anarchy"
and toward the reassertion of a leader as the individual in whose
shadow the institution will grow, or decline. The work of Mayhew
(1976), previously cited, and the example of John Silber of Boston
University are illustrations of the belief that leaders can make a
difference and affect change during the decline and retrenchment
of the 1980s.

Surely the use of the word "leadership" to describe these theories
does not mean that each writer speaks within the same context.
Leadership in one sense refers back to Carlyle's statement about
Great Men, while leadership with regard to changing a single
relationship with a subordinate refers to much of the work done
by organizational sociologists. While the term remains ambiguous
and differs from one study to another, the theories remain
grounded in the implicit assumption about how one studies
leadership. All of these works examine the leader and place the
individual on a hierarchical scale from which we perceive their
ability to affect change.

In contrast, the method for this work has been to construct how
the participants view their world and, within that world, how
leadership exists. Actors within an organization have performed
constructs of leadership and power. It is only when we incorporate
the natives' viewpoint within a larger framework that we grasp
the complexity and, ultimately, the consequence of leadership.
Generalizing the ways in which leaders should—or should not—
communicate with their constituencies was not the ultimate
purpose of this study. Rather, our purpose was to uncover the
dynamics by which leaders communicate.

As with Geertz, the task of this study was "to uncover the
conceptual structures that inform our subjects' acts, the 'said' of

social discourse, and to construct a system of analysis in whose terms what is generic to those structures, what belongs to them because they are what they are, will stand out against the other determinants of human behavior" (Geertz 1973, p. 27). The work has moved away from an individually oriented study and toward an understanding of leadership from within the organizational web. Instead of focusing on prespecified leadership variables or traits such as the ability of a leader to motivate followers, the study has integrated an organization's distinctiveness and ideology in order to determine how leadership arises from the data.

Measures and Values

The multiplicity of goals within which a university operates as well as the needed attention to the process that the institution takes to achieve those goals demands analysis. The study incorporates not only the outcomes of the organization, but also the intertwined process and values. We have seen how the College of Mother Mary's President struggled to achieve fiscal stability for the institution, but engendered harsh criticism from the faculty because of the process she used to implement those plans. There was no single unitary goal for the institution, such as there often is for a business that sees the profit margin as its measure of success. Indeed, CMM turned a half million dollar profit during the previous year, and the profit itself caused widespread anger and resentment.

The work of Michel Foucault provided a useful framework for the analysis of leadership in higher education. It is within Foucault's concept of "structuralist holism" that we viewed the actions of Sister Vera and the college. "Structuralist holism identifies elements in isolation and then asserts that the system determines which of the complete set of possible elements will be individuated as actual" (Dreyfus and Rabinow 1983, p. 55). The college structure depended upon the economic, political, institutional, and pedagogical practices which embody the meaning of the institution.

Thus, the organization of collegiate institutional processes and goals differs from businesses or sports teams. For example, a business presumably has a unitary measure—profit—whereby it can regard organizational success, or can disregard process. Institutional relations—and leadership is one of the relations—

come from the analysis of the larger processes at work in combination with the internal functioning of the organization. In turn, we use the interpretation of these processes and functions to understand organizational goals and values, and the routes the actors take to achieve those goals. In previous studies of leadership the reliance on goals as a unitary measure for effective leadership has lost sight of the importance of process in collegiate decision making.

METHOD

Ethnography is the proper tool to unearth the data necessary for an analysis of the kind mentioned here. Foucault's followers have called this methodological inquiry "interpretive analytics" in that the researcher utilizes the data "to analyze human seriousness and meaning without resort to theory or deep hidden significance" (Dreyfus and Rabinow 1983, p. 183). The necessity for "thick description" allows questions and hypotheses to arise from the research, rather than the researcher entering the field with preformed questions and theories that need to be validated or disregarded.

The data describe the minutiae of daily life of an organization and its president. The description of actions such as a city's tax assessment and activities like Executive Committee meetings and Commencement are examples not because they fit a preformed theory about how organizations operate or because they symbolize actions of power by leaders and followers that can be generalized across organizations and time. Descriptions of activities such as faculty meetings or presidential interactions get reported because they happened as repeated patterns, and it is out of these events and patterns that ideas of leadership evolve.

Necessarily, one must take into account the author function when one attempts such a method. That is, obviously all information cannot be reported within a single document by a single ethnnographer. Although preformed, routinized questions and steps do not exist, one can ask how the ethnographer goes about including and excluding information. Returning to the definition of ethnography, we see why the need arises for the researcher to be stationed "for a long period of intimate study in a small well-defined community, with a knowledge of the spoken language, and employ a wide range of observational techniques."

A full season in the field allowed the research itself to bring forth patterns that recurred. The smallness of CMM allowed for people to get to know me relatively quickly, as well as for me to become well acquainted with the practices of the institution. Knowledge of how liberal arts colleges function provided additional clues. Finally, structured and unstructured interviews, observations of a wide range of meetings and activities, participation in group events, and other activities created a variety of lenses with which to view the college and the participants' lives.

College of Mother Mary was not only small, but shared with other similar institutions a self-conscious struggle to achieve distinctiveness. CMM's ideology and inner fabric was one central issue of concern to faculty and administration throughout the year. As a Catholic college with a 116-year history, it struggled to shape an identity within the changing context of the 1980s. Not only had the institution defined itself by its Catholicism, but also by its curricula based on the liberal arts. The 1980s, however, saw the most popular major at the institution become business. Therefore, one issue of central concern was the saga of a college and how the personnel adapted to change.

The analysis of the data, the full "season" spent in the field, and the distinctiveness of the research site are in line with the kinds of methods needed for an "interpretive analytics." Dreyfus and Rabinow comment: "Interpretive understanding can only be obtained by someone who shares the actors' involvement, but distances himself from it. This person must undertake the hard historical work of diagnosing and analyzing the history and organization of current cultural practices. The resulting interpretation is a pragmatically guided reading of the coherence of the practices of the society" (1983, p. 124). Geertz's call for "thick description" is the method whereby we share actors' involvement, but do not live it.

The analysis forces us to realize the actors' humanness and moves the interpretation away from the discovery of great heroes who change the configuration of an organization. As we do not uncover heroes, so we do not find antiheroes or villains. The intertwining of actions, events, and actors propels us toward a holistic view of the web of leadership. Although no one individual exists who

creates change—to continue with the dramaturgical metaphor—
the primacy of the college President accorded her much time
onstage and, oftentimes, center stage. As Chapter I stated, the
problem is "how things happen." I chronicled the rise of crisis
at CMM throughout the year to portray "how things happened."
Events such as the extra half million dollars or the Administrative
Council's struggle to determine its future gave way to another
perspective through which we saw how things occurred—and did
not occur.

REFERENTS OF POWER

The integration of data about the institution made possible the
delineation of power and leadership. Rather than accept the
individuation of power within a set role or within an individual
endowed with this or that quality, we observed strategies employed
wherein power operated. "Power is everywhere: not because it
embraces everything, but because it comes from everywhere ...
Power is not an institution, nor a structure, nor a possession. It
is the name we give to a complex strategic situation in a particular
society" (Foucault 1977, p. 93).

Power is neither acquired nor lost. It comes to the forefront from
all angles in a constantly shifting environment. The relations of
individuals reside not only within a set of roles such as president
to vice president, but also from a variety of other relations such
as economic and social forces. Power is not found on an
organizational chart that outlines those who have it and those who
do not, which creates a hierarchical portrait of an organization.
Local interactions come into contact with the economic or
political processes which in turn create new opportunities,
conflicts, and possibilities for the organization.

This study aims for an intellectual result not unlike the
sedimentation in the ocean which over time drifts to the bottom
and presents, layer upon layer, a chronology of major geological
events. The attempt here is to record a multiplicity of events,
episodes, vignettes, and interactions with the hope that in
aggregate those events provide an institutional matrix comparable
to strata of coal containing fossil remains that help interpret the
past and present. If this simile is at all apt, then one can point

out the salient and particularly revealing data that serve as guide-posts along the way to understanding College of Mother Mary.

Thus, we do not find from power relations a causality for why things happened that one can attribute to an individual or group of individuals. Instead, we find the interlocking forces that come together in particular patterns to bring forth decisions and actions for the organization. As power resides throughout the institution, there will be resistance throughout the organization. At times we see the coalescing of resistance, but most often we observe individuals arrayed upon a transformable matrix wherein actors struggle over the consequences of power.

Two faculty members, for example, resigned in the fall to protest, in part, the use of power by the administration. The Faculty Senate eventually came together as a unified body to produce a six-page written statement that resisted the implicit use of power by the Academic Vice President. Because the institution was tuition driven and enrollment had declined, the economic atmosphere as perceived by the President demanded the quick implementation of policies without the consultation of constituencies.

Time

We have seen how the exploration of time came from a variety of perspectives. From the contextualization of history we have observed how the 1980s are a time of turmoil for the field of higher education in general and, specifically, for the College of Mother Mary. Declining enrollments, reduced financial support from the federal government, and a burgeoning administrative structure point to a radically different system than that of the 1950s and 1960s.

The analysis of formal and informal uses of time included observations of whom the President spoke with on a planned basis, whom she dropped in on, or who dropped in on her. Past events and future actions had an impact on the analysis of time insofar as present actions oftentimes had references to the past and future. The seasons generated activities so that we observed the school year "begin" in August with All-College Day and continue until May when the school year "ended" with Commencement. Finally, certain ceremonies came about because of the season, and other events occurred that were independent of seasons.

All of the aspects of time point this analysis away from a linear model of reality which places acts within set chunks of demarcated periods. A linear assumption that all organizations continue on a progressive continuum does not allow for change or decline except as the consequences of mistakes on the part of individuals. This analysis, however, viewed time as a series of pendulums created in social life by the participants as well as larger societal forces. The view accounts for how society tempers and mediates change, and how the inner processes of the organization focus time within these larger spheres. To not have included time as a referent point—as other studies have done—would have lessened our understanding of why the actors arrived at their conclusions and crises.

Space

As another referent point, space broadened the attempt to view the drama as the actors themselves did. We experienced what spatial difference meant to the participants. One individual bypassed the administration building—a spatial comment—so that the AVP could be avoided. Another individual noted anonymously to the President that she needed to come out of her office and meet with people on their own turf, and the President expressed astonishment that anyone feared entering her domain. Clearly, spatial arrangements provided meaning for the actors and, consequently, demanded analysis.

Public space connotes areas where groups of people come together for a variety of activities—to receive their mail, to have a meal, to conduct a conversation with one or more parties. The implication is that no one individual "owns" the space such as one owns his or her private office. Public space suggests areas of equality where different roles can be on the same terms, or that status differentials must come about in ways other than spatial. Sister Vera, for example, mentioned how she waited in line in the cafeteria, "just like everyone else," because her food card expired.

Private space refers to areas that the actors cede to one another or see as a particular individual's domain. The President's office was the best example of private space. People who stepped into the office realized they were not in their own sphere, and as the subcommittee to the Faculty Senate demonstrated, a group's powerlessness was in part confirmed by actors' use of space.

A variation of the private use of space is how individuals or groups used public space privately. A group of faculty met in the cafeteria oftentimes for lunch, and it was unstated but clear who could sit with the "lunch bunch" and who could not. At the Administrative Council Sister Vera often found herself sitting next to Sister Justin because Justin was aware of the public pressures placed on Sister Vera; Sister Justin's seat was a spatial comment of support. Conversely, the public use of private space most often found Sister Vera coming from behind her desk to sit with a guest in her office face-to-face rather than have the barrier of a desk between them. Gestures such as touching one's arm or hand were private gestures conducted publicly as signs of support for the individual with whom she spoke. An individual's clothes became public signals to people who had preconceived notions concerning how a Sister or President should dress.

Space receives mention as another form that connotes power and influences how people perceive one another's relationships. To enter the President's office—open door policy notwithstanding— demanded a degree of assurance that one was on good terms with the President, or that the individual had a specified reason for entering the President's office. The casual entrance into the office as had been done during the previous President's reign was nonexistent for two reasons. First, because BT walked throughout the campus, most actors saw the President's space not as an office, but as the entire campus. One individual commented, "Sometimes I felt like I was visiting some rich lady's home instead of a college. Her mark is everywhere." The ability to control the entire spatial surroundings allowed individuals to enter the President's office; that area was as public as the cafeteria or courtyard. Second, the movement of the President's desk from in front of the door to a hidden corner further supported the idea that the one area primary to the new President was her office.

Communication

The investigation of communication demonstrated that within the web of relationships of the college discursive forms and code underline collectively shared patterns and actions that produced "how things happen." "Discursive practices are not purely and simply ways of producing discourse. They are embodied in technical processes, in institutions, in patterns for general behavior, in forms for transmission and diffusion, and in pedagogical forms which, at once, impose and maintain them" (Foucault 1980, p. 200). Forms of discourse generated by the President communicate messages to her audience. These messages generate a bidirectional locality that come not merely as a simple statement understood to all, but rather as communication that produces differing patterns. These patterns can impose a new thought on the organization as well as maintain or lose control of a situation.

Jean Genet, in *Miracle of the Rose,* referred to this bidirectionality in the following way: "But words have the meaning one gives them, and the fact is that our language was a code, for the simplest exclamations sometimes signified complicated insults" (1967, p. 174). The "simplest exclamations," however, signify not only insults but a wide variety of discursive codes. We have seen the linguistic techniques used by the President in her speech patterns. The use of hedging statements or embedded imperatives produced mixed messages that allowed for a variety of interpretations from the audience. The audience could infer that the speaker was unsure of what she said, or perhaps that the speaker had a hidden agenda, or, possibly, the audience could be confused as to what to think.

Discourse comes not only by way of oral statements, but also from written communication. The six functionally defined uses of writing were: informational, news-related, historical, ceremonial, confirmational, and sanction. The means of expressing these functions varied from a public bulletin board to a letter to an individual, from the community's handbook to an accreditation agency's recommendations. The written information uncovered many messages that either reinforced or contradicted messages sent by other pathways—spatial, temporal, or verbal.

Communication, then, was another process whereby people formed meanings about the organization and one another. The processes used to form these meanings could be as dramatic as the keynote address by the President at All-College Day or a six-page statement of protest by the faculty to the President and Executive Committee. Yet these meanings could also come about from minute data such as the use of the pronouns "we" and "they" to demonstrate with whom the speaker's sentiments lay.

This study has worked from the premise that distinctive organizations such as a Catholic liberal arts college have a culture. Culture takes into consideration the larger economic and social processes as well as the more microscopic activities of individuals during the course of a day. The assumption throughout this work has been that a knowledge and understanding of these processes and activities is one way to unpack leadership. Historical perceptions and present-day circumstances circumscribe the way we think about leadership and determine in part the way an individual who resides in a functionally defined leadership role operates. The use of various investigations provided for a set of formations that determined what was said within a particular discourse at any given time.

Leadership can only be understood as a web of symbolic action and language. When leaders are unconscious of this web, this interplay of forces, their own leadership is hindered. It is caught in gossamer strands that seem invisible yet surprise us with their strength. Effective leadership is only possible when leaders are aware of this web and when they can shape it themselves by spinning actions and discourse on a symbolic level. Symbols often influence us in ways that we cannot control. Nevertheless, knowledge is power, and to ignore the symbolic forces at work in an organization is to condemn oneself to misunderstanding leadership. Again, the point is not that an individual must use this or that trait as an effective leader. This study is a call for an internalized understanding and interpretation of the forces at work in an organization so that the leader can then utilize this understanding to weave and move within his or her own web of leadership.

Ultimately, then, the study calls for a new way of analyzing leadership. It requires a shift in perspective that parallels the method for this study. The answer applies to any web of leadership, such as those at state universities or community colleges, insofar as we view leadership within the transformable matrix used here. To use this analysis one necessarily must come to grips with the determinants of power—time, space, and communication—not as preformed constructs, but rather as the actors conceive of them.

As this study has demonstrated, we can flesh out our understanding of different webs, their nodes and strands, and it is possible to comprehend why a leader feels caught within the web. Answers lie not on the level of actions and symbols per se, but in an actor's proactive stance, in awareness, in an active, ongoing interpretation of leadership and organizational culture.

The leader emerges not merely as both subject and object of the drama, but also as part organizer in the spectacle which occurred. The ambiguity appears through the existence of an individual both as an object of knowledge and as a subject who knows: enslaved sovereign, observed bystander. Anyone who fills the role of college president will move through particular leadership scenes. The individual must attend Board of Trustees meetings, for example, and the President will undoubtedly sit at the head of the table next to the chairperson. Yet the presidency and leadership is available only to certain individuals in certain situations. Most importantly, particular relations of discourse in situations of leadership become available to people moving through leadership scenes by the myriad of relations that create organizational culture. These relations make for the thick description of this study so that we see how the actors themselves defined leadership and how they came to believe and act the way they did.

One wonders how coordinates shift when a variable such as size of the institution increases, or how actors in a public institution without a hundred-year history conceive of their organization and leadership. Further work needs to be done concerning those coordinates—large and small, public and private, two-year, four-year, and research, to name but a few such institutional types. It is not yet time to build a theory or model of leadership based on a single study, but rather to move toward an ethnology of leadership in higher education from a cultural viewpoint that takes into account interwoven organizational webs.

Appendix A

A Note on Method

Chapter I outlined the kind of institution needed for this study: a distinctive college with a specified mission. In addition, the college—and in particular the President—had to be willing to grant me access and time. In June 1983 a colleague who knew the President, Lewis B. Mayhew, sent a cover letter to Sister Vera with a two-page enclosure describing the proposed research. Within a week's time the President had spoken over the phone with Mayhew and had an interview with me. During the interview I further outlined what I wanted to do. Sister Vera mentioned, "I've consulted with my Vice Presidents and they are in agreement to have you here next year. I look forward to your research." At that time neither I nor the President had any idea that the crises and conflicts for College of Mother Mary during 1983/84 would occur. In August I began my research and approached the institution with neither a hidden agenda nor preformed hypotheses that I wanted to test.

Observation and Study

I began the research August 14 and ended May 25. Except for two weeks during Christmas break I spent, on an average, 30 hours per week at College of Mother Mary. After May 25 I returned four times to interview the President, reconfirm findings, and visit with friends. My last official visit to the college was July 12, 1984.

I pursued four distinct tasks as an ethnographer. First, I undertook an historical study of the college and a detailed reading of the current history of CMM. Because the first hundred years of the institution were so closely allied with the religious order that founded it, I also studied the history of the Sisters of Mother Mary. Fortunately, the archives of the Order are on the college grounds and they afforded a wealth of material concerning the origin of the Sisters, their arrival in California, and the initial attempts to start a place of higher learning in the state capital in 1868. Journals, letters, and first-hand accounts as well as historical books provided an initial frame for understanding the historical context from which the college evolved.

The college also has kept a well-documented accounting of its life, and a perusal of the Board minutes, committee meetings, and various correspondence gave the immediate frame of reference. I interviewed older members of the religious community who gave oral accounts of the college 30 years ago. Sister Vera succeeded Sister Barbara Therese, who reigned for 24 years. Sister Barbara resigned in the spring of 1980, but remained on campus in the office of Chancellor in Belchamp Hall. She provided an abundance of information regarding the transition of the college from a two-year to four-year, and single sex to coed, institution and the addition of an evening division and a graduate division. Sister Barbara recently had her oral history published, which provided a wealth of data concerning a leader's view of the recent past. The previous Academic Dean, Sister Mary Therese, held office for 30 years; she too remains on campus and was interviewed on several occasions.

The present administration is meticulous about maintaining written records and documents. I reviewed virtually all correspondence sent to or from the Office of the President since Sister Vera took office. Committee notes, minutes, letters, memoranda, and a host of reports reside in the President's office. Thus, I conducted a thorough review of the written documents regarding the history of the college and background information concerning the present situation. I undertook the historical work throughout the year, but I did most of the reading in early August before the school year began and during Intersession in January, which was a slow time for the college.

A second task performed was the attendance at a variety of different meetings. In my initial discussion with the President she accepted my request that I be allowed to attend meetings that I deemed necessary. On only five occasions did the President ask me to absent myself from a meeting due to sensitive personal issues to be discussed. Otherwise, my access to the formal networking channels of the college was extraordinary. I was a constant observer of the "behind closed doors" Executive Committee meetings of the three Vice Presidents, the Chair of the Faculty Senate, and the President. I attended every Board of Trustees meeting, the Executive Task Force on budgetary planning, the Administrative Council, Directors' meetings, and meetings between the city of Rosewood and the college. In addition to attending meetings where the President resided as chair or participant, I attended meetings when the President skipped them, as well as meetings such as the Faculty Senate or Curriculum Committee of which she was not a member. I kept a daily record of the President's calendar so that I was aware of any individual meetings she had with the faculty, staff, or outsiders. On occasion I accompanied the President off-campus when she attended a conference.

A third task was the recording of informal encounters with the President, or in various contexts within the college community. In observing the President I either sat immediately outside of her office or in her office in a corner (see Appendix B). These two situations allowed for the recording of unplanned occurrences such as phone calls, interchanges with persons who dropped in on her unexpectedly, and observations detailing what she did when she was by herself. With regard to the college environment as a whole, I attended social gatherings such as end-of-month parties, wine receptions, basketball games, cultural nights, musical and theater productions, and other activities.

I spent a large amount of time sitting in public places such as the quadrangle, cafeteria, and the Inn. I had a mailbox in the mailroom and received any public information that other individuals received such as the *CMM News*, memorandum, and the student newspaper. I also used my trips to the mailroom as a means to meet people and frequently set up times to talk with them later. I sat in public places so that unstructured conversations and interviews could occur, and I could participate in group conversations over lunch or coffee.

Finally, I spent a good deal of time interviewing actors within the setting—faculty, staff, alumni, Board members, and other pertinent individuals. These interviews most often came about by my requesting an interview with an individual, but on occasion someone approached me and asked when he or she would get the chance "to tell my view of things." All interviews lasted at least a half hour, with some interviews continuing as long as two and a half hours. I interviewed many people more than once. There was a certain calculated haphazardness to those whom I interviewed. I sought out those people who spoke up at meetings, such as Joe Calabrese, and people recognized as "leaders" at the college such as Sue Ann Simmer and Dan Blue-Smith. At the same time, I sought people who played a moderating role at CMM, and those people who seemingly had little to do with the life of the college.

The interviews were open-ended and allowed individuals a wide range of response and reaction to their surrounding environment. Gradually, themes and patterns occurred repeatedly; reference to how the previous President ruled and the present President's shortcomings often received mention. The use of particular terms, events, or nicknames appeared in many people's stories of CMM. Particular traditions from the college's past were consistently singled out as benchmarks on which the college graded itself. At the end of each interview I paraphrased what the individual told me to ensure accuracy. If, after reviewing my notes, or with the passage of time, questions remained or another interview seemed warranted about a specific topic, one was arranged.

When I began the research I shared an office with the assistants to the Vice-Presidents for Academic Affairs and Development. The office was close to a main thoroughfare in the administration building and was an easy way for individuials to stop by and introduce themselves to either myself or the two new assistants. By midyear, however, we had to be relocated because of the planned office change of Admissions and the Computer Center. From January until the end of my research I had a private office in Belchamp Hall at the opposite end of campus. Although this office was more isolated, it provided me with easy access to individuals who did not normally cross my path in the other office. I was almost next door to the Chancellor's office and to Dan Grant, the Director of Finance. As I became more acquainted with these indivdiuals, I had many unplanned conversations about the activities of the college.

Throughout the year I found that being able to talk about sports and politics was a convenient way to "break the ice" with people.

Specifically, as the year progressed and the tension grew, one noncollege topic that Dr. O'Connell was quite fascinated by was the Democratic presidential campaign. Sister Vera was an avid football fan of a local professional team. Further, while there was no dress code at the college I was keenly aware of what kinds of clothes not to wear and, on special occasions, what clothes to wear. At Board of Trustees meetings all men wore suits; normal attire was a pair of slacks and open-necked shirt.

Method of Transcription/Analysis

I used various methods of transcribing the actions that occurred. Prior to using a tape recorder I asked the participants if it was possible to record them. I was never without a clipboard and pencil, and took notes wherever I went. After a meeting, interview, or informal observation, I returned to my campus office and wrote a summary of the event and filed it. At the end of each day I wrote a journal entry which reflected the tenor of the day, and problems confronted. At the end of each month an analysis of these records allowed for a continual reevaluation of clues, hypotheses, and points for future reference. By the end of the year I had close to two hundred files that contained information about individuals, events, or specific themes such as "body language."

I kept copies of literacy artifacts generated from the college in the President's name. The President's secretary, Sally, kept a current file on her desk for me filled with outgoing correspondence and Sister Vera's rough draft copies of letters to be typed. The Alumni Office, Office of Public Relations, and other college departments did the same. The President allowed me to review any files that existed in her office so that I was kept abreast of the informational flow not only from the oral perspective of meetings, but also through written reports, internal memos, and other documents.

As time passed I found patterns that occurred time and again. The analysis of my field notes and transcripts of various interactions provided me with much of what appears in Chapters III and IV. Spatial sketches and the analysis of body language lent an additional way to gain understanding of leadership within a collegiate environment. As Spradley (1980) suggests, I began writing the field notes into a coherent form—at midyear. By the end of fieldwork, I had finished the first draft of half of the chapters.

All of the events and dialogue presented in this study occurred while I conducted my research. At times I have condensed dialogues in order to present a more readable document. All of the actors presented acutally exist. In Chapter IV the section on a "day in the life" was compacted from many days to illustrate different themes and points that often occurred. The college, town, and actors, however, all remain anonymous.

The Ethnographer as Friend

Throughout the year I had to be careful of two potential problems: the revelation of secrets and sharing my opinion of events. Because I was privy to confidential information from meetings or interviews I had to make sure I told no one about what I heard. The half million dollar surplus, for example, I found out about in the fall while the rest of the college did not discover it until spring. I learned two weeks prior to anyone else that a popular faculty member would resign because of disagreements with the administration.

I stressed to everyone that I was not a channel for information and I was not doing an evaluation of the college. Fortunately, during the year no one ever accused me of telling secrets or presenting information that might change opinions. I was also careful to keep a distance from trying to solve practical problems for them. In the spring, for example, an administrator approached me and asked if I would write a grant for them to a foundation. She offered to pay me as a consultant; the grant concerned the acquisition of computers. I politely declined saying I did not want to jeopardize the research. There were many opportunities like the example given which I did not take.

Because I undertook neither a psychological analysis of leadership, nor a bibliography of individuals, I stayed away from personalized data. At the same time it would have been very strange for me to have spent 30 hours a week for a year at an institution and not have developed friendships with people. I made—and remain—friends with many people at the college. In one sense I was something of a mascot to people. They enjoyed talking with me, and encouraged me as I began the process of writing. I have been to some individuals' houses for supper, they held a surprise birthday party for me, and many people expressed an interest in reading this work when it reaches the library.

As an ethnographer who has left the field I necessarily had to ask the question: had I changed anything at the college? If I had not spent a year at CMM would any events have occurred in a different manner? The answer is no, nothing would have been different. Although I doubtlessly changed things in that I talked with many people, no events or problems occurred because of me. At the Executive Task Force meeting on November 16 I asked Joe Calabrese if my presence had changed the meeting. He said, "Oh no. I didn't even notice you were there. You were sitting opposite me so sometimes I caught your eye, but otherwise I wouldn't have known you were there. You are very good at being anonymous." At one point during the year Sister Vera made introductions of people at a meeting and skipped over me. When someone reminded her that she had forgotten me, she said, "Oh Bill ... that's what happens when you have a shadow. You forget he's there. He's studying us, me, for a year. I guess I'm his specimen." Toward the end of the year Sister Joan said to me, "It's been good you were here. We, I, needed someone to unburden to every now and then. I hope you don't forget us."

Obviously I could not have undertaken this research without the support of many individuals at the college, and, specifically, Sister Vera. The access she granted me to files, meetings, background information—especially in a year of crisis—was extraordinary. A goal of this ethnography has been to enable the reader to step into the place of the performer(s) and know the rules of behavior so well that the reader can become the performer. Furthermore, I have struggled to present the human side of events so that we see not only roles acting out parts, but realize that human beings fill those roles. To the extent that the study presented crisis and conflict, I portrayed individuals caught in the midst of a quite difficult period for the organization and the individuals involved. I built the analysis upon observed patterns of discourse and communication that used the events from the college's year to portray the "web of leadership."

Appendix B

Spatial Diagrams

President's Office

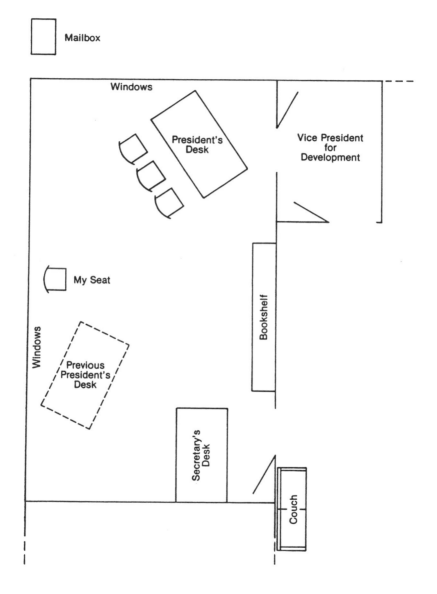

Administrative Offices

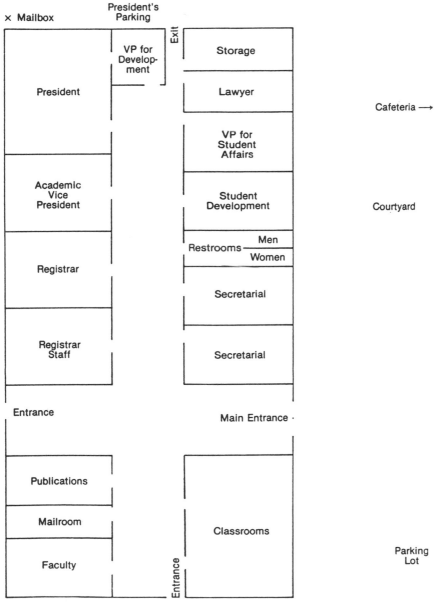

Campus

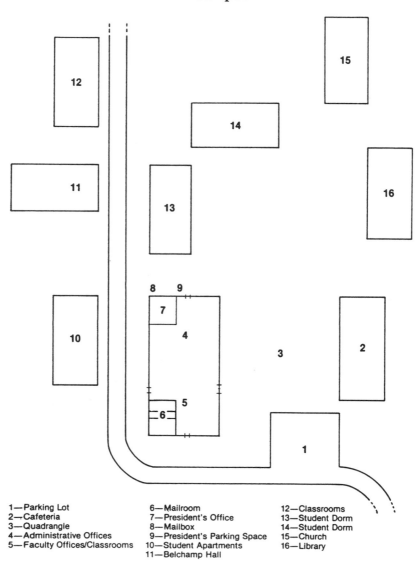

1—Parking Lot
2—Cafeteria
3—Quadrangle
4—Administrative Offices
5—Faculty Offices/Classrooms

6—Mailroom
7—President's Office
8—Mailbox
9—President's Parking Space
10—Student Apartments
11—Belchamp Hall

12—Classrooms
13—Student Dorm
14—Student Dorm
15—Church
16—Library

References

Adams, H. 1976. *The Academic Tribes.* New York: Liveright.

Agee, J. 1980 [1939]. *Let Us Now Praise Famous Men.* Boston: Houghton-Mifflin.

Baker, C. 1958. *A Friend in Power.* New York: Scribner.

Barnhard, R., J. Chilcott, and H. Wolcott, eds. 1979. *Anthropology and Educational Administration.* Tucson: Impresora Sahuaro.

Basso, K. 1974. "The Ethnography of Writing." In *Explorations in the Ethnography of Speaking,* edited by R. Bauman and J. Sherzer. Cambridge: Cambridge University Press.

Bateson, G. 1972. *Steps to an Ecology of the Mind.* New York: Ballantine Books.

Bauman, R. and J. Sherzer. 1974. "The Ethnography of Speaking." In *Explorations in the Ethnography of Speaking,* edited by R. Bauman and J. Sherzer. Cambridge: Cambridge University Press.

Bavelas, A. 1977. "Leadership: Man and Function." In *Psychological Foundations of Organizational Behavior,* edited by B. Staw. Glenview, IL: Scott Foresman.

Becker, H. 1961. *Boys in White.* Chicago: University of Chicago Press.

Belshaw, C. 1976. *The Sorcerer's Apprentice: An Anthropology of Public Policy.* Elmsford, NY: Pergamon Press.

Benedict, R. 1948. "Anthropology and the Humanities." *American Anthropologist* 50:585-593.

_____. 1959 [1934]. *Patterns of Culture.* Boston: Houghton-Mifflin.

Berger, P. 1976. *Pyramids of Sacrifice.* Garden City, NY: Doubleday.

Berger, P. and T. Luckmann. 1966. *The Social Construction of Reality.* Garden City, NY: Doubleday.

Berger, P., B. Berger, and H. Kellner. 1974. *The Homeless Mind.* New York: Random House.

Berlow, D. 1977. "Leadership and Organizational Excitement." In *Psychological Foundations of Organizational Behavior,* edited by B. Staw. Glenview, IL: Scott Foresman.

Berte, N. and E. O'Neil. 1980. "Managing the Liberal Arts Institution." *Educational Record* 61(3):25-33.

Bourdieu, P. 1977. "Systems of Education and Systems of Thought." *International Social Science Journal* 19(3):338-358.

————. 1979. *Outline of a Theory of Practice*. Cambridge: Cambridge University Press.

————. 1981. "Men and Machines." Pp. 304-317 in *Advances in Social Theory and Methodology*, edited by K. Knorr-Cetina and A. Cicourel. Boston: Routledge & Kegan Paul.

Bridges, E. 1977. "The Nature of Leadership." In *Educational Administration: The Developing Decades*, edited by L. Cunningham, W. Hack, and R. Nystrand. Berkeley: McCutchen.

Bridges, E. and W. Tierney. 1985. "Leadership." In *International Encyclopedia.* Elmsford, NY: Pergamon Press.

Brim, J. and D. Spain. 1974. *Research Design in Anthropology*. New York: Holt, Rinehart & Winston.

Brown, J.D. 1969. *The Liberal University*. New York: McGraw-Hill.

Burns, J. MacGregor. 1978. *Leadership*. New York: Harper & Row.

Bushnell, J. 1960. "Student Values." In *The Larger Learning*, edited by M. Carpenter. Dubuque, IA: Brown.

Calder, B. 1976. "An Attribution Theory of Leadership." In *New Directions in Organizational Behavior*, edited by B. Staw and G. Salancik. New York: Wiley.

Carlyle, T. 1897 [1841]. *Heroes and Hero-Worship*. London: Chapman & Hall.

Cazden, C., V. John, and D. Hymes. 1972. *Functions of Language in the Classroom*. New York: Teachers College Press.

Chaffee, E. 1983. *Case Studies in College Strategy*. Boulder, CO: National Center for Higher Education Management Systems.

Charters, W.W. 1964. "Teachers Perception of Administrator Behavior." Office of Education, U.S. Department of Health, Education, and Welfare, Cooperative Research Project No. 929.

Clark, B. 1970. *The Distinctive College*. Chicago: Aldine.

————. 1971. "Belief and Loyalty in College Organization." *Journal of Higher Education* 42(6):499-520.

————. 1980. "The Organizational Saga in Higher Education." In *Readings in Managerial Psychology*, edited by H. Leavitt, L. Pondy, and D. Boje. Chicago: University of Chicago Press.

Conklin, H. 1968. "Ethnography." In *International Encyclopedia of the Social Sciences*, Vol. 5, edited by D. Sills. New York: Macmillan.

Corson, J. 1975. *The Governance of Colleges and Universities*. New York: McGraw-Hill.

Cotton, E. 1926. *The Life of Charles Eliot*. Boston: Small.

Cunningham, L. and W. Gephart. 1973. *Leadership: The Science and the Art Today*. Itasca, IL: Peacock.

Deal, T. and A. Kennedy. 1982. *Corporate Cultures*. Reading, MA: Addison-Wesley.

Dimen-Schein, M. 1977. *The Anthropological Imagination*. New York: McGraw-Hill.

Dodds, H. 1962. *The Academic President: Educator or Caretaker?* New York: McGraw-Hill.

Dreyfus, H. and P. Rabinow. 1983. *Michel Foucault: Beyond Structuralism and Hermeneutics.* Chicago: University of Chicago Press.

Douglas, M. 1973. *Natural Symbols.* New York: Random House (Vintage Books).

Ervin-Tripp, S. 1964. "An Analysis of the Interaction of Language, Topic, and Listener." *American Anthropologist* 66(2)2:86-102.

Feldman, M. and J. March. 1981. "Information in Organizations as Signal and Symbol." *Administrative Science Quarterly* 26:171-186.

Fiedler, F. 1964. "A Contingency Model of Leadership Effectiveness." In *Advances in Experimental Social Psychology,* edited by L. Berkowitz. New York: Academic Press.

_____. 1967. *A Theory of Leadership Effectiveness.* New York: McGraw-Hill.

_____. 1976. "Validation and Extension of the Contingency Model of Leadership Effectiveness." *Psychological Bulletin* 71:128-148.

Fiedler, F. and W. Meuwese. 1963. "Leaders Contribution to Task Performance in Cohesive and Uncohesive Groups." *Journal of Abnormal and Social Psychology* 67:83-87.

Foucault, M. 1972. *The Archaeology of Knowledge.* New York: Random House (Vintage Books).

_____. 1973. *The Order of Things.* New York: Random House (Vintage Books).

_____. 1977. *Language, Counter-Memory, Practice.* Ithaca, NY: Cornell University Press.

_____. 1979. *Discipline and Punish.* New York: Random House (Vintage Books).

_____. 1980. *Power/Knowledge.* New York: Pantheon Books.

_____. 1982. *Madness and Civilization.* New York: Random House.

Gandhi, M.K. 1957 [1929]. *An Autobiography.* Boston: Beacon Press.

Geertz, C. 1968. *Islam Observed.* Chicago: University of Chicago Press.

_____. 1973. *The Interpretation of Culture.* New York: Basic Books.

_____. 1983. *Local Knowledge.* New York: Basic Books.

Genet, J. 1967. *Miracle of the Rose.* New York: Grove Press.

Germain, C. 1979. *The Cancer Unit: An Ethnography.* Wakefield, MA: Nursing Resources.

Gibb, C. 1968. "Leadership: Psychological Aspects." In *International Encyclopedia of the Social Sciences,* Vol. 5, edited by D. Sills. New York: Free Press.

Giddens, A. 1978. *Central Problems in Social Theory.* Berkeley: University of California Press.

Gluckman, M. 1962. *The Ritual of Social Relations.* Manchester, England: University of Manchester Press.

Goffman, E. 1959. *The Presentation of Self in Everyday Life.* Garden City, NY: Doubleday (Anchor Books).

_____. 1961. *Asylums.* Garden City, NY: Doubleday (Anchor Books).

_____. 1963. *Behavior in Public Places.* New York: Free Press.

_____. 1964. "The Neglected Situation." *American Anthropologist* 66(6)2: 133-136.

————. 1967. *Interaction Ritual.*New York: Pantheon Books.

————. 1971. *Relations in Public.* New York: Basic Books.

————. 1974. *Frame Analysis.* New York: Harper & Row.

Gold, R. 1958. "Roles in Sociological Field Observations." *Social Forces* 36:217-223.

Goldschmidt, W. 1972. "An Ethnography of Encounters." *Current Anthopology* 13:69-78.

Grant, G. and D. Riesman. 1978. *The Perpetual Dream.* Chicago: University of Chicago Press.

Gregor, T. 1977. *Mehinaku.* Chicago: University of Chicago Press.

Halpin, A. 1966. *Theory and Research in Administration.* New York: Macmillan.

Heath, S. 1978. "Teacher Talk: Language in the Classroom." In *Language in Education: Theory and Practice.* Arlington, VA: Center for Applied Linguistics.

————. 1978. "An Outline Guide for the Ethnographic Study of Literacy and Oral Language." NIE Report.

————. 1979. "The Context of Professional Languages: An Historical Overview." In *Language in Public Life,* edited by J. Alatia and G. Tucker. Washington, DC: Georgetown University Press.

————. 1980. "The Functions and Uses of Literacy." *Journal of Communications* (Winter):123-132.

————. 1981. "Ethnography in Education: Toward Defining the Essentials." In *Children in and out of School: Ethnography in Education.* Washington, DC: Center for Applied Linguistics.

————. 1982. "Protean Shapes in Literacy Events: Ever-shifting Oral and Literate Traditions." In *Spoken and Written Language,* edited by D. Tannen. Norwood, NJ: Ablex.

————. 1983. *Ways with Words.* New York: Cambridge University Press.

Helsabeck, R. 1973. *The Compound System: A Conceptual Framework for Effective Decision-making.* Berkeley: University of California Press.

Higham, J. 1974. "Hanging Together: Divergent Unities in American History." *Journal of American History* 61:5-28.

Hodgkinson, H. and L. Meeth. 1971. *Power and Authority on University Campuses.* San Francisco: Jossey-Bass.

Hollander, E. and W. Julian. 1968. "Leadership." In *Handbook of Personality Theory and Research.* Chicago: Rand McNally.

House, R. 1971. "A Path Goal Theory of Leader Effectiveness." *Administrative Science Quarterly* 16:321-338.

Hymes, D. 1961. "Functions of Speech: An Evolutionary Approach." In *Anthropology and Education,* edited by F. Gruber. Philadelphia: University of Pennsylvania Press.

————. 1964. "Toward Ethnographies of Communication." *American Anthropologist* 66(6):1-34.

————. 1973. "Speech and Language." *Daedalus* (Summer):59-85.

————. 1974. *Reinventing Anthropology.* New York: Random House (Vintage Books).

Jarrell, R. 1952. *Pictures from an Institution.* New York: Knopf.

Jencks, C. and D. Riesman. 1977. *The Academic Revolution.* Chicago: University of Chicago Press.

Jones, E. and K. Davis. 1978. "From Acts to Dispositions: The Attribution Process in Person Perception." In *Cognitive Theories in Social Psychology,* edited by L. Berkowitz. New York: Academic Press.

Keeton, M. 1971. *Shared Authority on Campus.* Washington, DC: American Society for Higher Education.

Kelly, H. 1972. *Causal Schemata and the Attribution Process.* Morristown, NJ: General Learning Press.

Knapp, D. 1969. "Management." *Educational Record* (Winter):55-59.

Kroeber, A. 1957. "Ethnographic Interpretations." *University of California Publications in American Archaeology and Ethnography* 47(3):236-240.

Kuhn, T. 1962. *The Structure of Scientific Revolutions.* Chicago: University of Chicago Press.

Lehman, B.H. 1928. *Carlyle's Theory of the Hero.* Durham, NC: Duke University Press.

Lieberson, S. and J. O'Connor. 1972. "Leadership and Organizational Performance." *American Sociological Review* 37:117-130.

Lindbloom, C. 1959. "The Science of Muddling Through." *Public Administration Review* 19:79-88.

March, J. 1980a. "How We Talk and How We Act." Paper presented at the Henry Lecture on Administration at the University of Illinois.

———. 1980b. "Footnotes to Organizational Change." Program Report No. 80-a6 for NIE.

March, J. and M. Cohen. 1974. *Leadership and Ambiguity.* New York: McGraw-Hill.

Mayhew, L. 1970. "Governance: Context for the '70's." Unpublished manuscript.

———. 1976. "Administration and Governance of the University." Unpublished manuscript.

———. 1977. *Legacy of the Seventies.* San Francisco: Jossey-Bass.

———. 1980. *Surviving the Eighties.* San Francisco: Jossey-Bass.

McCall, M. and M. Lombardo. 1978. *Leadership: Where Else Can We Go.* Durham, NC: Duke University Press.

McNamee, M.D. 1959. *Wilamette Interlude.* Palo Alto, CA: Pacific Books.

———. 1967. *Light in the Valley.* Berkeley, CA: Howell-North Books.

McWilliams, W.C. 1973. *The Idea of Fraternity in America.* Berkeley: University of California Press.

Metzler, K. 1973. *Confrontation: The Destruction of a College President.* Los Angeles: Nash.

Millett, J. 1975. "Higher Education Management Versus Businesss Management." *Educational Record* 56:221-225.

Mintzberg, H. 1980. *The Nature of Managerial Work.* Englewood Cliffs, NJ: Prentice-Hall.

Moore, K. et al. 1983. "The Structure of Presidents' and Deans' Careers." *Journal of Higher Education* 54(5):500-515.

Moore, W. 1971. *Blind Man on a Freeway.* San Francisco: Jossey-Bass.

Mother Mary [Sisters of]. 1926. *In Harvest Fields by Sunset Shores.* San Francisco: Gilmartin.

Mulhauser, F. 1975. "Ethnography and Educational Policy." *Human Organization* 34(3):311-319.

Pfeffer, J. 1977. "Power and Resource Allocation in Organization." In *Psychological Foundations of Organizational Behavior,* edited by B. Staw. Glenview, IL: Scott Foresman.

———. 1978. "The Ambiguity of Leadership." In *Leadership: Where Else Can We Go?,* edited by M. McCall and M. Lombardo. Durham, NC: Duke University Press.

———. 1981. "Management as Symbolic Action." In *Research in Organizational Behavior,* Vol. 3, edited by L. Cummings and B. Staw. Greenwich, CT: JAI Press.

Pondy, L. 1978. "Leadership is a Language Game." In *Leadership: Where Else Can We Go?,* edited by M. McCall and M. Lombardo. Durham, NC: Duke University Press.

Pratt, M. 1977. *Toward a Speech Act Theory of Literary Discourse.* Bloomington: University of Indiana Press.

Reiss, S. 1982. *A Native Daughter's Leadership in Education.* Berkeley: University of California Press.

Rist, R. 1977. "On the Relations Among Educational Research Paradigms: From Disdain to Detente." *Anthropology and Education Quarterly* 8(2):42-49.

———. 1979. "On the Utility of Ethnographic Case Studies for Federal Policy." Paper presented at the annual meeting of the American Educational Research Association, Washington, DC.

Rosaldo, R. 1980. "Doing Oral History." *Social Analysis* (September):89-99.

Schmidt, G. 1930. *The Old Time College President.* New York: Columbia University Press.

Scriven, M. 1972. "Objectivity and Subjectivity in Educational Research." In *Philosophical Redirections in Educational Research.* Chicago: National Society for the Study of Education.

Sheriden, A. 1982. *Michel Foucault: The Will to Truth.* New York: Tavistock.

Socolow, D. 1978. "How Administrators Get Their Jobs." *Change* 10(5).

Spindler, G., ed. 1974. *Education and Cultural Process.* New York: Holt, Rinehart & Winston.

———. 1982. *Doing the Ethnography of Schooling.* New York: Holt, Rinehart & Winston.

Spradley, J. 1980. *Participation Observation.* New York: Holt, Rinehart & Winston.

Stoke, H. 1959. *The American College President.* New York: Harper & Row.

Szwed, J. 1980. "The Ethnography of Literacy." In *Variations in Writing,* edited by M. Whiteman. Hillsdale, NJ: Erlbaum Associates.

Tedlock, D. 1971. "On the Translation of Style in Oral Narrative." *Journal of American Folklore* 84:114-133.

Thompson, R. 1954. *The Impending Tidal Wave of Students.* Washington, DC: American Council of Education.

Tierney, W. 1983a. "Governance by Conversation: An Essay on the Structure, Function, and Communicative Codes of a Faculty Senate. *Human Organization* 42(2).

———. 1983b. "The Tenure Drum: An Investigation of Ritual Violence in the Modern University." *Resources in Education* 83:ED230157.

———. 1985. "Ethnography: An Alternative Evaluation Methodology." *Review of Higher Education* 8(2).

Tolstoy, L. 1966 [1869]. *War and Peace*. New York: Norton.

Tyack, D. and E. Hansot. 1980. "From Social Movement to Professional Management: An Inquiry into the Changing Character of Leadership in Public Education." *American Journal of Education* 88:291-319.

———. 1982. *Managers of Virtue*. New York: Basic Books.

Veysey, L. 1965. *The Emergence of the American University*. Chicago: University of Chicago Press.

Vroom, V. 1977. "Leadership Revisited." In *Psychological Foundations of Organizational Behavior*, edited by B. Staw. Glenview, IL: Scott Foresman.

———. 1980. "A Normative Model of Leadership Style." In *Readings in Managerial Psychology*, edited by H. Leavitt, L. Pondy, and D. Boje. Chicago: University of Chicago Press.

Walker, D. 1979. *The Effective Administrator*. San Francisco: Jossey-Bass.

Wax, M. 1971. *Anthropological Perspectives on Education*. New York: Basic Books.

Wax, R. 1971. *Doing Fieldwork: Warnings and Advice*. Chicago: University of Chicago Press.

———. 1972. "Field Methods and Techniques." *Human Organization* 11(3).

Weber, M. 1976 [1904]. *The Protestant Ethic and the Spirit of Capitalism*. New York: Scribner.

Weick, K. 1976. "Educational Organizations as Loosely Coupled Systems." *Administrative Science Quarterly* 21:1-19.

Wilcox, K. 1980. "The Ethnography of Schooling: Implications for Educational Policy-making." Project Report No. 80-a10 for NIE.

Wolcott, H. 1970. "An Ethnographic Approach to the Study of School Administrators." *Human Organization* 29:115-122.

———. 1973. *The Man in the Principal's Office: An Ethnography*. New York: Holt, Rinehart & Winston.

Whyte, W.F. 1961. *Street Corner Society*. Chicago: University of Chicago Press.

Subject Index

Administrative council
   function, 129
Alumni, 114-17

Board of trustees, 79-83
Bourdieu, 15, 21
Budget and finance meeting, 76-78
   executive committee, 96-109

Clark, 28-29
Cohen and March, 170-72, 208
College of Mother Mary, 31
   beginnings, 36-39
   ceremonies and traditions, 205
   move to Rosewood, 39-42
   present circumstances, 45-53
   recent past, 42-45
   tax assessment, 83-85
Communication, xxii, 20
   address forms, 156, 198
   agenda, 133, 135, 197
   apologize, 199
   ceremonial, 196
   confirmational, 196
   difference, 198
   distancing, 200
   documents, 153
   greetings, 200
   heading, 135-36
   hedges, 198
   historical, 140-41, 145, 195, 197

humor, 163, 199
imperatives, 198
informational, 194-95
in-group language, 199
ledges, 198
metaphors, 200
news-related, 195
nonverbal, 160
oral, 132-33, 197-201
overstatement, 199
ownership of problem, 198
pronouns, 200-01
sanction, 197
small talk, 199
speech patterns, 133-34
with constituents, 162
written, 132, 139, 165, 194-97

Dodds, 11
Dramaturgical metaphor, xxi

Ethnographer, 24-28, 210-12, 219-225
   ethnographer as friend, 224-25
   informal encountering, 221
   interviewing, 221-22
   method of transcription, 223-24
   observation, 219-20
   thick description, xviii
   written records, 220
Executive committee, xx, xxi

239

Faculty, 85-96
  senate, 86-93
Fiedler, 9-10
Foucault, 22-23, 205, 210, 212
Founder's day, 60-1

Geertz, 27, 29, 203, 206, 208-09
Genet, 216
Goffman, 25

Halpin, 8-9
History, xviii
Honors day, 60-61

Leadership, xxi-ii, 5, 217-18, 203
  alternative framework, 15-24,
    66
  ambiguity of concept, 13-14
  collegial theory, 10-12
  contingency theory, 9
  general theory, 8-10
  historical context, 12-13, 204-
    05
  organizational theory, 8-10
  previous research, xxi
  Sister Vera's definition, 178-79
  values, 14, 209

MacGregor Burns, 7, 207
March, 10
Mission, xix

Organizations, xxi

Power, 22-23
  referents of, 212-18
  rule of continuous variations,
    23
  rule of double conditioning, 23
  rule of immanence, 23
  rule of the tactical polyvalence
    of discourses, 23

Presidency
  authority, 170
  Catholic, 172
  path to presidency, 170-71
  theories of, 10-12
  traits of college presidents, 170

Space, xxii, 19, 214-55
  office space, 159-60
  physical space, 127
  private space, 149-50, 193-94
  public space, 157-60, 192-93
  seating, 132
  spatial gestures, 160
Sister Barbara, 43-44, 55, 58, 60
  governance, 205
  selection as president, 173
Sisters of Mother Mary, 32
  California, 35
  first American unit, 33
  move to the west coast, 34-35
  Oregon, 34
  present context, 111-14
Sister Vera, 45-48, 57-60
  applying to CMM, 177
  definition of leadership, 178-79
  education, 175
  enjoyment of job, 178
  hobbies, 175
  life as a woman and nun, 175-
    76
  meeting with admissions
    director, 73-74
  meeting with director of
    finance, 74-76
  meeting with facilities man-
    ager, 69-73
  meeting with Faculty Senate,
    93-95
  office, 149-50, 157-60
Staff, 121-23
Students, 117-20

Time, xxii, 213-14
 ceremonial, 127, 190-92
 history, 189-90
 informal, 159-65, 189

 formal, 151-52, 189
 seasonal, 127, 161, 190-92
Total institutions, 25